658.1 dtt

Understanding Business and Finance

An active-learning approach

Jill Hussey (General Editor)

Roger Hussey (Section 1)
Mark Sutcliffe (Section 2)
Jill Hussey (Section 3)
Judith Jordan (Section 4)
Sally Howe (Section 5)
Monica Hall (Section 6)
Peter Cox (Section 7)
Geoffrey Heaven (Section 8)
Paul Goodwin (Section 9)

DP Publications Ltd
Aldine House
142/144 Uxbridge Road
London W12 8AW

1991

Acknowledgements

I would like to thank Dick Chapman of DP Publications for initiating and commissioning this book; Roger Hussey for his valuable support and guidance during its writing; the students of Bristol Polytechnic who over the years have enabled the contributing authors to gain a wide experience of teaching business and finance; and Stephen Thacker, LLM, for his help on business law.

JILL HUSSEY

A CIP catalogue record for this book is available from the British Library

First edition 1991

ISBN 1 870941 74 8

Copyright © DP Publications 1991
Cartoon illustration copyright © Richard Dearing 1991
Captions to cartoons by Catherine Chadwick, Dick Chapman, Jill Hussey and Claire Wright

Typeset by
Kai, 21 Sycamore Rise
Nottingham

Printed by
The Guernsey Press Co. Ltd
Vale, Guernsey

Contents

iii

List of Figures and Tables

Figures

Table

Preface

Aim of the book

Understanding Business and Finance is written for students of BTEC Higher National Certificate and Diploma in Business and Finance. It will also be of considerable value to students on other courses which include the study of business and finance.

It is not intended to be an instructional book, but a companion to the course text; it is a combined reference manual and activity book. It provides a skeleton outline of all business and finance core subjects, including essential definitions, checklists, formulae and explanation of key points. The book gives a summary and overview of the entire BTEC course and through the inclusion of tasks and assignments assists the student in developing knowledge and skills through problem identification, problem-solving, discussion and activities.

Structure of the book

Understanding Business and Finance is divided into nine major sections representing the core subjects of business and finance for the entire course. These sections have been given titles which are in common use. Recommended texts, chosen for the quality of their explanation of the subject at this level, are given at the beginning of each section. Each core subject section is divided into a number of subsections. These are arranged in a logical sequence, although it is possible to omit parts without detriment to the whole.

Tasks are set at frequent intervals. These can be completed by the student or used as a basis for discussion or group work. In addition, each subsection contains a formal assignment on that particular topic. Appendix A contains seven integrated assignments which draw on the skills and knowledge acquired from the study of each core subject.

Using the book effectively

Understanding Business and Finance can be used effectively in a number of ways:

Planning At the start of a course the book can be used to give an overview of the entire course and thus a guide to the topics covered in each core subject. This will enable students to appreciate the interrelationship between the core subjects as well as how knowledge is developed and ordered.

Problem-solving Once the course is underway, students need to make use of knowledge and skills which relate to material studied earlier in the course or in another subject area. This book gives rapid guidance to the solution of problems by placing knowledge and skill requirements within a cohesive framework.

Activity development The tasks and assignments encourage the development of skills and knowledge through activity and discussion. Students can assess their progress in a particular subject area and in the entire course.

Revision and reference The comprehensive index makes this book an excellent reference source. Its unique structure can be used for revision and as a supplement to the student's own notes where there are deficiencies or omissions.

To obtain maximum benefit from *Understanding Business and Finance*, the following resources should be available to students and extensively used:

(i)   access to a good library containing up-to-date text books, current newspapers and periodicals, official statistics and research directories;

(ii) use of computing facilities, including standard software programs such as spreadsheets, databases and word processing;

(iii) the support of specialist lecturers to explain and expand upon the material in this manual.

A separate lecturer's supplement is provided free of charge by the publishers to lecturers recommending the book as a course text. This gives guidance on topics such as report writing and presentations by students, as well as detailed recommendations as to whether particular topics are best dealt with through discussion, group work, individual research by students or other means.

Understanding
Business and Finance

Section 1
Accounting and Finance

by Roger Hussey

*PhD, FCCA, NWIS, Professor of Financial Services and
Touche Ross Fellow in Financial Reporting at Bristol Business School*

Accounting in its broadest form is concerned with identifying, measuring, recording and communicating the economic transactions of organisations.

Recommended Reading

Bendrey, Mike, Hussey, Roger & West, Colston, *Accounting & Finance for Business Students*,
    DP Publications, 1989

Holmes, G., & Sugden, A., *Interpreting Company Reports and Accounts*, Woodhead Faulkner, 1986

Hussey, Roger, *Cost & Management Accounting*, Macmillan Professional Masters, 1989

Lee, T. A., *Company Financial Reporting*, Van Nostrand, 1982

Limack, J., *Financial Accounting and Reporting*, Macmillan, 1987

Robert hadn't got to grips with cash flow forecasts yet, but something told him he had a problem...

Contents

1.1 The Accounting Framework

1.1.1 Accounting

The two main subdivisions of accounting are *financial accounting* and *management accounting*. These can be further broken down into activities such as bookkeeping, auditing and costing.

Task

Obtain a number of definitions of accounting from text books. What are the similarities and differences?

1.1.2 Financial Accounting

The classification, measurement and recording of business transactions are the concern of financial accountants. After a specified period of time, normally a year but often more frequently, the information is communicated by means of *financial statements*. The main financial statements are the *profit and loss account* and the *balance sheet*.

Financial accounting aims to present a *true and fair view* of business transactions and is conducted within a regulatory framework. It is based on concepts and conventions which have been established as general principles. The main categories of financial accounting are:

- *bookkeeping,* which is concerned with recording business transactions;

- *auditing,* which is the thorough examination of the financial records of an organisation to confirm that the financial statements give a true and fair view (an audit is legally required for limited companies);

- *corporate recovery*, which is an increasingly important area of accounting and covers the provision of insolvency services and advice to companies in financial difficulty;

- *taxation,* which is governed by legislation and involves individuals and businesses.

Task

Classify the articles in a selection of accounting journals into the various main accounting activities. Show the results in the form of a pie chart.

1.1.3 Management Accounting

Management accounting uses a range of financial and statistical techniques and methods to provide information to managers. It is not governed by legislation or other regulations. The information management accountants provide is of value to managers with responsibility for controlling and planning business activities and decision-making.

Cost accounting is part of management accounting. It is concerned with establishing budgets and standard costs, and the actual costs of operations, processes, departments or products.

Task

From a selection of advertisements for management accountants in the financial press, select any technical terms used and look up their meanings. Construct a segmented bar chart to illustrate their relative frequency.

1.1.4 The Accounting Profession

A person who is generally recognised as a qualified accountant is normally a member of one of the following professional bodies:

- Institute of Chartered Accountants in England and Wales
- Institute of Chartered Accountants in Ireland
- Institute of Chartered Accountants in Scotland
- Chartered Association of Certified Accountants
- Chartered Institute of Management Accountants
- Chartered Institute of Public Finance and Accountancy

Members of the different professional bodies can work in professional practice (for a firm of accountants), in industry, commerce or financial and public administration. A member of one of the professional bodies is entitled to use the appropriate designatory letters after his or her name.

Task

Obtain publicity brochures from the professional bodies, or information from a library, and decide which professional bodies are best for the following work:

- an accountant in a professional practice;
- a management accountant in industry;
- a treasurer in a local authority;
- an accountant in an area health authority.

1.1.5 Sources of Financial Information

The main and most comprehensive source of financial information on a limited company is its *annual report and accounts*. In recent years *computer databases* have also become a major source of financial information for those with sophisticated requirements.

As a general guide, the following are the better known, widely available sources of printed information:

- *Investors' Chronicle* is a weekly publication containing in-depth reviews on companies and industries.
- *Kompass* is a two-part publication. Volume 1 is a classified catalogue of products and services giving the names of manufacturers, wholesalers and distributors. Volume 2 contains information on over 30,000 companies.
- *The Stock Exchange Year Book* contains information on the operation of the Stock Exchange and on companies' directors, accounts and dividends.

5

- *Who Owns Whom* is annual directory in two parts. Volume 1 lists parent companies and gives their subsidiaries; Volume 2 lists the subsidiaries by name and gives the parent companies.

- *Extel* cards are available in many libraries and provide comprehensive financial information on companies.

Task

Prepare a word processed guide for students on the financial reference sources available in your local or college library and how to use them.

1.1.6 Potential Users of Financial Information

Limited companies are required by law to give shareholders certain financial information. The potential users of financial information are:

- shareholders and prospective shareholders;
- lenders;
- trade unions and employees;
- business contacts, including suppliers, customers and competitors;
- analysts and advisers.

Task

Obtain a copy of any company's annual report and accounts, and identify the information of greatest interest to the above groups.

1.1.7 Accounting Concepts

On a day-to-day basis accounting is conducted using generally accepted principles. These are called *accounting concepts* or *conventions*. The main concepts are:

- the concept of *going concern*, which states that the profit and loss account, and the balance sheet should be prepared on the assumption that the business will continue to trade in the future;

- the *matching (accruals)* concept, which allows for the preparation of financial statements of a company in which profits, losses, costs and expenses are recognised as they are earned or incurred, rather than when cash is received or paid;

- the concept of *consistency*, which states that items of a similar nature should be treated in the same way within any accounting period and from one accounting period to another;

- the concept of *prudence,* which prevents profits or revenues being anticipated except where there is a high degree of certainty; (provision is made for all costs and losses whether the amount is known for certain or is only a best estimate);

- the concept of *non-aggregation*, which states that the amount of each individual asset or liability must be ascertained separately before calculating the aggregate amount.

Tasks

(i) Explain the impact on the financial statements of a company if the going concern concept was not used.

(ii) Describe a situation in which two of the accounting concepts might be in conflict.

1.1.8 Measuring Income and Capital

In accounting there are a number of ways in which *income* (meaning profit) and *capital* can be measured. *Historical costing* is a traditional method in which the values of income and capital are derived from bookkeeping entries of actual transactions. The method has the advantage of being objective, understandable and simple to operate, but suffers from many deficiencies, particularly in periods of inflation.

In *current entry value (replacement cost) accounting* , the current entry value of an asset is represented by the cost of replacing the asset.

Current exit value (realisable value) accounting is based on the principle that profit or realisable income can be calculated using the following formula:

$$I = D + (R_t - R_{t-1})$$

where: I = realisable income;

D = the amount of distributions during the period

R_t = the net realisable value of the entity's net assets at the end of the period;

R_{t-1} = the net realisable value of the entity's net assets at the beginning of the period.

Current purchasing power is a method which makes adjustments to the historical cost accounts to allow for the general rate of price inflation.

Current cost accounting was a method put forward by Statement of Standard Accounting Practice 16 (Section 1.1.9), which was subsequently withdrawn. It is a system of current value accounting which uses a mixture of current entry value, current exit values and economic values. It also uses the capital maintenance concepts of maintaining the operating capability of a business.

Task

What are the advantages and disadvantages of current entry value accounting and current exit value accounting?

1.1.9 The Regulatory Framework

The accounting activities of limited companies are undertaken within a *regulatory framework*, the three elements of which are:

- company legislation;
- Statements of Standard Accounting Practice (SSAPs);
- Stock Exchange regulations.

The most recent *company legislation* is included in the *Companies Act 1989* which added to and amended the *Companies Act 1985*. The main requirements placed on every limited company are:

- to keep accounting records which show and explain the company's transactions;

• to prepare final accounts comprising a profit and loss account, balance sheet, auditor's report and directors' report and lay them before the *shareholders* (*members*) in general meeting. They must also be delivered to the Registrar of Companies.

Statements of Standard Accounting Practice (SSAPs) were issued by the Accounting Standards Committee until 1990 when it was replaced by the Financial Reporting Council (FRC) and the Accounting Standards Board (ASB). The FRC has some 25 members drawn from users, preparers and auditors of accounts and guides the ASB on policy. The ASB is responsible for devising new SSAPs and has an Urgent Issues Task Force to deal with any issues which are too urgent to leave to the normal standard-setting process. In addition there is a review panel which examines and questions departures from accounting standards by large companies.

Stock Exchange regulations apply to those companies which have a full listing (*quoted* companies). To obtain a listing for its securities, a company must conform with the regulations contained in the Yellow Book issued by the Council of the Stock Exchange.

Task

Take a set of accounts of a quoted company and identify the main disclosures of information under the three elements of the regulatory framework.

Assignment 1.1: Investigative journalism

A friend who is a trainee reporter on a local newspaper has been asked to write an article on local industry. He has no knowledge of business and has sought your help in collecting original data to use. He wants to cover some twelve local companies. The sort of information he requires is:

- Who owns the companies?
- What are their products?
- What have their profits been like?
- Can you buy shares in them?
- How many people do they employ locally?
- Are they part of a national or international group?
- Who are the directors?
- Have any stories been published about them in the national press within the last six months?

Student activities

(i)   Identify a number of companies in your locality.

(ii) If any of the companies are public limited companies, send for their annual report and accounts.

(iii) Using various sources of information, collect the data required by your friend.

(iv) With the financial and quantitative data you have collected, construct diagrams in the form of bar charts, pie charts, etc which your friend can use to illustrate his article.

1.2 Personal and Organisational Finance

1.2.1 Personal Financial Planning

Personal financial planning is concerned with:

- assessing your present financial resources;
- setting financial objectives to be achieved within a specified period of time ;
- deciding how objectives can be achieved;
- monitoring actual performance against objectives.

Task

Construct a schedule of your present financial resources, listing your financial objectives and the time period for each.

1.2.2 Main Sources of Personal Finance

The *main sources of personal finance* are savings, earnings and loans. *Savings* should be invested to obtain a return, taking the following criteria into consideration:

- the degree of *risk t*hat is acceptable;
- the *amount* available for investment;
- the degree of *access* required;
- the rate of *return* required.

Earnings are the main source of personal finance for most people. Earnings are subject to *taxation* and/or other deductions such as *National Insurance*.

There are two main forms of personal *loan* : short-term and long-term. Minors, those under the age of 18, are not legally bound by contracts for money borrowed.

Task

Draw a pie chart showing each source of your personal finance as a percentage of the whole.

1.2.3 Types of Personal Investment

Building societies have many different schemes all offering low risk and clearly defined interest rates.

Banks offer various types of deposit account with immediate access; also term and fixed notice accounts with higher interest rates.

The *Post Office* offers simple schemes and competitive rates of interest through the National Savings Bank and National Savings Certificates which have certain tax advantages.

Stocks, shares, debentures and bonds are securities issued by limited companies, local authorities, central government and other institutions.

Unit trusts are funds held on behalf of investors by trustees. These are usually banks, insur companies or other large financial institutions.

Task

Collect details of as many different building society schemes as possible. Suggest methods by which the information can be stored to allow easy retrieval of schemes according to their characteristics; for example, those requiring 90 days' notice of withdrawal and interest rates of 12 per cent and over.

1.2.4 Simple Interest

This is interest paid only on the amount invested (known as the *principal*) . To calculate the amount of *simple interest* the formula is:

$$I = P \times \frac{r}{100} \times n$$

where: I = simple interest

P = principal

r = percentage rate of interest per time period

n = time period

Tasks

What is the amount of simple interest receivable on:

(i)   a principal of £250 invested at 6.5 per cent per annum for a ten-year period?

(ii) a principal of £700 invested at 12 per cent per annum for a six-year period?

1.2.5 Compound Interest

This is interest paid on the original *principal* and on the interest that has been added to it. In this case the interest is not paid out but is automatically reinvested. To calculate the final amount of *compound interest* the formula is:

$$A = P \left(1 + \frac{r}{100} \right)^n$$

where: A = amount

P = principal

r – percentage rate of interest per time period

n = time periods

Alternatively, tables can be used to calculate the compound interest instead of applying the formula.

Tasks

What is the amount receivable on:

(i)   a principal of £500 invested at 8 per cent compound interest for four years?

(ii)   a principal of £1,000 invested at 11 per cent compound interest for three years?

1.2.6 Short-term Personal Loans

The purpose of a *short-term personal loan* is to remedy a deficiency when income is temporarily lower than expenditure. Sources include:

- *bank overdrafts*, where a borrowing limit is agreed on a current account;
- *credit cards*, such as Access or Barclaycard, or company specific cards such as Marks and Spencer Chargecard;
- *credit accounts*, where the purchaser pays a regular monthly amount to the retailer and can purchase items to a value in excess of the total amount saved.

Tasks

(i)   Collect details of credit accounts from a number of retailers and construct a bar chart showing the different interest rates by company.

(ii)   Write an short article for a students' magazine explaining the problems associated with the use of credit cards.

1.2.7 Long-term Personal Loans

The purpose of a *long-term personal loan* is to purchase an expensive item which otherwise could not be afforded. Sources include:

- a *personal loan* from a bank or building society to buy such items as a car, a boat or sports equipment;
- *hire purchase*, which is usually arranged by the retailer selling the goods;
- a *mortgage*, which is usually used to purchase a house or flat.

Task

Identify an expensive item of sports or leisure equipment you would like to own and calculate the difference in cost between an outright cash purchase and hire purchase over one, two and three years.

1.2.8 Annual Percentage Rate

The flat rate of interest on a loan is not the true rate of interest because of the timing of repayments. The true rate of interest is much higher. *The Consumer Credit Act 1974* (Section 3.8.6) requires all those who make credit available to the public to show in their advertisements, brochures and other literature the true *annual percentage rate (APR) of interest* .

> **Task**
>
> Compare the APR of various forms of credit and suggest why they may vary.

1.2.9 Income Tax

Different rates of *income tax* are charged according to the level of income received. There is a threshold below which no income tax is chargeable. Income includes pay, bonuses, tips, pensions, interest from investments etc. Anyone with a high enough income, whether working or not, is liable.

Personal allowances are announced by the Chancellor of the Exchequer in the government's annual budget. *Mortgage Interest Relief at Source (MIRAS)* is a system under which mortgage repayments are automatically adjusted for basic rate tax relief.

Tax avoidance is the term used to describe the legal arrangement of financial affairs in order to minimise liability to tax. *Tax evasion* is the term used to describe an illegal attempt to evade tax.

> **Task**
>
> Identify separately the advantages of taxation to both the individual and society.

1.2.10 Tax Forms and Documents

Tax returns are sent annually to individuals by the Inland Revenue and must be completed and returned within 30 days.

Tax tables are supplied by the Inland Revenue to employers to allow the correct deduction of tax. Each tax payer is issued with *Notice of Coding* which gives details of the tax allowances given by the Inland Revenue and the code the employer should use to when calculating the amount to be deducted.

Form P45 is given to the employee by the employer when employment is terminated and gives details of earnings, tax and other deductions in that employment, together with the employee's tax code. *Form P60* is given to the employee by the employer at the end of each tax year and gives details of earnings, tax and other deductions in that employment for that particular tax year.

> **Task**
>
> What are the main personal allowances currently given? What changes would you wish to see in personal allowances and why?

1.2.11 Other Deductions

Apart from income tax, a number of other legally required contributions and deductions, some of which are voluntary, are made from earnings. These include:

- *National Insurance Contributions* at different rates according to level of income and employment status, which are legally required from all employed and self-employed persons;

- *superannuation* contributions, which may be due if the employer operates a contributory pension scheme;
- *union membership* subscription, which may be payable if the employer operates a check-off system.

Task

Design a questionnaire to ascertain people's interest in and knowledge of pension schemes.

1.2.12 Types of Organisational Finance

Type of finance	Source	Example of purpose
Long-term (20 years +)	Mortgage	Purchase of business premises
	Venture capital	Purchase of new technology
Medium-term	Hire purchase	Purchase of cars
	Lease	Lease of plant and machinery
	Loan	Improvements to premises
Short-term	Factoring	Credit to customers
	Overdraft	Short-term cash deficit

Task

Collect brochures from a number of banks on the different types of loans offered. Classify each scheme according to its suitability for different purposes.

1.2.13 Sources of Organisational Finance

These include:

- *banks* which offer businesses mortgages, overdrafts and both medium and long-term loans, usually at different rates to personal borrowers;
- *venture capitalists* who offer finance in excess of 100,000 to sound businesses for a high rate of return;
- *hire purchase* agreements with retailers which are available to both individuals and organisations to buy such items as cars and equipment;
- *factoring organisations* (and some banks) offer a service whereby debts owed by customers to a business are taken over for a fee.

Limited companies can raise finance by issuing shares and small businesses in particular may be able to obtain funds from local and central government operated schemes.

Internal finance can sometimes be obtained by a department or subsidiary of an organisation from another division.

Tasks

(i)   Prepare a publicity brochure to explain the features and advantages of factoring.

(ii)   Design a leaflet giving the main details of government assistance schemes available in your area.

Use a desktop publishing package to produce the brochure and leaflet.

1.2.14 Cash Flow

Cash flows in and out of an organisation. The term *cash* includes coins, bank notes and cheques, which can be held as cash within the organisation or in an account.

Cash in (receipts) is *positive cash flow*. Cash out (expenditure) is *negative cash flow*. The difference between cash in and out is *net cash flow*. More cash in than out results in a *cash surplus*. More cash out than in results in a *cash deficit*.

A *cash flow forecast* is a financial statement which:

• predicts the amount of cash coming in and out;

• identifies the timing of cash flows;

• can be used for planning and control;

• is an essential management tool for *business plans*.

Task

Suggest what difficulties may arise when predicting the timing of cash flows and how they can be overcome.

1.2.15 Constructing a Cash Flow Forecast

A *cash flow forecast* can be constructed by drawing a matrix showing time intervals across the top of the columns and dividing the rows into detailed headings under *Cash in* and *Cash out*. The amounts and times of cash flows are entered allowing the monthly and cumulative cash position to be calculated.

Example

Keith Whitaker has a business supplying and erecting garden fencing. He has £1,200 in his business account at 31 December 1990 and is owed £780 by his customers for sales during that month. He owes £370 to his trade suppliers for goods in November and £240 for December. He has a telephone bill of £84 outstanding which he intends to pay in January.

He estimates that his turnover for the first quarter of 1991 will be £800 per month, rising to £950 per month for the second quarter. His normal credit allowed is one month. He is planning to sell garden ornaments on a commission basis and hopes to receive £50 per month from this venture starting in January.

He estimates that his purchases each month will be £440 and he obtains two months' credit from his suppliers. He rents storage space at £75 per quarter, payable at the end of each quarter. His next telephone bill, estimated at £90, is due in March and he expects to pay it in April. His transport expenses total £100 per month and are payable in the month in which they occur. In addition he has miscellaneous expenses of £18 per month also payable in the month in which they occur. His annual insurance premium of £500 falls due in March.

Monthly cash flow forecast for Keith Whitaker for the six months ending 30 June 1991

	Jan £	Feb £	Mar £	Apr £	May £	Jun £	Total £
Cash in:							
Turnover	780	800	800	800	950	950	5,080
Commission	50	50	50	50	50	50	300
Subtotal	830	850	850	850	1,000	1,000	5,380
Cash out:							
Goods	370	240	440	440	440	440	2,370
Insurance	–	–	500	–	–	–	500
Storage	–	–	75	–	–	75	150
Telephone	84	–	–	90	–	–	174
Transport	100	100	100	100	100	100	600
Miscellaneous	18	18	18	18	18	18	108
Subtotal	572	358	1,133	648	558	633	3,902
Balance b/f	1,200	1,458	1,950	1,667	1,869	2,311	1,200
Monthly surplus/ (deficit)	258	492	(283)	202	442	367	1,478
Balance c/f	1,458	1,950	1,667	1,869	2,311	2,678	2,678

Task

Poppy Patel opens a market stall on 1 January selling dried flowers. She estimates that all the sales will be for cash and will average £600 a month for the first three months and £900 per month thereafter.

The cost of the flowers and other materials will be 60 per cent of the monthly sales figure per month; the supplier will allow one month's credit. The rent of the stall will be £1,200 per annum, payable quarterly in advance on the first of each quarter. Advertising will cost £200 in the first month and £25 per month subsequently, payable within the month. Miscellaneous expenses will be £30 per month for the first quarter and £45 per month thereafter, paid two months after the month in which they were incurred.

How much cash will be available at the end of each month for Poppy Patel?

Assignment 1.2: A windfall

You have won £10,000 and intend to invest it for three years, after which you hope to buy a sports car. There are a number of alternative investments you might choose, but you have reduced them to the following:

1. *Invest the money in a building society for three years.*

2. *Invest the money in an existing business for three years.* A relative has a successful business and has offered you 12 per cent compound interest to invest your windfall in his business for three years, with his house as security.

3. *Invest the money in a new business for three years.* A family friend intends to start a business manufacturing and selling water filters on 1 January and is looking for additional sources of finance. He already has £30,000 capital to invest. He has offered to pay you simple interest at a rate of 20 per cent per annum, payable at the end of each year. The main items in his business plan are:
   - Purchase of equipment: £21,000 to be paid on 1 January.
   - Factory rent: £6,000 per annum, payable quarterly at the start of each quarter.
   - Overheads: £2,500 per month, payable in the month following the month in which they are incurred.
   - Materials: £4,000 per month for the first quarter, increasing to £5,000 from April. Suppliers allow one month's credit.
   - Wages and salaries: £5,000 per month for the first six months, increasing to £6,000 per month from July, payable in the month in which they occur.
   - Sales: £12,000 per month for the first quarter, increasing to £15,000 per month from April. Customers are given two months' credit.

Student activities

(i) Collect information on building society accounts and decide which would be the most suitable for the investment of your windfall.

(ii) Calculate the total amount of your investment at the end of the first year under Alternative 2.

(iii) Construct a cash flow forecast for Alternative 3 to ascertain whether the business will have sufficient cash to pay interest and repay the loan and the end of the three years.

(iv) Decide where you would invest the simple interest you would receive each year under Alternative 3.

(v) Compare the three alternatives and select the investment you consider is most suitable for your windfall and give your reasons.

1.3 Recording Financial Information

1.3.1 Prime Documents

The transactions undertaken by a business generate documents, known as *prime documents*, which serve as the basis for entries made in the books of accounts. They include sales invoices, purchase invoices and cheque counterfoils.

Task

Collect some examples of prime documents. Identify the information that will be recorded in the accounts of the business.

1.3.2 Double Entry Bookkeeping

Traditionally accounts were recorded in large leather volumes known as *ledgers*, but today many businesses use computerised accounting systems. Whether manual or computerised, ledger accounts are normally maintained using a system of *double entry bookkeeping*.

Under this system every business transaction is recorded twice in the ledger accounts, a separate account being kept for each person, firm, liability or expense. Every debit entry is matched by a credit entry. Thus, at the end of the financial period the total of the debit entries equals the total of the credit entries as show by the trial balance (Section 1.3.8).

The rules of double entry bookkeeping are:

- *asset and expense accounts* show an increase by debiting the accounts and a decrease by crediting them;
- *liability, capital and revenue accounts* show an increase by crediting the accounts and a decrease by debiting them.

Example

During the month of January the following transactions take place:

1 January	Started business with £500 cash
1 January	Sales of £450 for cash
10 January	Sales of £290 to Arthur Brown on credit
15 January	Purchases of £330 from Lesley Stone on credit
18 January	Cash purchase of stationery for £35
21 January	Received part-payment of £90 from Arthur Brown
25 January	Cash payment of £200 to Lesley Stone as part-payment
28 January	Sales of £85 to Nigel Dean on credit

Sales account

		£			£
Jan 31	Balance c/d	825	Jan 1	Cash	450
			Jan 10	Arthur Brown	290
			Jan 31	Nigel Dean	85
		825			825
			Feb 1	Balance b/d	825

Cash account

		£			£
Jan 1	Capital	500	Jan 18	Stationery	35
Jan 1	Sales	450	Jan 25	Lesley Stone	200
Jan 21	Arthur Brown	90	Jan 31	Balance c/d	805
		1,040			1,040
Feb 1	Balance b/d	805			

Capital account

		£			£
			Jan 1	Cash	500

Arthur Brown

		£			£
Jan 10	Sales	290	Jan 21	Cash	90
			Jan 31	Balance c/d	200
		290			290
Feb 1	Balance b/d	200			

Purchases account

		£			£
Jan 15	Lesley Stone	330	Jan 31 Balance c/d		330
		330			330
Feb 1	Balance b/d	330			

Lesley Stone

		£			£
Jan 25	Cash	200	Jan 15	Purchases	330
Jan 31	Balance c/d	130			
		330			330
			Feb 1	Balance b/d	130

Stationery account

		£			£
Jan 18	Cash	35	Jan 31	Balance c/d	35
		35			35
Feb 1	Balance b/d	35			

Nigel Dean

		£			£
Jan 28	Sales	85	Jan 31	Balance c/d	85
		85			85
Jan 31	Balance b/d	85			

Trial balance as at 31 January

	Dr	Cr
	£	£
Sales		825
Cash	805	
Capital		500
Arthur Brown	200	
Purchases	330	
Lesley Stone		130
Stationery	35	
Nigel Dean	85	
	1,455	1,455

Task

Using the data in the task in Section 1.2.15, draw up the appropriate accounts using the double entry bookkeeping system.

1.3.3 Books of Prime Entry

As it is not practical to enter every transaction individually in the general ledger and therefore books of *prime entry* are used. These group together and summarise similar transactions, thus providing subtotals which can be entered in the general ledger, usually at monthly intervals. The books of prime entry are not part of the double entry bookkeeping system and can be manual or computerised. They comprise:

- the *sales day book* which lists sales invoices and gives the total sales;
- the *sales return day book* which lists credit notes issued and gives the total sales returns;
- the *purchase day book* which lists purchase invoices and gives the total purchases;
- the *cash book* which lists cash receipts and payments and any cash discounts received or allowed.

Task

Draw a diagram of a simple accounting system.

1.3.4 The Cash Book and Bank Reconciliation

Cash receipts and payments are recorded in a *cash book* which is a book of prime entry and part of the double entry bookkeeping system. The cash book is balanced regularly and the closing balances confirmed. Any deficiencies should be investigated immediately. These may be due to:

- omission of entries in the cash book;
- incorrect entries in the cash book;
- incorrect addition;
- theft or loss of cash.

Standard cash books can be bought from stationers. However, in some cases it is necessary to have the cash book specifically designed to meet the business's needs. Alternatively the business may use an accounting software package and keep the cash book on a computer.

Example

Angela Price starts a business on 1 January and the transactions for the first month are as follows.

January	1	£5,000 paid into a bank account by Angela Price
January	5	Pays office rent of £1,000 by cheque
January	8	Bought office furniture for £600 by cheque
January	12	Received £750 cheque from client
January	15	Paid £940 by cheque for advertising
January	21	Received £350 cash from client
January	21	Paid £200 cash into bank
January	24	Bought stationery for £120 cash
January	28	Paid £480 for advertising by cheque
January	28	Took £150 cash from bank for business use
January	31	Received £400 cheque from client
January	31	Paid electricity bill of £180 by cheque

Cash book

RECEIPTS				PAYMENTS			
Date	Details	Cash	Bank	Date	Details	Cash	Bank
		£	£			£	£
Jan 1	Capital		5,000	Jan 5	Rent		1,000
Jan 12	Sales		750	Jan 8	Office furniture		600
Jan 21	Sales	350		Jan 15	Advertising		940
Jan 21	Cash (contra)		200	Jan 21	Bank (contra)	200	
Jan 28	Bank (contra)	150		Jan 24	Stationery	120	
Jan 31	Sales		400	Jan 28	Advertising		480
				Jan 28	Cash (contra)		150
				Jan 31	Electricity		180
				Jan 31	Balances c/d	180	3,000
		500	6,350			500	6,350
Feb 1	Balances b/d	180	3,000				

A **bank reconciliation** is constructed to explain the differences between the bank balance as shown in the cash book and that shown on the bank statement. These may occur for the following reasons:

- errors in the cash book or on the bank statement;
- items recorded in the cash book but not on the bank statement;
- items shown on the bank statement but not in the cash book;
- timing differences.

The procedure for drawing up a bank reconciliation is as follows:

- Tick the cash book entries against those on the bank statement.
- Correct any errors in the cash book and recalculate the balance.
- Identify timing differences.
- Draw up the bank reconciliation statement.

Example

At the end of January Angela Price's bank statement showed a balance of £3,260. Investigation revealed that the cheque for £400 received on 31 January had not yet been processed and the cheques paid on 28 and 31 January for £480 and £180 had not yet been presented.

Bank reconciliation statement for Angela Price
for the month of January

	£
Balance as per bank statement	3,260
Add lodgements uncleared	400
	3,660
Less cheques unpresented	660
Balance as per the cash book	3,000

Task

Maintain a personal cash book of your financial transactions for next month and draw up a bank reconciliation statement at the end of the month.

1.3.5 Ledger Accounts

The main **ledger accounts** are:

- the **purchase** (or **bought**) **ledgers** and the **sales ledgers** which contain the personal accounts of firms, companies and individuals;
- the **general ledger** which contains real and property accounts such as stock, premises and machinery;
- the **nominal ledger** which contains accounts such as wages, electricity and commission received.

In a business of any size it is impossible to enter every individual debtor and trade creditor balance in the *trial balance* (Section 1.3.8). To overcome this *control accounts* are used. The balances on the control accounts represent the total trade debtors and the total trade creditors. Control accounts are part of the double entry bookkeeping system and the purchase and sales ledgers containing the individual customers' accounts are supporting records of transactions.

Task

Write an instructional leaflet for use by new clerks, explaining control accounts.

1.3.6 The Journal

The *journal* is a book of prime entry used to keep a record of the unusual entries made in the general ledger, which cannot conveniently be entered in any other book of prime entry. Such unusual entries include correction of errors, sales of fixed assets or bad debts which are to be written off.

The procedure is as follows:

- Each entry is dated.
- The general ledger code numbers of the relevant accounts are placed in the folio column.
- The title of the accounts and an explanation for the entry appears in the accounts column.
- The debit and credit columns are totalled for each entry to ensure that they agree.

Example

On December 31 a new office desk was purchased for £480 from Excel Supplies on credit. On the same date it was discovered that an earlier purchase of an office chair for £95 had been charged to stationery.

	Journal		
		£	£
Dec 31	Office Furniture Account	480	
	Excel Suppliers		480
	being purchase of new office desk		
Dec 31	Office Furniture Account	95	
	Stationery Account		95
	being correction of earlier entry		
	debiting purchase of office chair		
	to Stationery Account		

Task

On 31 March 1991 a business sells unwanted office equipment for £285 and writes off a debt owing from N Dawson of £75. Write up the journal and show the entries in the ledger accounts.

1.3.7 Accruals and Prepayments

As mentioned in Section 1.1.7, *the profit and loss account* is drawn up on an *accruals* basis. At the end of the financial period every item of expense recorded in the books is reviewed to ascertain whether any entries relate to future periods (*prepayments*) or any expenses have been incurred which have not yet been recorded (*accruals*).

The balance of prepayments is carried forward from the credit to the debit side of the expense account. It appears as a debit item in the trial balance and as a current asset in the balance sheet. The balancing figure remaining in the expense account appears as a debit item in the trial balance and is transferred to the profit and loss account.

The balance of accruals is carried forward on the expense account from the debit to the credit side. It appears as a credit item (accrual) in the trial balance and as a creditor due within one year in the balance sheet. The balancing figure on the expense account appears as a debt item in the trial balance and is transferred to the profit and loss account.

Task

A business makes up its accounts to 31 December 1991. Make the necessary entries for the following transactions.

- Annual charge of £1,000 for rent paid to 31 March 1992.
- Last quarterly insurance premium of £250 paid to 30 September 1991.

1.3.8 Trial Balance

A *trial balance* is a summary of all the balances in the ledger accounts, and is made at the end of the financial period. It is not part of the double entry bookkeeping system and is simply drawn up to check the accuracy of the credit and debit balances in the general ledger. From the trial balance a *trading and profit and loss* account and *balance sheet* can be prepared. Even though the trial balance may balance, hidden errors may be present, including errors arising in the prime documents.

Reasons for a trial balance failing to balance include:

- omission of entries from the ledger accounts;
- incorrect entries from the ledger accounts;
- incorrect balances brought forward from the previous period;
- the trial balance has been miscast;
- a ledger account has been miscast;
- incorrect addition.

After the trial balance has been prepared there are normally a number of adjustments to be made for transactions which have not yet gone through the books. It is important to ensure that these items are reflected twice in the final accounts. A good examination discipline is to tick each item on the trial balance and the adjustments when is it used in the final accounts. If every figure is correctly treated, each item in the trial balance will be ticked once and each adjustment will be ticked twice.

Example

The following is Nick Williams' year end trial balance. He is a sole trader.

Trial balance as at 31 December 1990

	Dr £	Cr £
Capital		20,000
Sales		51,000
Purchases	18,000	
Stock at 1 January 1990	4,000	
Salaries	14,500	
Insurance	1,500	
Fixed assets at cost	32,000	
Provision for depreciation		8,000
Debtors	6,600	
Drawings	6,000	
Creditors		5,200
Administration expenses	1,200	
Cash	400	
	84,200	84,200

Adjustments required:
Accruals on administration expenses of £200
Prepayments on insurance of £300
Bad debts written off of £400
Stock at 31 December 1990 of £6,000
Depreciation at 10 per cent on cost

Nick Williams
Trading and profit and loss account
for the year ending 31 December 1990

	£	£
Sales		51,000
Less cost of goods sold:		
Opening stock	4,000	
Purchases	18,000	
	22,000	
Less closing stock	6,000	16,000
Gross profit	35,000	
Less expenses:		
Salaries	14,500	
Insurance	1,200	
Administration expenses	1,400	
Bad debts	400	
Depreciation	3,200	20,700
Net profit		14,300

Balance sheet as at 31 December 1990

	£	£	£
Fixed assets		32,000	
Less depreciation		11,200	20,800
Current assets:			
Stock		6,000	
Debtors		6,200	
Prepayments		300	
Cash		400	
		12,900	
Current liabilities:			
Creditors	5,200		
Accruals	200	5,400	7,500
Capital employed			28,300
Represented by:			
Opening capital		20,000	
Add profit		14,300	
		34,300	
Less drawings		6,000	
Closing capital			28,300

Task

Identify the errors which can arise but will not be revealed by the trial balance.

Assignment 1.3: The new clerk

You have just been appointed as a clerk in an office and one of your duties is to maintain a simple bookkeeping system. This topic was not your strongest point as a student and you realise that you will have to do some revision before you start work. You consider it would be useful to have an aide memoire by your side when you start work.

Student activities

(i)   Revise double entry bookkeeping by identifying the main principles and those areas where you have particular difficulty.

(ii) Design a word-processed, two-page leaflet which will help you when you commence work.

(iii) Exchange leaflets with a fellow student and both of you suggest where improvements can be made.

1.4 The Main Financial Statements

1.4.1 Trading and Profit and Loss Account

A *trading and profit and loss account* records the financial performance of a business over a period of time. It can be constructed for any financial period, such as a week or a month, but it should always be drawn up for the financial year. The heading of the statement should always refer to the period covered.

The first part of a trading and profit and loss account calculates the *gross profit*. This is the difference between the sales and the costs incurred in putting the goods in a saleable condition in the financial period. In the second part of the statement the *net profit* is calculated by deducting from the gross profit all other costs incurred in the period. Any revenue earned in the period other than from main trading, such as commission or rent, is added to the gross profit before deducting the other costs.

The *cost of sales adjustment* is calculated to ensure that only the cost of goods actually sold is deducted from the turnover when arriving at the figure of gross profit. This entails adding the purchase of goods for the period to the opening stock and then deducting the closing stock to arrive at the cost of sales. The layout is as follows:

	£	£
Revenue		x
Cost of sales:		
Opening stock	x	
Add purchases	x	
Less closing stock	x	x
Gross profit		x

Tasks

Insert the missing figures in the following table:

	(i)	(ii)	(iii)	(iv)	(v)
Opening stock	100	?	550	27	970
Purchases	300	2,000	?	159	?
Closing stock	?	200	350	34	150
Cost of sales	350	2,400	2,350	?	11,920

1.4.2 Balance Sheet

The *balance sheet* is a statement of the financial position of a business at one point in time. It can be drawn up at any date but should always be prepared for the financial year end. The heading of the statement should always refer to the date for which it has been prepared.

The balance sheet is based on the accounting equation which states:

$$\text{Assets} = \text{capital} + \text{liabilities}$$

Assets are the resources owned by the business, such as land, buildings, machinery, stock and cash. *Capital* is the money invested by the owners of the business. *Liabilities* are the amounts owed by the business to long-term lenders such as banks, and short-term lenders such as trade creditors.

A balance sheet can be drawn up in a horizontal format. In the following example the structure and main headings are those used for a sole trader (Section 3.1.1).

Name of sole trader

Balance sheet as at (date)

	£		£	£
Fixed assets	x	Capital	x	
Current assets	x	Add profit	x	
			—	
			x	
		Less drawings	x	x
			—	
		Current liabilities		x
	—			—
	x			x
	==			==

The next example shows how the above balance sheet can be drawn up in a vertical form. This format is more usually adopted, particularly for *limited companies* (Sections 1.4.4 and 3.1.3).

Name of sole trader

Balance sheet as at (date)

	£	£
Fixed assets		x
Current assets	x	
Less current liabilities	x	
	—	
Net current assets		x
		—
Capital employed		x
		==
Represented by:		
Capital at start of year	x	
Add profit for year	x	
	—	
	x	
Less drawings	x	
	—	
Closing capital		x
		==

Tasks

Insert the missing figures in the following table:

	Assets	Capital	Liabilities
	£	£	£
(i)	?	3,000	2,000
(ii)	14,000	?	5,500
(iii)	750	350	?
(iv)	12,100	?	6,075
(v)	?	6,150	4,230

1.4.3 Partnership Accounts

In the absence of any agreement between the partners, the provisions of the *Partnership Act 1890* (Section 3.1.2) apply. The trading and profit and loss account and the balance sheet for a *partnership* follow the same principles and concepts as for a sole trader. The additional items shown are:

- *Salaries* paid to partners are not tax deductible and should be shown in the *appropriation account* rather than in the trading profit and loss account.

- *Interest on partners' capital,* which is a preferential allocation of the divisible profits, must be shown in the appropriation account.

- *Interest on partners' loans* above the agreed capital should be shown as an item in the main trading and profit and loss account.

- *Interest on drawings* is added to the net profit in the appropriation account.

- *Capital and current accounts* are normally maintained. The capital account is not altered unless there are changes in agreed capital contributions. The current accounts are used to show the adjustments arising from the appropriation account.

The procedure for preparing the *trading and profit and loss account* for a partnership is:

- Construct a trading and profit and loss account as for a sole trader.
- Carry the final net profit down to an appropriation account.
- Add any interest on drawings to the net profit figure.
- Deduct from this any partnership salaries or interest paid on capital.
- Divide the balance of the profit between the partners in the agreed ratio.

The procedure for preparing the *balance sheet* for a partnership is:

- Construct a balance sheet as for a sole trader.
- Show the partners' individual capital account balances.
- Show the partners' current accounts, commencing with the opening balance and giving details of all the items arising from the appropriation account.

Task

Pine & Tweedie are in partnership. In their first year, which ended on 31 December 1990, they made a net profit of £37,000. Pine has invested £8,000 capital in the partnership and Tweedie 12,000. Interest is paid at ten per cent. Each partner has made drawings of £8,000 and interest charged on drawings was £650 each. Pine receives a salary of £20,000 and profits and losses are shared equally. Prepare the appropriation account for the partnership and the partners' individual current accounts.

1.4.4 Limited Company Accounts

The trading and profit and loss account and the balance sheet of a *limited company* must be constructed in accordance with the provisions of the *Companies Act 1985* (Section 3.1.3), Statements of Standard Accounting Practice and, for listed companies, Stock Exchange regulations (Section 1.1.9).

The trading and profit and loss account and balance sheet for a limited company follow the same principles and concepts as for a sole trader. The additional items shown are:

- *share capital*, which is the amount subscribed by shareholders and is shown on the balance sheet at the nominal value;

- *debentures*, which are formal loans made to the company and the interest is charged to the profit and loss account (debentures normally appear on the balance sheet as a long-term liability);

- *dividends*, which are recommended by the company's directors (most dividends are shown as an appropriation);

- *corporation tax*, which is paid by limited companies (this figure is usually estimated at the time the final accounts are prepared).

Task

Obtain a copy of the published accounts of a limited company. Compare the structure of the balance sheet with the example given for a sole trader in Section 1.4.2. Explain the differences.

1.4.5 Public Sector Organisation Accounts

There are various types of *public sector organisation* (Section 3.1.7). *Local authorities* must publish an income and expenditure account annually for each of their main funds; for example the general rate fund, loans fund, superannuation find. In addition they must also publish a balance sheet for the combined funds.

The requirements for *nationalised corporations* are similar to those for limited companies; they must publish a trading and profit and loss account and a balance sheet. The main difference is that some nationalised corporations wholly or partly use *current value accounting* (Section 1.1.8). The accounts of nationalised corporations are published by HMSO.

The National Health Service is an example of a *central government organisation* and receives most of its funding from central government. Allocations are made to the regional health authorities for capital and revenue expenditure and expenditure is recorded on an *as incurred* basis.

Task

Obtain a copy of the accounts of any public sector organisation and compare them with those of a limited company. Explain the main differences in the content and structure.

1.4.6 Receipts and Payments Accounts

A club or society is usually formed for recreational and non-profit making purposes. The organisation may have many members and the main financial transactions are collecting subscriptions and paying expenses. These transactions are carried out by a *treasurer* who is usually unpaid.

It is normal for the treasurer to present an annual financial statement to the members, usually at the annual general meeting. This might be a *receipts and payments account* in which the following items are shown:

- balance of cash in hand and at the bank at the beginning of the year;
- cash receipts during the year, analysed by their source;
- cash payments made during the year, analysed by their nature;
- balance of cash in hand and at the bank at the end of the year.

The main points to note on a receipts and payment account are:

- It is prepared on a cash basis rather than an accruals basis.
- No distinction is made between capital expenditure and revenue expenditure.
- No balance sheet is prepared to give a full view of the financial position.

Because of the deficiencies of a receipts and payment account, a number of clubs and societies produce an *income and expenditure account and balance sheet*, using the same principles as the trading and profit and loss account and balance sheet used by a sole trader (Sections 1.4.1 and 1.4.2). As clubs and societies do not trade for profit, the balance sheet does not show capital but *accumulated fund*. This is the value of the net assets at any one time.

Task

Write a memo to a club treasurer advocating the merits of producing an income and expenditure account. Explain what steps should be taken to convert a receipts and payments account to an income and expenditure account.

1.4.7 Sources and Application of Funds Statement

Statement of Standard Accounting Practice 10 requires that the audited financial accounts of limited companies, other than those with a turnover of less than 25,000 per annum, include a *statement of sources and application of funds (funds flow statement)*. It shows the sources from which the business has obtained its funds during the financial period and how these funds were used. It is constructed from information contained in the balance sheets of the current and previous financial periods, and the profit and loss account for the current period.

Sources from internal operations should be distinguishable from external sources of funds; long and short-term sources of funds should also be differentiated. The main headings are:

- Net profit for the year
- Depreciation charged during the year
- Proceeds from sale of fixed assets
- Increases in capital
- Proceeds from sales of investments
- Increases in loans

The application of funds must show the detail of increases or decreases in working capital. The main headings are:

- Capital/shares repaid or redeemed
- Loans repaid
- New fixed assets purchased
- Dividends paid or drawings
- Taxation
- Increase/decrease in working capital

The difference between the sources of funds and their application results in an increase or decrease in *net liquid funds*. This is the final line of the statement. Net liquid funds are cash and cash-equivalents, such as short-term investments and borrowings including bank overdrafts.

To record the movement of working capital correctly as a decrease or increase, the following rules should be applied:

- working capital increases if current assets increase and/or current liabilities decrease;
- working capital decreases if current assets decrease and/or current liabilities increase.

Example

The following balance sheets are for a sole trader, Helen Pugh.

Balance sheets as at	31.12.90	31.12.89
	£	£
Fixed assets	7,200	2,500
Less depreciation	800	250
	6,400	2,250
Current assets:		
Stock	14,100	7,500
Debtors	16,300	5,400
Bank	8,700	12,300
Less current liabilities	(9,300)	(6,500)
Capital employed	36,200	20,950

Balance sheets as at	31.12.90	31.12.89
	£	£
Represented by:		
Opening capital	20,950	18,150
Add new capital	5,000	–
	35,950	18,150
Add net profit	23,180	16,900
	59,130	35,050
Less drawings	22,930	14,100
Closing capital	36,200	20,950

Notes
1. No fixed assets are sold during the year.
2. Taxation is ignored.

Sources and application of funds statement
for the year ending 31 December 1990

	£	£
Sources of funds:		
Net profit for period	23,180	
Add back depreciation	550	
Total generated from operations		23,730
Funds from other sources:		
New capital introduced		15,000
		38,730
Application of funds:		
New fixed assets	4,700	
Drawings	22,930	27,630
		11,100
Increase/(decrease) in working capital:		
Increase in stocks	6,600	
Increase in debtors	10,900	
Decrease in creditors	(2,800)	
Decrease in cash	(3,600)	11,100

Task

Obtain a copy of the published accounts of a limited company. Using the profit and loss account and the balance sheet, draw up a funds flow statement. Compare your statement with the one published by the company.

Assignment 1.4: A letter from Devon

You have recently received the following letter from a friend.

Ye Olde Gift Shoppe   31 December 1991
3 High Street
Dartmouth
Devon

Dear Jo

I need your help! As you know, for the last year I have been running a gift shop. Now I have to let the taxman know what profit I have made. Can you please do the accounts for me from the following information?

The rent of the shop is £5,000 per annum. On top of that I pay £900 per quarter for heating and lighting, and the bill for the telephone for the year was £720, of which I still owe £140. My total sales for the year amounted to £53,430, but I am owed £6,000 and I expect ten per cent of that will have to be written off as bad debts.

During the year I bought £28,000 worth of goods and I still owe the suppliers £4,620. At the end of the year I had stock left worth £2,900. During the summer I employed temporary staff at a total cost of £930. I have also paid for advertising in the local press; this came to £1,640 and I still owe the newspapers £210. My annual bank charges came to £430 and I had miscellaneous expenses which amounted to £310.

I started the business with £5,000 and I've now got £7,000 in the business deposit account and an overdraft of £860.

I do hope you'll be able to help. Thanks in advance.

John

Student activities

Reply to John's letter enclosing the following:

(i)   a profit and loss account;

(ii) a balance sheet;

(iii) a list of further information you will require to be satisfied that your figures are as correct as possible;

(iv) recommendations on what system your friend should adopt to ensure adequate accounting records are kept in future and any suggestions you can make on how the financial management of the business might be improved.

1.5 Analysing and Interpreting Financial Statements

1.5.1 Ratio Analysis

Ratio analysis is a method of describing and interpreting the relationships of certain financial data which would otherwise be devoid of meaning. It allows comparisons to be made between companies of different sizes, a particular company and the industry average, and the same company over a period of time. Ratio analysis is used for the following purposes:

- to assess a company's financial performance;
- to evaluate the financial stability of a company;
- to predict the future performance and stability of a company.

However, there are a number of limitations:

- There are no agreed definitions of the terms used.
- Data drawn from different sources may not be comparable.
- The deficiencies in the historical cost profit and loss account and the balance sheet are reflected in the ratios.

The following data extracted from the profit and loss account and the balance sheet of a company will be used to illustrate the calculation of the ratios.

	£'000
Turnover	191,302
Profit before interest and tax	15,874
Capital employed	101,272
Current assets	73,194
Current liabilities	55,800
Stock	20,980
Debtors	28,940

Task

Obtain a copy of the published accounts of a limited company. Identify any items on the profit and loss account and balance sheet that you consider are related.

1.5.2 Performance Ratios

There are a number of ratios which can be used to assess performance. In this section *return* is defined as profit before interest and tax; *capital employed* is defined as fixed assets plus current assets less current liabilities. The three main ratios are as follows.

The *prime ratio* measures the return on capital employed *(ROCE)*. The formula is:

$$\text{ROCE} = \frac{\text{Profit before interest and tax}}{\text{Capital employed}} \times 100$$

Using the data given in Section 1.5.1:

$$\text{ROCE} = \frac{15,874}{101,272} \times 100 = 15.7\%$$

The *profit margin* measures the return on sales (turnover). The formula is:

$$\text{Profit margin} = \frac{\text{Profit before interest and tax}}{\text{Sales}} \times 100$$

Using the data given in Section 1.5.1:

$$\text{Profit margin} = \frac{15,874}{191,302} \times 100 = 8.3\%$$

Capital turnover measures the level of activity of the business, as reflected in the sales, in relation to the capital invested. It is often expressed as the number of times rather than a percentage. The formula is:

$$\text{Capital turnover} = \frac{\text{Sales}}{\text{Capital employed}}$$

Using the data given in Section 1.5.1:

$$\text{Capital turnover} = \frac{191,302}{101,272} = 1.9 \text{ times}$$

Note that the profit margin multiplied by the capital turnover gives the prime ratio.

$$8.3\% \times 1.9 = 15.7\%$$

These three ratios are interrelated. A business can improve its prime ratio by reducing costs and/or raising prices, which will improve its profit margin, or increasing its sales volume and/or reducing its capital employed, which will improve its capital turnover.

Task

Ascertain which publications in your library give information on industry averages. Find the profit margins for six different industries and suggest reasons why they vary.

1.5.3 Liquidity Ratios

Liquidity ratios are intended to reflect the financial stability of a business and show how effectively the business is managing its working capital. The main ratios are set out below.

The *current test (working capital) ratio* , gives an overall view of the financial stability of a company. It is usually expressed as a ratio of x:1 rather than a percentage. In many industries there are benchmarks of what is considered acceptable. In general terms, if the ratio drops below 1.5:1 it may indicate illiquidity; a ratio of above 2:1 could indicate ineffective working capital management. However, it is essential to relate the ratio to the type of business and its trend over a period of time. The formula is:

$$\text{Current test ratio} = \frac{\text{Current assets}}{\text{Creditors: amounts due within one year}}$$

Using the data given in Section 1.5.1:

$$\text{Current test ratio} = \frac{73,194}{55,800} = 1.3:1$$

The *acid test (liquid capital) ratio* , is a more stringent test of liquidity than the current test ratio. A general dictum is that the ratio should not fall below 1:1. However, the type of business and the trend are all important.

The formula is:

$$\text{Acid test ratio} = \frac{\text{Current assets (excluding stock)}}{\text{Creditors: amounts due within one year}}$$

Using the data given in Section 1.5.1:

$$\text{Acid test ratio} = \frac{73,194 - 20,980}{55,800} = 0.94{:}1$$

The *debt collection period (credit) ratio*, measures the average time in days that debtors take to settle their accounts. It attempts to give an indication of the effectiveness of working capital management. The formula is:

$$\text{Debt collection period ratio} = \frac{\text{Debtors at the end of the year}}{\text{Sales}} \times 365$$

Using the data given in Section 1.5.1:

$$\text{Debt collection period ratio} = \frac{28,940}{191,302} \times 365 = 55 \text{ days}$$

Task

Suggest other ratios which might be constructed to permit an evaluation of the effectiveness of working capital management.

1.5.4 Gearing Ratios

Gearing is the relationship between the funds which have been borrowed to finance the business on which interest is payable and the investment by the shareholders. The figures for the *gearing ratio* are extracted from the balance sheet. This ratio gives an indication to bankers, lenders and shareholders of whether the company is over-geared. The formula is:

$$\text{Gearing ratio} = \frac{\text{Gross borrowing}}{\text{Shareholders' funds}} \times 100$$

The **income gearing ratio** analyses the relationship between interest charges and profit. It is usually calculated by expressing the interest charge as a proportion of the before-interest profit. The formula is:

$$\text{Income gearing ratio} = \frac{\text{Interest charges}}{\text{Profit before interest and tax}} \times 100$$

Task

Obtain a copy of the published accounts of a limited company. Calculate as many ratios as possible for two financial years. Suggest reasons for any changes in the ratios.

1.5.5 Investment Ratios

These relate a company's performance to the price of its shares. The most popular source of investment ratios is the Financial Times.

Earnings per share is the profit in pence attributable to each equity share. It is based on earnings which are the consolidated profit for the period after tax and the deduction of minority interest and preference dividends, but before extraordinary items. The figure for earnings is divided by the number of equity shares issued and ranking for dividend.

The *dividend yield* shows the return offered to an investor before income tax is deducted. The gross dividend is found by taking the net dividend and grossing up by the basic rate of income tax. The formula is:

$$\text{Dividend yield} = \frac{\text{Gross dividend per share}}{\text{Market price per share}} \times 100$$

Dividend cover is calculated by dividing the figure for profit after tax by the amount of the dividend payment. It demonstrates how secure the dividend payment is by showing the number of times it is covered by after-tax profit.

The *price earning (P/E) ratio* gives an indication of how highly investors value a company. The formula is:

$$\text{Price earnings ratio} = \frac{\text{Market price per share}}{\text{Earnings per share}}$$

Task

Obtain a copy of the latest published accounts of a limited company. Look up its share price in the Financial Times and show how the ratios have been calculated from the published accounts.

1.5.6 Mark Up and Gross Profit Margin

In retailing in particular, the gross profit figure is considered an essential feature of management control and a guide to pricing and purchasing policies. The *gross profit mark up* is an important ratio. The formula is:

$$\text{Gross profit mark up} = \frac{\text{Gross profit}}{\text{Cost of sales}} \times 100$$

The *gross profit margin*, also known as the *gross profit percentage*, is directed at the same activity. The formula is:

$$\text{Gross profit margin} = \frac{\text{Gross profit}}{\text{Sales}} \times 100$$

Because of the similarity of the ratios, it is important to remember that the mark up is where the gross profit is expressed as a percentage of the *cost of sales* and the gross profit margin is expressed as a percentage of *sales*.

Task

Calculate the gross profit mark up and the gross profit margins for the following:

	(i)	(ii)	(iii)	(iv)
	£	£	£	£
Sales	4,000	67,000	122,400	83,750
Cost of sales	1,000	49,000	97,310	61,420
Gross profit	3,000	18,000	25,090	22,330

Assignment 1.5: Trade union assistance

Your uncle is a shop steward in a company in the Manchester. His union members have asked him to give them a talk explaining the finances of the company, since there are rumours that some form of employee share purchase scheme is about to be launched.

He has enlisted your help in finding answers to the following questions he feels his talk should address:

- Is the company financially solvent?
- What is the dividend cover for the company and what does the term mean?
- What is the EPS for the company, what do these initials stand for and how is it calculated?
- What is the share price of the company? How has it fared over the last three months and how does that compare to the FT Index?
- Would you purchase shares in the company?

Student activities

(i) Obtain a set of published accounts of a quoted public limited company to represent your uncle's employer.

(ii) Calculate four accounting ratios for at least four years. Prepare flip charts or overheads for your uncle to use to explain the purpose of and interpret the ratios.

(iii) Prepare answers to the five questions, bearing in mind the likely level of financial sophistication of the audience.

(iv) Prepare a brief word processed handout covering the main points for distribution at the end of your uncle's talk.

1.6 Cost Classification and Control

1.6.1 Cost Units and Centres

Cost can be used as a verb or a noun. To cost means to calculate the cost of a specified thing or activity; a cost is the amount of actual or notional expenditure incurred on or attributable to a specified thing or activity.

The *output* of a business can be measured by devising some form of *cost unit*. This is a quantitative unit of the product or service in relation to which costs are allocated. The type of cost unit depends on the nature of the industry. A brick works, for example, may have a cost unit of 1,000 bricks; a hospital may have a cost unit of a patient-bed-occupied. In addition to attributing costs to cost units, they can be attributed to a cost centre. This may be a department, an item of equipment or an individual.

Task

Suggest appropriate cost units for the following businesses:
- a brewery
- an hotel
- a paint manufacturer
- a distribution company

1.6.2 Cost Classifications

The main *cost classifications* are:
- *direct costs*, which can be identified with a specific product or saleable service such as materials used in production, and *indirect costs*, which cannot be identified with any particular product or service but are shared, such as supervisors' salaries;
- *fixed costs*, which tend to remain the same in total irrespective of changes in the level of activity, and *variable costs*, which tend to change in total in direct proportion to changes in the level of activity;
- classification by the *nature* of costs such as material, labour and expenses, which can be further divided into such classifications as raw materials, maintenance materials, etc;
- classification by the *function* of costs such as production, administration, selling and distribution costs.

Task

Select an industry and suggest which of the above classifications the costs fall into.

1.6.3 Elements of Cost

The total *cost* of a product or service is built up as follows:

Direct materials which become part of the finished goods

plus

39

direct labour which converts direct materials into the finished goods

plus

direct expenses such as subcontracted work or special tools

gives the

prime cost

plus

production overheads which are the indirect costs
arising from the provision of the production resources

gives the

factory cost

plus

administration overheads, sales overheads and distribution
overheads which are the indirect costs analysed by function

gives the

total cost

Task

Select any well-known household item and describe the various elements of cost which may have been incurred in arriving at the total cost.

1.6.4 Costing for Materials

Materials represent a substantial cost in a business. The procedure for costing for materials should ensure that:

- the correct materials are delivered;
- materials are correctly stored and issued only with proper authorisation;
- production is charged with the cost of materials used;
- stored materials are correctly valued.

The main documents used are:

- a purchase requisition;
- a purchase order;
- a goods received note (GRN);
- a bin card and/or stock record card;
- a materials requisition note.

Although adequate records may be maintained, proper control is exercised through a physical examination and count of materials in store known as *stock-taking*. This may be periodic or continuous. In a perpetual inventory system a stores record card is maintained to give the quantity of each item in store as a balance after each issue and receipt has been physically checked.

Task

Draw a diagram showing the flow of documents used in controlling the movement of materials.

1.6.5 Pricing Material Issues

The main methods are:

- *first in, first out (FIFO)*, which uses the price of the first delivery of materials for all issues from store until that particular consignment has been exhausted, followed by the price of the subsequent consignment;

- *last in, first out (LIFO)*, which uses the price of the last delivery of materials for all issues from store until that particular consignment has been exhausted, followed by the price of the previous consignment;

- *replacement price method*, which uses the replacement price on the day of issue to value materials issued from store;

- *average price method*, which uses either a simple average or a weighted average price for all issues from store;

- *standard price method*, which uses a predetermined standard price for all issues and returns of materials from store.

Task

Show the difference in issue prices and stock valuation between FIFO and LIFO from the following data.

DATE	DETAILS
January 1	Received 200 kg of materials at £3.00 per kg
January 2	Received 250 kg of materials at £3.60 per kg
January 3	Issued 180 kg of materials
January 4	Issued 110 kg of materials

1.6.6 Costing for Labour

Labour costing is closely related to the method of remuneration operated by the organisation. Methods include:

- *time-based schemes*, where workers are paid a basic rate per hour;

- *performance-based (incentive) schemes*, where workers are paid on the basis of output;

- *straight piecework schemes*, where workers are paid an agreed amount for each unit produced or piecework time is paid for each unit produced;

- *premium bonus schemes*, where a time allowance is given for each job and a bonus is paid for any time saved.

The documents used in labour costing depend largely on the method of payment used. The main ones used are:

- *clock cards*, which record attendance time;
- daily or weekly *time sheets*, countersigned by a supervisor, which record how workers have spent their time;
- *job cards*, which refer to a batch or single job and record how long each task takes to pass through the production process;
- *piecework tickets*, which refer to each stage of manufacture.

Task

Describe two work situations where you consider it would be preferable to adopt the time rate method of remuneration rather than an incentive scheme.

Assignment 1.6: Leather losses

You have been appointed as a management trainee with a small company which manufactures high quality leather gifts. For a a number of years there have been high stock losses, both of raw materials and finished goods. The managing director has asked you for your views on how the problem should be investigated and to suggest a good system for controlling materials.

Student activities

Send a word processed report to Colin Eaves, the managing director, covering the following points:

(i)   the documentation to be used for controlling materials;

(ii) the requirements for effective store keeping and stock-taking;

(iii) possible methods for pricing material issues from store and your recommendation;

(iv) the possible reasons for the stock losses and how you suggest they should be investigated.

1.7 Financial Information for Decision-Making

1.7.1 Absorption Costing – Allocation and Apportionment

In absorption costing all the costs of an organisation are charged to the cost unit to arrive at the total cost (Section 1.6.3). Direct materials, labour and expenses can usually be identified with the cost unit by analysing invoices, store issue notes, time sheets etc. However, indirect overheads must be charged through a process of *allocation, apportionment* and *absorption*. If the exact amount is known, production overheads can be allocated to the cost centres incurring the overhead. If the overhead has been incurred by more than one cost centre, it should be apportioned between them in proportion to the estimated benefits received.

When all the production overheads have been charged to all the cost centres, service cost centres must be charged to the production cost centres. Where there are reciprocal services, with two or more services departments providing services to each other as well as to production cost centres, a suitable method of charging must be used. Under the *elimination* method the cost effects of their reciprocal services are ignored. Under the *repeated distribution (continuous allotment)* method, the overheads are continuously reapportioned to each service department until the amount remaining in any one service department is insignificant. Under the *algebraic* method an equation is constructed for each service department to show the total overhead cost for that department.

Task

Suggest what you consider to be a fair basis for apportioning the following overheads:

- rent;
- depreciation of machinery;
- supervisors' salaries;
- indirect materials;
- heat and light.

1.7.2 Absorption Costing – Bases of Absorption

The method of charging production cost centre overheads to the cost units that pass through them is known as *absorption*. An *overhead absorption rate* is calculated by taking the overhead for a particular cost centre and dividing it by the number of units of the absorption base. The budgeted overheads and the budgeted units of base are used to allow a predetermined overhead rate to be calculated at the beginning of a period and applied throughout. This usually leads to an under or over-absorption of overheads. The main absorption bases are:

Cost unit overhead absorption rate

$$\frac{\text{Production cost centre overheads}}{\text{Number of cost units}}$$

Direct labour hour overhead absorption rate

$$\frac{\text{Production cost centre overheads}}{\text{Number of labour hours}}$$

Machine hour overhead absorption rate

$$\frac{\text{Production cost centre overheads}}{\text{Number of machine hours}}$$

Direct wage percentage overhead absorption rate

$$\frac{\text{Production cost centre overheads}}{\text{Direct wages}} \times 100$$

Material cost percentage overhead absorption rate

$$\frac{\text{Production cost centre overheads}}{\text{Direct materials}} \times 100$$

Prime cost percentage overhead absorption rate

$$\frac{\text{Production cost centre overheads}}{\text{Prime cost}} \times 100$$

Once the overhead absorption rate has been calculated it can be applied to the cost unit. Non-production overheads, such as administration and selling, must also be charged to arrive at the total cost. Administration overheads can be apportioned between production and selling before the total production cost centre overhead is calculated. A *selling overhead absorption rate (SOAR)* can be calculated using the following formula:

$$\text{SOAR} = \frac{\text{Total selling overheads}}{\text{Total factory cost of sales}} \times 100$$

Task

In an assembly department a material cost percentage overhead absorption rate is currently used. Write a memo to the departmental manager recommending other absorption rates which might be adopted. Justify your proposals.

1.7.3 Marginal Costing

Marginal costing is a method by which only the variable or marginal costs of production are charged to cost units. The unit selling price less the unit variable costs gives the contribution per unit. The advantage of marginal costing over absorption costing is that it recognises that costs behave differently as activity changes. Total *fixed* costs tend to remain the same despite changes in levels of production or sales activity. Total *variable* costs tend to increase or decrease in line with production or sales activity. *Semi-variable* costs contain both fixed and variable cost elements and must be analysed so that the fixed cost elements can be added to other fixed costs and the variable cost elements to the other variable costs.

Marginal costing is useful for a number of short-term decisions including the following:

- setting the selling price of products, particularly in times of trade depression and when introducing new products;
- deciding whether it is preferable to manufacture a component or buy it;
- evaluating the proposed closure or temporary cessation of part of the business;
- deciding the value of accepting a special contract or order;
- comparing the cost implications of different methods of manufacture.

Example

L & M Grant Ltd manufactures models of the Tower of London for the tourist trade. The materials cost 60 p and the labour costs are 30 p per unit. The presentation boxes cost 15 p per unit. The selling price is £2.30 each. The total weekly overhead costs for the business are £850 per week. The normal weekly output is 1,000 units.

Marginal cost statement for one week

Output	1,000 units		Per unit	
	£	£	£	£
Sales		2,300		2.30
Variable costs:				
Materials	600		0.60	
Labour	300		0.30	
Packaging	150	1,050	0.15	1.05
Contribution		1,250		1.25
Less overheads		850		
Profit		400		

The break-even point is $\dfrac{£850}{1.25}$ = 680 models (approximately)

Task

Write a brief word processed report explaining why marginal costing is more useful than absorption costing for decision-making in a seasonal industry. Construct simple numerical examples to illustrate your argument.

1.7.4 Contribution and Limiting Factors

A *limiting factor* is a key factor which constrains the growth of an organisation. Examples are sales or shortages of materials or labour. The limiting factor should be identified and production arranged so that the contribution per unit of limiting factor is maximised. Alternative products should be *ranked* to show the most profitable using one of the following methods.

- *Ranking by contribution per unit:* If there is no limiting factor, the absolute size of the unit contribution can be used.

- *Ranking by profit/volume ratio:* If there is a maximum sales income which can be achieved from any of the alternative products, the profit/volume (P/V) ratio should be used. The formula is:

$$\frac{\text{Contribution}}{\text{Selling price}} \times 100$$

- *Ranking by total contribution*: If sales in units for alternate products are unequally limited, ranking should be by the total contribution.

- *Ranking by limiting factor*: If a limiting factor is in operation, the contribution per unit of limiting factor should be used for ranking.

Task

A company has a choice of manufacturing two products. Which product is most profitable if sales of £100,000 can be achieved of either Product A or Product B?

	Product A	Product B
	£	£
Selling price per unit	30	60
Direct materials per unit	10	25
Direct labour per unit	8	20

1.7.5 Break-Even Analysis

Break-even analysis is an extension of marginal costing and is used to identify the *break-even point* of a business; this is the level of activity where it makes neither a profit nor a loss. The break-even point can be determined graphically or by applying either of the following formulae:

$$\text{Break-even point in units} = \frac{\text{Total fixed costs}}{\text{Contribution per unit}}$$

$$\text{Sales value at break-even point} = \frac{\text{Total fixed costs} \times \text{sales value}}{\text{Total contribution}}$$

If the organisation has a specific target profit, the level of activity that will achieve it can be found by applying the following formula:

$$\text{Selected level of activity in units} = \frac{\text{Fixed costs} + \text{target profit}}{\text{Contribution per unit}}$$

The difference in activity levels between the break-even point and the selected level of activity is known as the *margin of safety*.

Break-even analysis makes the same assumptions about the behaviour of fixed and variable costs as marginal costing. These assumptions hold true only within a certain range of activity known as the *relevant range*. *Cost-volume-profit (C-V-P) analysis* is a term sometimes used instead of break-even analysis in order to emphasise the changes in the relationship between costs, volumes and profits at different levels of activity.

Task

A company manufactures a single product with a maximum production capacity of 3,000 units. The products sell at £21 each. Variable costs are £9 per unit and fixed costs are £18,000 for the financial period. Draw a graph to show the break-even point for the business and check the answer using the formula.

1.7.6 Capital Investment Appraisal

Organisations use a number of capital investment appraisal techniques to evaluate the financial worth of investing in long-term projects. The principal techniques are:

- *payback technique*, in which the payback period is calculated by predicting the cash inflows and cash outflows associated with the project, including the initial investment;

- *accounting rate of return (ARR)*, which is calculated by expressing the average profits after depreciation as a percentage of the capital invested;

- two main methods of calculating the *discounted cash flow*: *net present value (NPV)* and *internal rate of return (IRR)*, which both use cash flows. The main concept is the conversion of future cash flows into equivalent present time values, usually by using discount tables (Appendix B).

Task

A company has the choice of two project, each with a life span of four years. Both require an initial investment of £120,000. The discount rate is 10 per cent and the net cash flows for the two projects are as follows. Use NPV to select the best project.

Year	Project A £	Project B £
1	40,000	70,000
2	60,000	60,000
3	60,000	70,000
4	80,000	20,000

Assignment 1.7: Reducing prices and increasing costs

You are an assistant management accountant in a manufacturing company which uses absorption costing. The company has been suffering considerably in the economic recession. The production manager is worried because his total cost per unit is increasing despite the strict cost controls he exercises.

The marketing manager is complaining that in order to maintain sales volume, the selling price per unit must be reduced. This may take it lower than the increasing cost per unit.

Student activities

Write a word processed report addressed jointly to the production and marketing managers explaining:

(i)   why the total cost per unit increases as production decreases;

(ii) why marginal costing may be more appropriate than absorption costing for decision-making in times of recession;

(iii) what other accounting methods might assist the marketing manager in making decisions.

1.8 Financial Information for Planning and Control

1.8.1 Budgetary Control

Budgetary control is an accounting technique which assists in the *planning* and *control* of a business organisation. It requires the setting of departmental *budgets*. A budget is a quantitative and/or financial statement. It is prepared prior to the start of a financial period and sets out the objectives, activities and policies to be follow by management during that period. Through regular comparison of actual achievement against the budget, managers can see where action should be taken to achieve the original objective, or where revision of policy should take place.

Financial budgets on an accruals basis are prepared for the different functions in the organisation. Non-financial budgets for *capital expenditure* and *cash flow* are also prepared. The individual budgets are incorporated into a *master budget* which includes the *budgeted profit and loss account* and *budgeted balance sheet*.

Task

You have been asked by the local Chamber of Commerce to give a talk entitled Budgetary Control – Its Advantages and Limitations. Prepare suitable speech notes.

1.8.2 Types of Budget

A *fixed budget* is one which is established and not adjusted when actual activity levels differ from those set. A *flexible budget* is one which is established, but this type of budget is adjusted to allow for the behaviour of *variable costs* at different levels of actual and budgeted activity. A *zero-based budget* is prepared on the assumption that the function does not already exist. It is set by adding increments of cost and increments of benefit.

Task

Write a word processed report to Miss Christie, a departmental manager, recommending that she changes from a fixed budget to a flexible budget. Include some simple numerical examples in your report to reinforce your argument.

1.8.3 Standard Costing

Standard costing is a technique which allows the comparison of predetermined levels of costs and sales with the actual costs and sales achieved. Any *variances* can then be investigated. The predetermined costs are known as *standard costs*. These are the costs which are incurred under defined working conditions. It is usual to measure the time required to complete a certain volume of work in *standard hours or minutes*.

Any variances are analysed to reveal their constituent parts so that sufficient information is available to permit management investigation. *Favourable variances* are those which improve the predetermined profit. *Adverse variances* are those which reduce the predetermined profit.

Task

It has been established in a department that a hundred units can be made in one standard hour. In a eight-hour day, 950 units are produced. Will this give rise to a favourable or adverse variance? Suggest reasons for this being so.

1.8.4 Direct Material Variances

Standards are set for the quality and the quantity of material to be used for a specific volume of production and the price to be paid per unit of direct material. The total variance can be divided into a *usage variance* and a *price variance*. The *total direct material variance* is calculated using the following formula:

Total direct material variance = (Standard units × standard price) – (Actual units × actual price)

The *usage variance* is the difference between the standard quantity specified for the actual production and the actual quantity used at standard price. The formula is:

Usage variance = (Standard quantity for actual production × standard price)

– (Actual quantity × standard price)

The *price variance* is the difference between the standard and actual purchase price for the actual quantity of materials purchased or used in production. The formula is:

Price variance = (Actual quantity × standard price) – (Actual quantity × actual price)

Task

To produce one unit, a standard usage of 10 litres of direct material has been set with a standard price of £6.20 per litre. In the period, 80 units were made and 880 litres of material consumed at a cost of £5.95 per litre. Calculate all the relevant material variances and suggest possible reasons for them.

1.8.5 Direct Labour Variances

Standards are set for the rate per hour and the time required to complete a certain volume of work. This is usually measured in *standard hours or minutes*. The *total direct labour variance* formula is:

Total direct labour variance = (Standard direct labour hours produced × standard rate per hour)

– (Actual direct labour hours × actual rate per hour)

The total variance can be broken down into a *rate variance* and an *efficiency variance*. The *direct labour rate variance* is the difference between the standard and actual direct labour rate per hour for the actual hours worked. The formula is:

Direct labour rate variance = (Standard rate × actual hours) – (Actual rate × actual hours)

The *direct labour efficiency variance* is the difference between the actual production achieved, measured in standard hours, and the actual hours worked, valued at the standard labour rate. The formula is:

Direct labour efficiency variance = (Standard hours produced × standard rate per hour)

– (Actual hours worked × standard rate per hour)

Task

To make one unit, the standard hours are six and the standard rate is £8 per hour. The actual production is 900 units and this took 5,100 hours at a rate of £8.30 per hour. Calculate all the relevant labour variances and suggest possible reasons for them.

1.8.6 Overhead Variances

Fixed overheads are charged to production on the basis of the *fixed overhead absorption rate (FOAR)*, which is calculated from budgeted figures. The *fixed overhead total variance* is the difference between the standard cost of fixed overheads charged to production and the actual fixed overheads for the period. The formula is:

Fixed overhead total variance = (Standard hours production × FOAR) – Actual fixed overheads

The *fixed overhead expenditure variance* is the difference between the budgeted fixed overheads and the actual overheads incurred. The formula is:

Fixed overhead expenditure variance = Budgeted fixed overheads – Actual fixed overheads

The *fixed overhead volume variance* is the difference between the overheads absorbed in the production achieved and the budgeted fixed overheads for the period. The formula is:

Fixed overhead volume variance = (Standard hours production × FOAR) – Budgeted fixed overheads

Variable overheads fluctuate according to the level of production. Once the predetermined *variable overhead absorption rate (VOAR)* has been calculated, the original budget figures are no longer relevant.

The *variable overhead total variance* is the difference between the actual variable overheads incurred and the actual variable overheads absorbed for the period. The formula is:

Variable overhead total variance = (Standard hours production × VOAR) – Actual variable overheads

The *variable overhead expenditure variance* is the difference between the variable overheads allowed for the actual hours worked and the actual overheads incurred. The formula is:

Variable overhead expenditure variance = (Actual hours worked × VOAR) – Actual variable overheads

The *variable overhead efficiency variance* is the difference between the variable overheads allowed for the actual hours worked and the variable overheads absorbed in production. The formula is:

Variable overhead expenditure variance = (Actual hours worked × VOAR)

– (Standard hours production × VOAR)

Task

A company has the following budget:

Variable overheads	£200,000
Standard hours of production	40,000

The actual variable overheads for the period are 186,000 and 32,000 hours are actually worked to produce 38,000 standard hours of production. Calculate the relevant variances.

1.8.7 Sales Margin Variances

The *total sales margin variance* is the difference between the budgeted margin and the actual margin, the cost of sales being at the standard cost of production. The formula is:

Total sales margin variance = (Actual sales in units × actual margin per unit of sales)

– (Standard sales in units × standard margin per unit)

The *sales margin price variance* is the difference between the actual margin per unit and the standard margin per unit, multiplied by the actual sales volume. The formula is:

Sales margin price variance = (Actual margin – standard margin) × Actual sales volume in units

The *sales margin volume variance* is the difference between the actual sales volume and the standard or budgeted sales volume, both measured in units, multiplied by the standard margin per unit of sales. The formula is:

Sales margin volume variance = (Actual sales in units – standard sales in units)

× Standard margin per unit of sales

Task

The sales director of your company has complained recently that it is easier to control costs than it is to control income. Write him a report explaining how sales margin variances can be used for controlling income.

Assignment 1.8: Budgeting for failure

The director of a small publishing company recently introduced a budgetary control system. A young accountant was appointed who drew up budgets for the advertising and editorial departments based on the actual results for the last three years. At the end of the first month of the new financial period the actual total revenue was higher than planned, but the total advertising department costs were also higher than the budget. The editorial department actual costs were the same as those budgeted and the actual profit for the period was higher.

On receiving the first month's results the director immediately threatened to dismiss the advertising manager for exceeding the budgeted costs. The advertising manager has retaliated by threatening to resign unless the budgetary control system is scrapped. The accountant has resigned to join another company.

Student activities

You are an assistant in a firm of consultants who have been called in to advise the company. Your immediate superior, a senior consultant, asks you to prepare a preliminary word processed report covering the following:

(i)   an analysis of the problems and how you think they have arisen;

(ii) guidelines for the operation of a successful and effective budgetary control system;

(iii) recommendations as to what action the director of the client company should now take.

Section 2
Business Environment

by Mark Sutcliffe

BA (Hons), Lecturer in Economics and Sociology at Bristol Polytechnic

Business environment is the study of those factors which influence business decision-making and policy in an environment of economic and political change.

Recommended Reading

Beardshaw, J, & Palfreman, D, *The Organisation in its Environment*, Pitman, 1990
Donaldson, P & Farquhar, J, *Understanding the British Economy*, Pelican, 1988
Farnham, D, *The Corporate Environment*, Institute of Personnel Management, 1990
Glew, Matthew, Watts, Michael, & Wells, Ronald, *Business Organisations and Environment*, Heinemann, 1987

*I thought I'd planned for every eventuality ...
now what's holding me back?*

Contents

2.1 Principles and Assumptions of Different Economies

2.1.1 The Problem of Scarcity

All economic systems face the ***problem of scarcity***, although they vary in the way they attempt to resolve this problem. The term *scarcity* in an economic sense means limited in supply. People's wants are many: more consumer durables, more holidays etc. But the *resources (factors of production)* required for producing things to satisfy these wants are themselves limited in supply. Therefore a *choice* must be made as to how the resources should be used and which of the consumers' wants are the most pressing.

Factors of production are the basic inputs used in the production of goods and services. They are classified as:

- land
- labour
- capital
- enterprise

The supply of land is fixed and the supply of raw materials limited. Human resources such as labour are limited both in quantity and in skills. Capital refers to the number of factories, machines etc that are used in the production process. Enterprise is the process whereby land, labour and capital are combined and organised to produce output. Such entrepreneurial ability may be classified as a scarce resource.

Task

Can you think of any goods or resources which are not scarce in an economic sense?

2.1.2 Classifying Economic Systems

Economic systems are distinguishable from one another on the basis of government involvement in the economic decision-making process. There are three broad categories of economic systems:

- free market economy
- planned economy
- mixed economy

Within each category, producers, consumers and the state make distinct contributions to the running and operation of the economy.

In a free market economy the consumer dictates what is produced; in a planned economy the state dictates what is produced and allocates resources accordingly.

Task

Make a list of economic decisions taken by consumers, producers and the state in the British economic system.

2.1.3 Planned Economy

A *planned economy* is associated with the socialist/communist economic system. Under this system the state plans, controls and allocates society's resources as follows:

- between present consumption and future investment;
- between industries and firms;
- between consumers (for example, output is distributed on criteria of need or possibly on how much each individual produces).

The *advantages* are:

- resources can be more fairly distributed amongst the population;
- the state can plan for the future;
- problems like unemployment and inflation can be controlled.

The *disadvantages* are:

- the task of planning is highly complex and inefficient due to poor information concerning what resources are available and in what quantities;
- prices set by the state do not reflect the relative scarcity of goods and services;
- without worker and producer incentives, such as profits and wage bonuses, production is inefficient and suffers from both low productivity and quality;
- there is limited consumer choice.

Task

How might you set about improving the efficiency of a planned economy without introducing market forces?

2.1.4 Free Market Economy

A *free market economy* is associated with the capitalist economic system. In such an economy the price mechanism determines supply and demand, and the subsequent allocation of resources between competing goods and services. *Prices* act as:

- a reflection of a goods or services scarcity;
- a source of information for buyers and sellers;
- an incentive to produce or consume.

The *advantages* are:

- the market mechanism operates automatically and responds quickly to changes in demand and supply;
- competition leads to efficiency;
- there is freedom of consumer choice.

The *disadvantages* are:

- competition between firms is limited since the large firms have market power and the ability to set rather than respond to prices;
- it will not produce certain goods and services known as *public goods*, because it might prove unprofitable or impractical to do so;

- it will under provide certain goods and services known as *merit goods* which are of benefit to society as a whole;
- the prices of goods and services do not take account of the external costs of production, such as pollution etc;
- output is distributed on the ability to pay and not need;
- markets tend to be constantly fluctuating which makes it difficult to plan for the future.

Task

Classify the following list of goods and services into merit goods and public goods. Consider how far in each case the market is or is not capable of providing such goods and services.

- a lighthouse
- national defence
- a meals on wheels service
- public housing
- education
- health

2.1.5 Mixed Economy

Most, if not all, economies in the world are of this type. A *mixed economy* attempts to combine the efficiency of a free market and price mechanism with the equity and stability of a planned economy. State intervention can include:

- the direct provision of goods and service, such as the nationalised industries;
- the use of economic policy to manage the economy.

Task

Make a list of the ways that the UK government intervenes in the running of the economy.

2.1.6 Objectives of Economic Policy

Economic policy is the action taken by the government to regulate, alter and adjust economic activity within the economy. It attempts to influence such decisions as how much producers supply to the market and how much consumers demand. A successful economic policy would achieve a range of economic objectives:

- a low rate of unemployment;
- a high or expanding rate of economic growth;
- a low rate of inflation;
- a position of surplus or balance in foreign trade.

Most governments aim to achieve such objectives and they are widely seen as indicators of economic success. However, these objectives may not be their only aims. *Income distribution, environmental protection* etc may also be seen as important and given equal priority in the policy process. The selection of objectives is as much a reflection of political differences between governments as a response to the economic problems a country might face. This is also true of the types of policy that a particular government might use.

Task

The table below outlines the performance of the British economy over the last ten years. What can you say about the achievement of the policy objectives cited in Section 2.1.6.

Year	Economic growth (real GDP %)	Unemployment (%)	Inflation (%)	Balance of payments current account (£bn 1985 prices)
1980	-2.44	6.2	17.9	4.4
1981	-1.20	9.4	11.9	8.8
1982	1.52	9.6	8.6	5.5
1983	3.39	10.4	4.6	4.3
1984	2.60	10.7	5.0	2.1
1985	3.67	10.9	6.1	3.2
1986	3.58	11.2	3.4	-0.1
1987	4.83	10.3	4.2	-3.5
1988	4.25	8.3	4.9	-12.9
1989	2.10	6.5	7.8	-16.8

2.1.7 Types of Economic Policy

Governments can adopt a range of *economic policies* to attempt to manage the national economy. The two main types are *fiscal policy* and *monetary policy*.

Fiscal policy attempts to control economic activity by regulating the level of tax raised and the amount of revenue spent. If the level of government spending exceeds revenue raised from taxation (a *budget deficit*), this will have a net expansionary effect on the economy. Overall demand will grow. Alternatively, if the government runs a *budget surplus* in which revenue from taxation exceeds expenditure, the economy will contract. Overall the level of demand will fall.

If the government runs a budget deficit for any length of time, it may be forced to borrow money to finance its spending. The difference between government's tax revenue and spending is called the *public sector borrowing requirement (PSBR)*. Such debt is financed by the government selling bonds to the general public. The stock of such bonds is known as the *national debt*.

Monetary policy involves a control over economic activity by influencing the amount of money in circulation and the cost of borrowing. If the quantity of money in circulation increases and the cost of borrowing (the rate of interest) falls, the economy will expand and grow. Conversely, if the amount of money in circulation falls and the cost of borrowing rises, economic activity in the economy will contract.

Although the government has full control over the level of taxation and the amount it spends, it does not have full control over the supply of money. The banks have significant influence over the quantity of money in circulation. The government can only indirectly influence their activities by imposing restrictions on how much they can lend to customers or by influencing their level of reserve requirements for example.

Other policies a government can adopt tend to be more selective in their targets and focus on particular areas *(regional policy)*, or on particular sectors of the economy *(industrial policy)*. Recently there has been increased emphasis on *supply side policy*. These policies focus on the supply of factors to the market place, in particular labour. Supply side policies place greater emphasis on market forces and the government plays a minimal role in the policy-making process.

Tasks

You are the manager of a small electrical components business in the north of England. Consider the effects on the performance of the business and the likely business decisions you will have to take after the following government policy decisions:

(i) a rise in interest rates;

(ii) an increase in corporation tax;

(iii) a fall in personal income tax;

(iv) the government orders a new range of machines from one of your customers to whom you supply components;

(v) the government reduces grants to small businesses in the north of England.

Assignment 2.1: Changing economic policy

You have been asked by your local Chamber of Commerce to give a brief talk on the impact of changes in economic policy on local business.

Student activities

(i) Select two local businesses to use as your examples and prepare suitable speech notes, diagrams and illustrations for your presentation.

(ii) What resources are being used in the production of each business's product or service.

(iii) What changes in economic policy are likely to have an impact on the performance of each business?

(iv) In what important respects do your two businesses differ from each other in terms of points (i) and (ii) above?

2.2 Business Organisations

2.2.1 Types of Business Organisation

A *sole proprietor* or *sole trader* (Section 3.1.1) is a one person business. It tends to be small, with few employees. Such businesses are easy to set up and only require limited capital investment. They tend to be very responsive to changing market conditions. However, they have only a limited scope for expansion, and the owner is personally liable for any losses that the business might make.

A *partnership* (Section 3.1.2) can be owned by two but no more than 20 people. With more than one owner, there is greater scope for expansion. More finance can be raised and the partners can each specialise in different aspects of the business. Partners have unlimited liability. Where large amounts of capital are required, the risk of business failure can be very high for the individual partners.

A *limited (joint-stock) company* (Section 3.1.3) is legally separate from its owners. Any debts are its debts, not the owners, the owners having limited liability. This means that if the company goes bankrupt, the owners only lose the amount of money they have invested in the company.

There are two types of limited companies: public and private. *Public limited companies* are so called because they can offer new shares publicly. They are often quoted on the Stock Exchange. The price of these shares is determined by demand and supply. A *private limited company* can only offer its shares privately. This makes it more difficult for private limited companies to raise finance and consequently they tend to be smaller then public companies. They are often family businesses. Private companies are easier to set up than public companies.

Public corporations (Section 3.1.7) are state-owned enterprises such as the BBC, the Bank of England and the nationalised industries (British Rail, the Post Office etc). They have a legal identity separate from the government. However, the board appointed to run the corporation by the relevant government minister must act within various terms of reference laid down by statute.

Task

What disadvantages are there for a public limited company listed on the Stock Exchange?

2.2.2 Aims of Business Organisations

Traditional theory assumes that the principal *aim* of a business organisation is one of *profit maximisation*. Although firms have other objectives, such as improved working conditions, better salaries etc, they are of secondary importance.

The theory of sales *revenue maximisation* works on the assumption that sales are frequently used as a means of bonus payments. Therefore salaries, power and prestige within the organisation may well depend upon ability to sell.

Growth maximisation is a long-term objective. A large firm generates certain managerial advantages, such as expanding promotion prospects, greater power, and the satisfaction of being part of a growing organisation. Growth can be achieved externally through merger or internally through investment and product diversification.

Behavioural theories suggest that an organisations' objectives are varied and complex. Different departments within the firm are likely to have conflicting interests and targets. These are determined by compromise and negotiation. Behavioural theories suggest that to use a simple model to explain the actions and policies of a manager is not realistic; reality is far more complex and difficult to predict.

Task

The development of alternative theories of the business grew as a result of the gradual separation of the ownership of the business from its management. What reasons might explain why such a division emerged? What advantages and disadvantages do you think such a division will have for the business and its performance?

2.2.3 Production Decisions

A business manager must make a series of *decisions* concerning the production of the goods or services supplied to the market. The decision to produce depends on a range of considerations determined by the market within which the organisation operates, as well as overall managerial objectives. Such decisions might focus on:

- whether the demand for the goods/service is growing, constant or declining;
- the price to be charged;
- the impact on costs and revenue of selecting alternative levels of output.

Task

List a range of other decisions that a business manager needs to take into account prior to and during the process of production. Consider factor markets as well as product and service markets.

2.2.4 The Production Decision: Demand and Supply

The *demand* for a product or service is represented by a simple inverse relationship. As the price of the product falls, the quantity demanded increases. Alternatively, a high price causes the quantity demanded to fall. However, price is not the only determinant of demand. Other factors are:

- consumer tastes;
- the number and price of *substitute products;*
- the number and price of *complementary products;*
- the level of income;
- fashion and advertising;
- expectations of, for example, future price changes or supply shortages.

Traditional consumer theory assumes that the individual consumer takes all the above conditions into consideration when making a purchasing decision. The consumer is assumed to be perfectly informed about the quality of the products on offer, the price and availability of substitutes and complements, and will use this information to maximise *satisfaction (utility).*

More modern approaches to consumer theory suggest that factors other than price, such as quality, reliability, design and performance, after-sales etc play a significant part in determining consumer decisions. If price is not the only thing that consumers are interested in, managers must think carefully about how they market and present their goods and services.

The relationship between price and quantity and the decision to *supply* is a direct one. The higher the price of a product or service, the greater the amount supplied to the market. Conversely, the lower the price, the less will be supplied. However, price is not the only determinant of supply. Other factors include:

- the costs of production, including the application of a particular type of technology;
- the objectives of producers, for example, profit maximisers will reach
- different supply decisions to sales maximisers;
- expectations of future price changes, for example, producers may reduce current supply by stockpiling goods if a price rise is expected in the future.

Before producers can decide what level of output to supply and what price to charge, they require additional information concerning the cost structure of producing the product at particular levels of output, and some confirmation that the price is not too high or too low.

Tasks

(i) Draw a graph of the demand and supply curves from the data given below.

Price (£)	10	20	30	40	50	60	70
Quantity supplied (tons)	20	40	75	90	120	150	180
Quantity demanded (tons)	200	180	160	140	120	100	80

(ii) What is the equilibrium price?

(iii) What happens if the government fixes a maximum price of £40? Would this lead to a market surplus or a shortage? Explain what would happen to the price of the product in such a situation?

(iv) Assume supply increases by 55 units at every price due to a new production method. What would be the new equilibrium price and output?

(v) What would happen to the demand curve if the price of a substitute product fell in price?

2.2.5 The Production Decision: Elasticity

Managers not only need to know whether a price rise or fall will lead to a change in demand, but also by how much. The term *elasticity* is used to describe the responsiveness of a change in demand to a change in price. The more responsive demand is to a change in price, the more elastic the product. A product or service that is unresponsive to a change in price is called *inelastic*. Whether it is elastic or inelastic depends on a number of factors:

- the availability or closeness of substitutes (the more substitutes, the more elastic);
- the proportion of income spent on the goods (the larger the proportion, the more elastic);
- the period of time over which consumer decisions are allowed to change (the longer the time, the more elastic).

One of the most important applications of elasticity concerns the relationship between a change in price and its effect on the organisation's sales revenue. Figure 2.1 shows two demand curves. In (a) the curve is elastic, in (b) the curve is inelastic.

In (a), prior to a price increase, the firms total revenue (TR) is equal to areas A and B. Following a rise in price, the new total revenue area is equal to A and C. Area B is greater than area C, thus showing that the price rise has led to a fall in revenue. With an elastic demand curve, price and total revenue move in opposite directions. Conversely, with an inelastic demand curve, as price rises so total revenue rises. In this case price and total revenue move in the same direction.

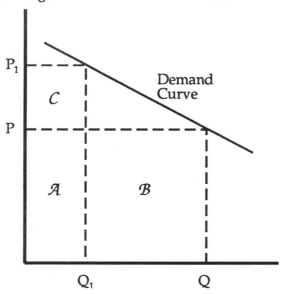

Figure 2.1(a) Elastic Demand Curve

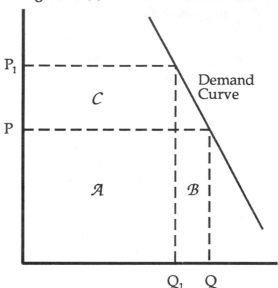

Figure 2.1(b) Inelastic Demand Curve

Even if we could estimate the demand curve for a product, simply to look at the curve may not fully reveal the goods' elasticity. This is particular true when analysing a product whose elasticity varies along its length. Therefore a simple mathematical technique can be used to estimate an elasticity coefficient, the value of which tells us whether the product is elastic or inelastic and the strength of this condition.

$$\text{The price elasticity of demand} \ = \ \frac{\text{Proportionate } \Delta Q}{\text{Proportionate } \Delta P}$$

where Δ means *change in*.

A proportionate change in Q is measured by dividing the change in Q by Q, that is, $\dfrac{\Delta Q}{Q}$.

A proportionate change in P is measured by dividing the change in P by P, that is, $\dfrac{\Delta P}{P}$.

Thus price elasticity of demand can be calculated using the following formula:

$$\frac{\Delta Q}{Q} \div \frac{\Delta P}{P}$$

With this formula, a value greater than 1 illustrates an elastic demand curve, whereas a value less than 1 shows an inelastic demand curve.

Tasks

(i) Calculate the elasticity of demand for each of the price ranges given in the following table.

(ii) From your results indicate whether the curve is elastic or inelastic, and assess the impact such a price change would have on the organisations total revenue.

P (£)	10	8	6	4
Q	15	25	35	45

2.2.6 The Production Decision: Costs

A business organisation's *costs* are directly related to the factors of production it uses to produce a given level of output. *Fixed costs* are those which do not vary with output, for example rent. *Variable costs* are those which do vary with output, such as raw materials. È₁ are the sum of these fixed and variable costs.

The *average cost* of production is found by dividing the total costs by the quantity produced. In the process of selecting a point of profit maximisation it is useful to further distinguish *marginal cost*, which is the change in total costs divided by the change in quantity.

In order to locate the profit maximisation point, in addition to the cost curves we need to analyse the revenue curves. *Total revenue* is simply total earnings from a particular level of output. *Average revenue* is the amount the organisation earns from each unit of output. In this case, the goods' price. The average revenue curve is the same as the demand curve. The *marginal revenue* curve is the additional revenue from one more unit of the product.

The profit maximisation point can be located by using the total cost and total revenue figures, or the marginal cost and marginal revenue curves. The amount of profit to be made at this point can be calculated by deducting total revenue from total costs. In the case of the marginal curves, the addition of the average cost and revenue curves are required. Average revenue or the demand curve locates the price to be charged. The cost of this unit is determined by average costs. The difference is the *profit per unit*.

Tasks

You have been given the following information:

Q	0	1	2	3	4	5	6	7
P	15	14	13	12	11	10	9	8
TC	4	9	12	15	20	30	42	55

(i) Work out the business's AC, MC, TR, AR and MR curves.

(ii) Construct diagrams from these calculations to illustrate the point of profit maximisation and the level of maximum profit.

Assignment 2.2: Celtic Threads

Celtic Threads is a small woollen textile company. It was established in 1987 and expanded rapidly. In fact, the company enlarged their premises and introduced power looms to meet demand. The business is located in a small town which prior to the 1970s had an established textile industry. However, the widespread use of cheap synthetic fibres saw the collapse of many of the woollen mills.

It was a risky venture for the founders of Celtic Threads to set up business in what was at the time a contracting industry. However, with new design ideas and an attractive financial package from the regional development agency, the firm weathered the difficult start-up period.

Student activities

You have been appointed by Celtic Threads to advise the company on a number of matters concerning its future.

(i)   Prepare a brief word processed report giving an outline of the actual and potential problems which face a small business when expanding operations. Assess those factors which may be directly relevant to the textile industry.

A large fashion house which uses Celtic Threads' weave is about to embark on a major advertising campaign to launch a new range of garments. If the campaign is successful, the demand for weave will increase greatly. Celtic Threads wants to be able to respond to the increased demand, but requires an estimate of how large the rise is likely to be. You have been given the results of a survey conducted by the fashion house into sales of the new range of garments, which are as follows:

Price	Old range Demand per month (actual)	New range Demand per month (estimated)
£50.00	4,500	6,500
£55.00	3,000	6,250
£60.00	2,000	5,750
£65.00	1,300	5,500
£70.00	900	5,250

The old range retailed at £55.00 per garment; the new styles will be priced at £65.00.

(ii) Show the increase in the fashion firm's revenue following the advertising campaign and price increase by plotting the demand curves.

(iii) Explain why the demand curve might shift to the right and become more inelastic as a result of advertising.

(iv) What advice would you give Celtic Threads concerning the likely increase in new output of weave prior to the advertising campaign being launched? Assume that six garments can be cut from a single 20 metre roll.

2.3 Business Structure and the Market

2.3.1 The Four Market Structures

The level of competition a business faces has an important influence over its decision-making considerations. For example, the price to set, the level of output to produce, whether to introduce new products. Four distinct *market structures* can be determined on the basis of the level of competition:

- perfect competition
- monopolistic competition
- oligopoly
- monopoly

2.3.2 Perfect Competition

Perfect competition is a theoretical environment in which production is assumed to take place in ideal conditions. This allows a more accurate study of the influences on production in real-world competitive situations. It assumes:

- A large number of business organisations.
- Each business only produces a small fraction of the industry's total output.
- The businesses are price takers.
- There are no barriers preventing new businesses from entering the market.
- All firms in the industry produce an identical product; there is no branding or advertising.
- Producers and consumers are assumed to have perfect knowledge.

Certain agricultural markets come close to achieving perfect competition.

Task

Consider the markets for the following goods and assess the ways in which they meet the assumptions of perfect competition:

- rhubarb
- steel
- pork
- pine tables
- sports cars
- economics textbooks

2.3.3 Monopolistic Competition

Monopolistic competition is a form of imperfect competition. It occurs when:

- There are a large number of business organisations.
- Each has only a small share of the market.
- There is freedom of entry into the industry.
- Businesses produce distinct products from their rivals.

They have a downward sloping demand curve (elastic) which gives them some control over the price of the product.

An example of monopolistic competition is found in the retail trade. A comparison of a business operating in monopolistic competition with another operating in an environment of perfect competition would show that the former charges a higher price and produces a lower level of output than the latter. In addition, the former is less efficient and may operate at less than full capacity.

Task

What conditions facilitate the formation of a market structure of monopolistic competition?

2.3.4 Oligopoly

Oligopoly is a form of imperfect competition. It occurs when:

- There are few business organisations in the industry.
- Each has a significant market share, although such shares need not be equal.
- There are barriers preventing new businesses from entering the market.
- Businesses produce distinct products from their rivals and spend large amounts on advertising and branding.
- Businesses are interdependent and must take account of rival's actions when making decisions.
- They face an inelastic demand curve and have a high degree of control over the price of their products.

Under oligopoly the behaviour of industries is difficult to predict owing to the variety of ways in which firms can respond to changes in the economic environment. The uncertainty faced by firms can be reduced by *collusion*, either in the form of a *cartel* or by more tacit or informal agreements if cartels are illegal. The possibility of collusion within a market is influenced by:

- the number of businesses in the market: the fewer the number, the easier it is for collusion to take place;
- the lack of secrecy concerning costs and production methods;
- similar cost and revenue structures;
- the potential threat of new entrants into the market;
- a stable market structure;
- little government interference in the affairs of business.

Task

In groups, debate the following motion: Collusion between businesses is a good thing.

2.3.5 Monopoly

In its strictest sense a *monopoly* occurs when:

- There is only one business organisation.
- Its demand curve is the industry's demand curve.
- It is a price setter.

- There are barriers preventing new businesses from entering the market.
- There is very little branding or advertising as the firm produces a single product.

There are very few examples of monopoly, although this is determined by how narrowly a product or market is defined. For example, British Gas plc has a monopoly over gas but not over energy sources. As with the model of perfect competition, monopoly represents an ideal with which to compare reality.

Task

Monopolies have a number of barriers to entry which they can use to prevent other firms entering the market. Make a list of as many barriers to entry as you can, giving examples.

2.3.6 Non-price Competition

Even though businesses may collude over certain aspects of business policy such as what price to charge, they may still compete on non-price terms. This might involve competition over *product development* and *advertising*.

Product development is an attempt to produce a product that is clearly distinct from its main rivals. Advertising aims to increase sales of a brand and increase brand loyalty. Advertising is very prominent under conditions of monopolistic competition and oligopoly. The following functions of advertising are said to be of benefit to the consumer:

- It provides information.
- It launches new products and creates consumer awareness.
- It increases sales allowing business to gain economies of scale and lower costs.

Critics suggest that advertising has the following disadvantages:

- It can mislead consumers as they have imperfect information.
- It costs money and can lead to higher costs.
- It can create a barrier to entry by establishing strong brand loyalty, reducing competition and efficiency.

Task

In groups, debate the following motion: Advertising is good for the consumer.

Assignment 2.3: The Big Six

There are approximately 200 brewers in the UK, of which the top six control over 75 per cent of the market. The following table gives a breakdown of the number of breweries, pubs and brands owned by the top six brewers.

Brewer	Number of breweries	Number of pubs	Number of brands
Bass	13	7,190	100
Allied-Lyons	6	6,678	107
Grand Metropolitan	5	6,419	114
Scottish & Newcastle	6	2,287	66
Whitbread	6	6,483	57
Courage	3	5,002	45

Student activities

You are a research student working for the Monopolies and Mergers Commision and have been asked to write a word-processed report to include the following:

(i)   What market structure best fits the brewing industry? Justify your answer using the information above.

(ii) How might this industry operate against the public interest?

(iii) The Big Six have recently been instructed by the Monopolies and Merger Commission to sell off over 22,000 pubs. What impact will this have on the structure of the industry?

2.4 National Economic Change and Business Activity

2.4.1 Economic Growth and the Business

In looking at *economic growth* it is important to distinguish between *actual growth* and *potential growth*. Actual growth is measured by what is actually produced over a given period. Potential growth is a measure of what the economy could produce given the efficient use of resources available. The major influence on the actual rate of growth is the level of *aggregate demand*. The potential growth of the economy is determined by the availability of resources and the level of technology being used.

In the short-term a business may be concerned with and respond to changes in the actual growth rate within the economy. In the long-term the business needs to consider issues related to potential growth, since these restrict the actual growth that the firm could achieve in the future; for example, the need to invest in new machinery or new technology.

Tasks

(i)   What factors influence the investment decision of the business?

(ii) How could the government set about influencing a business's level of investment in order to ensure the future expansion of the national economy?.

2.4.2 Economic Growth and Aggregate Demand

Aggregate demand (AD) refers to the level of spending within the economy. It consists of four elements:

- consumer spending (C);
- investment spending by firms (I);
- government spending (G);
- spending on UK exports by foreigners, including foreign investment (X).

To find the total level of spending in the economy we must subtract spending on imports (M) which represents a flow of spending abroad. AD can be shown as:

$$AD = C + I + G + X - M$$

If AD rises, businesses will respond by expanding production. Conversely, if AD falls, businesses will have to cut back on output levels. Thus, a rising level of AD is associated with an expanding or growing economy, whereas a falling level of demand is a characteristic of an economy with declining economic activity.

Actual growth tends to fluctuate from year to year. At certain points in time the economy may be experiencing a boom in economic activity. At other times the economy may be in decline and business activity in a slump. The economy tends to go through a cycle of booms and slumps. Although the length and intensity of the various phases of the cycle are unpredictable, the direction in which the economy is moving is very important in influencing the business decision-making process. For example, a business that observes a falling rate of economic growth or a steady decline in orders will be reluctant to invest in new machinery or recruit additional workers. Such decisions will contribute to a fall in business activity.

Task

Whether the economy is expanding or contracting not only influences the level and direction of growth that the economy is facing, but also the other principal economic variables in the economy: unemployment, inflation and the balance of payments. Assess each of these variables and describe and explain the state of the economy in each phase of the cycle.

2.4.3 Economic Growth and Economic Policy

The government can have significant influence over the *rate of economic growth* within the economy. It may attempt to manage the level of demand by manipulating consumer spending through various *fiscal* and *monetary* measures, such as personal taxation or interest rates. Alternatively it may attempt to regulate other aspects of aggregate demand, such as its own spending. The government may turn to the *supply side* and offer a range of incentives to encourage businesses to invest or increase research and development, both of which would have direct impact upon the level of potential growth.

Tasks

Assess whether economic growth will expand or contract as a result of the following the policy changes:

(i)   a reduction in tax benefits on company cars;

(ii)   the imposition of quota restrictions on imports;

(iii) a cut in defence spending;

(iv)   the expansion of education;

(v)   an agreement with the unions that wages will be index-linked to inflation.

2.4.4 Aggregate Demand and the Circular Flow of Income

The *circular flow of income* diagram in Figure 2.2 illustrates a simple model of the economy and shows the flow of money between households and consumers.

In the inner flow households receive factor payments such as wages, rent and interest payments from businesses. Households spend part of these earnings on products produced by businesses. This represents *consumer spending* (C). However, households do not spend all their earnings on the consumption of domestically produced products: part may be *saved* (S), part will be taken in *taxation* (T) and part spent on foreign *imports* (M). S, T and M are called *withdrawals* (W) from the circular flow.

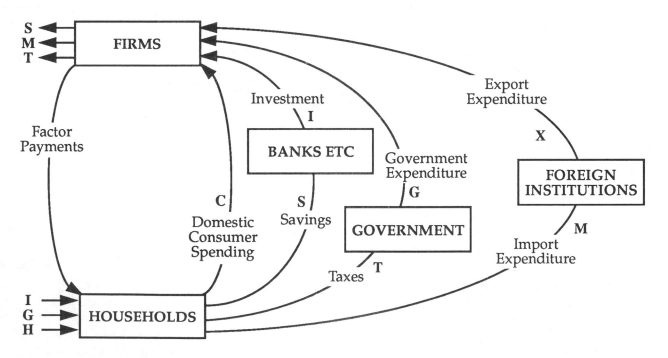

Figure 2.2 The Circular Flow of Income

Not all money flowing into businesses comes from consumer spending. *Investment* (I) by banks or other financial institutions, expenditure by *government* (G) and the spending by foreigners on domestic *exports* (X) are all *injections* (J) into the circular flow.

Consequently the level of demand within the economy at any particular time depends upon the level of injections and/or withdrawals. If withdrawals are greater than injections, there is a net outflow of money from the circular flow. Businesses will experience a falling level of demand for products. But if injections are greater than withdrawals, this will have a stimulating effect upon the economy and businesses will experience rising levels of demand.

Tasks

What would happen to the level of demand in the domestic economy in the following situations?

(i)   Building societies and banks increase interest rates on savings accounts.

(ii) VAT is reduced from 15 per cent to 10 per cent.

(iii) Business expectations are that the economy is on the verge of recession.

(iv) The pound falls in value against a number of competitors' currencies.

(v)   The government decides to expand the existing motorway network.

2.4.5 Aggregate Demand and the Multiplier Effect

The *multiplier effect* is what a given change in either the level of injections or withdrawals has on the level of income. For example, the government increases its level of spending: *aggregate demand* is now higher. Business organisations respond by employing more resources in the production of goods and services, thus paying out more in factor incomes to households. Households spend a fraction of this new income on consumption, causing demand to rise yet again. Businesses respond by expanding output further and generating yet more income.

Each time this process is repeated a fraction of income is withdrawn from the inner flow, and the effect on demand gets smaller and smaller. What is apparent however, is that for a given rise or fall in the level of aggregate demand there will a multiplied effect on the level of economic activity within the economy.

Task

Using a local economy based on a small fishing village as an example, describe the effect of the discovery of oil off the coast and its subsequent exploration would have on local goods markets, service markets and factor markets.

2.4.6 Inflationary and Deflationary Gaps

An *inflationary gap* is where the level of spending exceeds the level of output that can be produced causing prices to rise. A *deflationary gap* is one where the level of spending is less than the level of output being produced. Therefore resources are not used to their full potential, and there may be unemployment and machinery may be run under capacity.

The multiplier effect has important implications for governments attempting to control the level of demand and thus correct such gaps. If there is unemployment, the government may find it desirable to stimulate demand to create more employment. It can do this either by raising injections or by reducing withdrawals.

However, the multiplier effect means that only a slight change in one of the components of aggregate demand may be sufficient to remove the unemployment problem. Excess spending will simply over stimulate the economy and lead to inflationary pressures. Alternatively, if the government is attempting to reduce demand, excess cuts in the level of injections or increases in withdrawals may simply reduce economic activity such that businesses cut back on the level of production making resources, such as labour, redundant.

Tasks

If the level of demand is to be changed in order to correct high unemployment or high rates of inflation, the government will want to adjust the level of AD by exactly the right amount. It is very important that the government knows the size of the multiplier in order to achieve this. The following formula can be used to calculate the multiplier:

$$k = \frac{1}{mpw}$$

where: $mpw = \frac{\Delta W}{\Delta Y}$

and mpw is the marginal propensity to withdraw or the fraction of every pound that is not spent on consumption. The larger the mpw, the smaller the effect of a change in demand.

(i)   Calculate the multiplier effect if the mpw is known to be a quarter.

(ii) If the economy were to experience an injection of £150m government spending, what impact would this have on the level of income?

(iii) Calculate the multiplier effect if the change in consumption from an increase in income of £8,000m was £2,550m.

(iv) Which would have the greater effect on income: a rise in government spending or a cut in taxation?

2.4.7 Types and Causes of Unemployment

Unemployment is a sign of economic inefficiency. It typifies an economy that is operating below its full potential. There are a number of different reasons why and how people become unemployed including the following:

- *Demand deficient or cyclical unemployment* is caused by a lack of demand within the domestic economy.

- *Real wage or classical unemployment* is the result of market imperfections which prevent wages from falling to their market clearing levels.

- *Frictional unemployment* is caused as people move from job to job.

- *Structural unemployment* is the result of a mismatch between the skills of the workforce and the jobs available.

- *Seasonal unemployment* is determined by the time of the year.

- *Technological unemployment* is caused by the introduction of new systems of production.

Task

Given the types of unemployment described in Section 2.4.7, outline a range of policies a government might adopt to remove or reduce the unemployment problem.

2.4.8 Inflation and Business

The rate of *inflation* measures the annual increase in prices. It is usually expressed as a percentage change and is calculated from a measure of retail prices compared over a twelve month period. Inflation is a problem for business in two important respects.

- *Uncertainty*: When the rate of inflation fluctuates from year to year, businesses find it very difficult to predict their costs and revenues, and consequently their profits. They may respond to this uncertainty by reducing their level of investment. If all businesses were to behave in this way, economic growth would fall.

- *Competition and the balance of payments*: If the rate of inflation is higher in the UK than abroad, UK goods will be both less competitive overseas and on domestic markets. Exports will fall and imports rise. This would lead to a deterioration in the balance of payments.

Task

Why is inflation a problem for consumers?

2.4.9 Types and Causes of Inflation

There are a number of different *types of inflation*:

- *Demand pull inflation* is caused by a rise in the level of aggregate demand.

- *Cost push inflation* results when the costs of production rise independently of the level of demand. Part of this cost is passed on to the consumer in the form of higher prices. Under this type of inflation the main causes of cost push are:

    ○ wage push inflation

    ○ profit push inflation

    ○ import push inflation

    ○ tax push inflation

    ○ the exhaustion of natural resources push inflation

- *Inflation and expectations*: Making decisions such as what wage level to demand will require some expectation of the future level of prices. If high rates of inflation are anticipated, higher wage settlements will be demanded. The anticipated inflation rate becomes the actual inflation rate as wages rise in line with expectations and companies put up their prices to recover the higher costs of production. In the next round of wage negotiations this new rate of inflation becomes the basis of expectations. This process is known as the *wage/price spiral*.

Task

What policies might a government adopt to tackle the problem of inflation?

Assignment 2.4: Economic forecasts

You work for a firm of economic advisors and have been asked to prepare a report and make a verbal presentation on the state of the state of the British economy to a new client, a furniture manufacturer and retailer.

Student activities

(i)   Write a word processed report describing the current key UK economic variables and assessing the potential effects such variables are likely to have on your client's competitive position. You should also make some general forecasts for the economy over the next two years, and clearly state some of the problems in doing this.

(ii) Prepare a set of speech notes for your presentation, together with visual aids to highlight your main findings.

2.5 British Political Parties and Pressure Groups

2.5.1 The Political System and Business

Britain has a mixed economy which operates within a democratic *political system*. The term *democracy* is difficult to define. However, it is common to refer to a democratic system as one in which key freedoms exist such as the freedom of speech, expression and choice, and the government is responsible to and elected by the people.

Decisions made within the political arena not only have an important influence on the society in which people live, but also affect the environment in which businesses trade. The decisions taken by government are assumed to be in the interests of society and business, and reflect their demands. Within this decision-making process, pressure groups are able to voice their interests and concerns, and thus influence the policy of government.

In the UK there are three levels of government:

- *Local government* can influence the business environment by planning decisions and offering incentives such as competitive land costs and grants for example.

- *Central government* has the greatest impact on the business environment by enacting laws, dictating macroeconomic policy and providing key services such as education.

- The influence of *European government* has grown as Britain has become integrated into the European Community. Community-wide policies such as the *Social Charter* are intended to establish a series of workers' rights which affect the rights and obligations of workers and businesses.

Task

Compile a list of government business undertaken during a particular week from television, radio or a quality newspaper.

2.5.2 The Institutions of Government

The main *institution of government* in the UK is *Parliament,* which comprises the *House of Commons,* the *House of Lords* and the *Crown.* It is the ultimate legislative authority in the land and fulfils four main functions:

- It creates the laws of the land.
- It carries out policy programmes.
- It acts as a check on individual and government actions.
- Through its elected members it represents the views of the electorate.

The House of Commons, the lower chamber, is the most influential and dominant part of Parliament. It consists of 650 elected members representing a similar number of constituencies throughout the UK. The political party with the majority of seats forms a government. It elects a leader or *prime minister* who forms a cabinet of ministers to run the affairs of government ministries.

The House of Lords, the upper chamber, consists of 1,200 members drawn from hereditary peers, life peers and the clergy. Their main role is to provide a forum for debate on proposed government legislation and to offer amendments to bills. If a bill is rejected by the Lords, it can lead to serious delays in implementing government policies. However, the influence of the House of Lords is limited.

The Crown's role in parliamentary affairs is more ceremonial than a position of power. The monarch must give royal assent to all acts of parliament before they become law and appoint cabinet ministers on recommendation of the prime minister. Other functions include the opening of Parliament and offering a speech outlining the government's intended proposals for the next parliamentary session.

Task

Television coverage of the House of Commons in session is a relatively novel feature of the parliamentary process. However, the debate of parliamentary matters in the Press and on radio and television current affairs programmes has long played an important part in keeping the public informed of the issues. In small groups, devise a current affairs programme role play. You will need a presenter, a reporter and at least two Members of Parliament from different political parties.

2.5.3 The Policy Process, Public Opinion and Government

The British political system is frequently referred to as *cabinet government* as the running of the country and the creation of future government policy is developed and decided upon by the cabinet. The policies pursued are presented in the government's election manifesto and are shaped by the perceived concerns of the public, as gained from opinion polls etc, and the influence of pressure groups.

Public opinion can be expressed in a variety of ways such as:

- opinion polls
- by-election results
- media reports and public issues
- pressure groups

Pressure groups represent an organised expression of opinion. They can be very influential in certain areas of government policy. There are two types of pressure group. *Interest groups* represent sectional concerns, such as those of a particular occupational group, for example trade union members or management. Such pressure groups are well established and have long-term aims and objectives. *Promotional pressure groups* are usually formed for a specific cause or issue. They have a wide base of support from people of different social backgrounds. Environmental groups and many charities are promotional pressure groups. Pressure groups can use a variety of measures to influence decisions, such as:

- providing sponsorship;
- offering support to government in return for government support;
- influencing the media and thus wider public opinion;
- holding specialist knowledge of an issue;
- organising civil disobedience.

Once public opinion has been considered and more detailed considerations taken into account, the government prepares a *bill* or a *draft statute*. A *Green Paper* represents the discussion stage of the bill. A *White Paper* is the bill presented in its final form to Parliament. Before a bill can become an act of Parliament it must pass through a number of stages:

- At the *first reading* the House of Commons is told of the bill's existence and the date of the second reading and debate.
- The *second reading* involves a limited debate on the bill's main points.
- At the *committee stage* the bill is assessed in detail and proposals for amendments and changes are made.
- At the *report stage* the amended bill is returned to the House of Commons where notification is given of any changes made.
- The *third reading* is the final opportunity for debate before the bill is accepted or rejected. •
- *'Another place'* is the stage at which the bill passes to the House of Lords to go through the same procedures. If the Lords decide to amend or reject a bill, it is returned to the Commons for further debate.
- Once the Commons and Lords have decided on the final form of the bill, it becomes an *act of Parliament* only by *royal assent* and takes effect.

Task

Conduct an opinion poll of class members on a number of topical political issues. You might ask whether they agree or disagree with a decision or policy. You might ask what issues they see as important and how they feel the government is dealing with the problem. Present your findings.

2.5.4 Political Parties, their Aims and Objectives

Political parties play a number of roles:

- communicating with and representing the electorate;
- formulating and seeking support for policies;
- providing individuals to run the country.

British politics have been dominated since 1945 by two main political parties. In the 1987 general election, parliamentary seats were distributed as follows:

Conservative	376
Labour	229
Liberal	19
Social Democrat	3
Plaid Cymru	3
Scottish Nationalists	3
Others	17

The *Conservative Party* is considered by many to have moved away from its paternalistic style of the past, although certain fundamental values and beliefs remain. Conservatives believe that a common goal shared by all members of society justifies the existence of a hierarchy of authority which seeks to maintain order and individual freedom, not only in society and politics but also in the economic market-place. They dislike the influence of the trade unions and argue that government's role in the economic process should be as limited as possible, ensuring only that markets remain free and unrestricted. The *New Right* of the Conservative Party emphasises the old values and advocates that the state should play a more central role in ensuring such values are supported and enforced.

The *Labour Party* grew out of the union movement and as a result is often referred to as the party of the working man. The Labour Party holds a broadly socialist set of values which stress the importance of community and co-operation as a means of achieving individual liberty and freedom. Members believe that the role of government is to protect those least able to protect themselves, both in society and in the economic market-place. Labour Party philosophy includes working closely with the trade union movement and business, and sees an active role for itself in promoting investment, education, training and efficiency. The more radical policies of nationalisation and social ownership play a less central role than in the past.

Over the last few years the *Liberal Democratic Party* has been searching for a new identity as Labour policies have become less radical and closer to the middle ground of British politics. The former Liberal Party has had a long tradition in British politics and was at the height of its powers at the turn of the century. However, the Liberal Democratic Party of today is less influential and treads an uneasy path between its rivals, striving to create an alternative political view. It stresses the role of citizenship, the decentralisation of power, and an economic perspective which emphasises the future rather than the short-termism of recent government policy.

The remaining political parties are predominantly national parties representing the people of Scotland, Wales and Northern Ireland. In the case of the *Scottish Nationalist Party* and the *Welsh Nationalist Party* their principal aim is to achieve freedom to run their own affairs. In addition there are other political movements which do not have parliamentary representation. The most influential at present is the *Green Party*. Through its crusades on environmental issues, it has begun to develop a new approach to social and economic life, questioning the virtues of economic growth and the costs of increased prosperity.

Task

Obtain a copy of the current manifestos of the three main political parties in the UK. Make a separate list of their economic and social policies and compare the different values and philosophies behind them.

Assignment 2.5: Setting up a political party

You are setting up your own political party.

Student activities

(i) Decide upon a manifesto of policies including economic as well as social objectives. Remember that you must pay for what you spend and you will have to attract support from a wide variety of social groups to get elected.

(ii) If a number of groups are available, try criticising each other's manifestos in the form of a political debate.

2.6 The International Dimension

2.6.1 Imports, Exports and the Terms of Trade

In an *open economy*, where foreign trade is an important part of business activity, the economic decision-making process, both within business and within government, must consider international economic relations. In recent years, as international trade has expanded, economies world-wide have become more interdependent. Economic change in one part of the world has a dramatic effect on business activity elsewhere.

Countries are linked via the *import* and *export* of goods, services, commodities and capital. Whether such trade is benefiting a country can be assessed by reference to a country's *terms of trade*. This is the quantity of foreign goods a country can get in exchange for a given quantity of its own goods. If a country gets more imports for a given quantity of its own exports, the terms of trade are moving in its favour. The terms of trade are calculated by dividing the price of exports by the price of imports.

Task

Using the formula

$$\frac{\text{Index of average price of exports}}{\text{Index of average price of imports}} \times 100$$

calculate from the data below the terms of trade for the UK economy and assess whether trade is moving in Britain's favour or not.

Year	Export unit value index	Import unit value index	Terms of trade
1980	70.7	69.4	
1981	75.3	73.3	
1982	80.6	79.2	
1983	87.4	87.5	
1984	94.0	95.2	
1985	100.0	100.0	
1986	101.4	100.8	
1987	105.3	103.7	
1988	108.9	104.2	

2.6.2 The Balance of Payments

The *balance of payments* is an account which records all the monetary transactions between the UK and the rest of the world over a given period of time, usually a year. It is divided into a *current account* and a *capital account*. The current account comprises a further two sections: trade in goods or *visible items* and trade in services or *invisible items*. The difference between the level of visible exports and visible imports is known as the *balance of trade* and represents the largest section of the balance of payments account.

The invisible balance looks at trade in travel, financial services, and the payments of profits and dividends. The capital account balances aspects of investment and borrowing between countries. It includes monies used in short-term capital movement for speculation, and long-term capital investments. It also includes debits and credits in the UK's reserves of gold and foreign currency which change in response to government intervention in the foreign exchange market.

The current account and the capital account should balance when they are added together. However, omissions and errors which may occur can be accounted for by using a *balancing item*. Depending on whether there is a balance of payments *surplus* (exports greater than imports) or a balance of payments *deficit* (imports greater than exports) this will have implications for government policy, the exchange rate and ultimately the performance of business overseas.

Task

Using the following data, write a brief report on the performance of the British economy overseas.

Year	Visible balance	Invisible balance	Current balance	Capital balance	Balancing item
1979	–3,343	2,794	–548	–742	1,095
1980	1,357	1,441	2,797	–3,930	953
1981	3,252	3,390	6,641	–7,436	637
1982	1,910	2,698	4,608	–2,589	–2,019
1983	–1,537	5,303	3,796	–4,551	755
1984	–5,336	7,123	1,956	–7,900	5,944
1985	–3,345	6,293	3,165	–7,419	4,254
1986	–9,485	9,318	–45	–10,105	10,150
1987	–11,223	6,552	–4,352	–3,908	8,260
1988	–21,078	5,855	–14,960	5,465	9,495
1989	–23,840	4,045	–19,067	4,043	15,024

2.6.3 The Balance of Payments and the Exchange Rate

The *exchange rate* is the rate at which one currency can be traded for another. The rate of exchange is determined by the demand and supply of a particular currency on the foreign exchange market. If foreigners want to buy British goods, they will demand sterling to do so. They can buy sterling by selling their own currency for it. The rate of exchange determines how many pounds they will get for their money. If the exchange rate is £1 = $1.89, an American would need to give $1.89 for every £1 purchased.

However, if we are in the UK and wish to purchase imports or invest overseas, we would need to supply sterling to the market. If there is an excess supply of sterling, the exchange rate falls; if there is excess demand, the exchange rate rises.

The *advantages* of a high exchange rate are:

* It keeps import prices low as we get more foreign goods for every £1.
* High prices for British exports force British business to be more competitive and more efficient in order to trade overseas.

The *disadvantages* of a high exchange rate are:

* The balance of payments moves into deficit.
* British goods and services becomes less competitive. Some organisations may be forced out of business which could lead to rising unemployment in the long-term.

The *advantages* of a low exchange rate are:

* Increased competitiveness abroad could stimulate business investment and expansion in the domestic economy.

- Domestic products are relatively cheaper than imports which could stimulate domestic demand.
- The balance of payments moves into surplus.

The *disadvantage* of a low exchange rate is that high import prices cause costs to rise and lead to rising levels of inflation.

In a system of *floating* exchange rates, exchange values are determined by market forces. This not only ensures that the demand and supply of sterling are equal, but also that debits on the balance of payments are equal to the credits.

However, most foreign exchange rates are not left to the market. Governments frequently intervene to solve balance of payment disequilibria and regulate exchange rate fluctuations to improve the decision-making environment for business by reducing uncertainty when trading abroad. There are a variety of ways in which government can intervene and attempt to *fix* the rate of exchange.

- *Short-term intervention,* such as using reserves of gold and foreign currency to buy and sell pounds on the open market; raising or lowering interest rate to persuade or dissuade investors to deposit money in the economy.
- *Long-term intervention,* such as direct controls on the flow of goods, services and capital both into and out off the country through the use of tariffs, quotas and exchange control regulations for example; introducing deflationary/reflationary measures which regulate the level of domestic spending; undertaking devaluation/revaluation which may be possible in a system of fixed exchange rates. By devaluing or revaluing a currency, the price of foreign currency is adjusted and the competitive position of the country improves or deteriorates.

Tasks

What will happen to the exchange rate under the following circumstances?

(i)   The UK inflation rate is higher than abroad.

(ii)   There is a fall in the level of income in the UK.

(iii)   UK interest rates rise.

(iv)   American interest rates rise

(v)   Business expectations are that the UK economy is entering a recessionary period.

2.6.4 Preferential Trading

Even though intervention is an important part of modern international trade, the move towards the creation of free trade areas, has important implications for business and its foreign trading environment. A *common market* has the following features:

- no tariffs and quotas between member countries;
- a common system of taxation;
- a common system of laws and regulations concerning, for example, product specifications and standards, health and safety at work, mergers and restrictive practices, and labour and union rights;
- the free movement of labour and capital between member countries;
- common economic policies and full monetary union (a single currency and a single central bank).

The *European Community (EC)*, although not a perfect example of a common market, possesses many of its features. Integration between member countries has grown over the last 10 to 15 years and is set to expand with the *Single European Act* in 1992 which removes many of the remaining barriers to trade. The following benefits are expected:

- There will be an expansion of trade.
- There will be a fall in business costs as trade barriers are removed and businesses are able to gain greater economies of scale from expansion.
- Increased competition will encourage businesses to be more efficient, and encourage product innovation and technological developments.

However, a number of potential problems may arise:

- Radical economic change may be highly disruptive and costly for industry and many business may be unable to compete.
- Not all countries will benefit equally; those on the edge of the community may see a decline in economic activity as businesses locate more centrally in the new market.
- There will be a greater opportunity for monopolistic and oligopolistic firms to develop, destroying gains to the consumer.
- Governments will ultimately lose control over economic policies and be less able and less effective in managing their domestic economies.

Monetary union within the European Community involves the operation of a semi-fixed or pegged exchange rate. The European *Exchange Rate Mechanism (ERM)* allows currencies to fluctuate within a narrow band of exchange values (2.25% for most member countries). A country's exchange rate with non-member countries is allowed to float freely. The advantages of this system are:

- The more stable the exchange rate, the greater the incentive to trade between member countries.
- The combined reserves of member countries help to stabilise the fluctuation in their exchange rates with the rest of the world.

As with greater trade integration, monetary integration is seen to restrict governments' economic policy options. Moves to extend such integration may result in the further decline of a country's autonomy.

Task

Draw up a list for discussion of the advantages and disadvantages for business of membership of the European Community. Distinguish between the short-term and the long-term.

2.6.5 International Trade and International Co-Operation

Following the turmoil of the Second World War, the desire to establish a new, stable economic system quickly resulted in the creation of two new institutions to help manage world economic affairs.

The *International Monetary Fund (IMF)* was established under the Bretton Woods Agreement 1944 initially to help manage the fixed exchange rate or adjustable peg system. It was to hold a fund of reserves contributed by members and to act as a lender in times of crisis. Its role today is not fundamentally different, although its importance in international affairs has declined significantly since the 1970s. Today the IMF's role centres around the management of Third World debt, acting either as a direct provider of funds or as a middleman between debtor nations and creditors.

The *International Bank for Reconstruction and Development (IBRD)*, popularly known as the *World Bank*, was established under the same agreement as the IMF, although it was not formally operational until 1947. Its initial role was to aid in the post-war reconstruction of Europe by supplying loans and credit for development projects. As with the IMF, the World Bank is financed via funds from member countries. Whereas the IMF's role has changed over time, the World Bank remains the provider of funds for development projects, although its operations are increasingly based in less developed countries.

Political and financial constraints have restricted the effectiveness of the IMF and the World Bank. With the liberalisation of capital and financial markets, it is becoming increasingly easy for countries to arrange commercial credit for themselves.

One international body which has proved to be more effective is the *General Agreement on Tariffs and Trade (GATT)*. It was established in 1948 with the aim of reducing tariffs as an aid to increasing the volume of international trade. Although initially successful, more recently many countries have returned to protectionist policies. In addition, international trade is not helped by the establishment of trading blocs, such as the European Economic Community, which are frequently inward looking. Many countries have adopted hidden forms of protectionism, such as product specifications, which can be just as effective in restricting the level of imports and the extent of overseas competition.

Task

Outline a range of economic arguments that could be used to support the adoption of protectionist policies. Why, in the long-term, might protectionism prove to be costly for all countries concerned?

Assignment 2.6: Mason & Stanworth

You are employed by Mason & Stanworth, a firm of investment consultants specialising in international markets and investment opportunities.

Student activities

You have been asked by a client to write a report on the long-term prospects for business in a number of overseas markets. Your assessment of these markets will form an important part of their long-term business strategy. Your brief is as follows:

(i) Assess the opportunities for business and investment in South Korea, Italy and Brazil.

(ii) Compare these three countries on selected criteria which you consider to be the most significant and influential in shaping the long-term performance of these economies.

(iii) Decide which country offers the best opportunities and support your conclusions.

(iv) Outline some of the more general problems that businesses may face if they seek to expand their business activities overseas.

Use a word processing package to write your report.

Section 3
Business Law

by Jill Hussey

Author and editor specialising in corporate and academic texts

The business environment is heavily regulated and there is pressure for more regulation. The study of business law helps future managers and others seeking a career in commerce and industry appreciate the legal problems faced by businesses and understand when it is necessary to seek legal advice.

Recommended Reading

Abbott, K.R., & Pendlebury, N., *Business Law,* 5th Edition, D P Publications, 1991

Cole, Bill, Shears, Peter, & Tiley, J., *Law in a Business Context,* Chapman & Hall, 1990

Doughty, A., Holmes, A., & Kelly D., *Business Law,* Letts, 1989

Keenan, Denis, & Riches, Sarah, *Business Law,* Pitman, 1990

Marsh, S. B., & Soulsby, J., *Business Law,* McGraw Hill, 1989

Price, T., *Mastering Business Law,* Macmillan, 1989

One way of finding out if goods are of merchantable quality...

Contents

3.1 Legal Organisations of Business

Business organisations can be classified into two basic legal forms: *unincorporated bodies* and *corporate bodies*. An unincorporated body is an individual or a group of individuals who pursue a common business purpose; for example a *sole trader* or a *partnership*. A corporate body, or corporation, also comprises individuals who pursue a common business purpose, but by the process of legal incorporation they have created a legal entity; for example *limited liability companies* or *public sector organisations*.

3.1.1 Sole Traders

A *sole trader* is a *self-employed* individual (Section 3.3.1) managing a business alone with a view to making a profit, possibly employing full-time or part-time staff. There are no specific legal formalities relating to the formation of a one-person business and like other individuals the sole trader can sue and be sued or prosecuted. In addition, the sole trader has *unlimited liability* and is personally liable for any debts the business may incur. This extends beyond any original investment and could mean the loss of personal property.

As an employer, the sole trader is subject to the law relating to employment (Section 3.3). As a supplier of goods or services the sole trader must comply with consumer law (Section 3.7).

Under the *Business Names Act 1985* a business operating under a name other than that of its owner(s) must:

- normally display the name of the owner and business or other address in Great Britain;
- show this information when writing business letters, orders, receipts invoices and demands for payment.

A sole trader can terminate the business voluntarily at any time, subject to the payment of all business debts. The death of a sole trader does not necessarily terminate the business; it can be bequeathed to a beneficiary. If there is no will, under the rules of intestacy the business can pass to the sole trader's successor(s) in title.

Insolvency is the inability to pay debts. It may eventually lead to the cessation of a business. If insolvency is a temporary situation, creditors may be willing to wait for payment, but if no improvement looks likely, the individual(s) may be sued. Insolvency can lead to *bankruptcy*. An act of bankruptcy is deemed to have been committed if an individual or organisation performs an act with the intention of defeating or delaying creditors, or fails to comply with a bankruptcy notice served by a creditor to pay a debt ordered to be paid by the courts.

Task

Draw up a list of the legal advantages and disadvantages of trading as a sole trader.

3.1.2 Partnerships

The *Partnership Act 1890* defines a *partnership* as the relation which subsists between persons carrying on business in common with a view to profit. There are no specific legal formalities relating to the formation of a partnership, but the *Companies Act 1985* lays down that there should be a maximum number of twenty partners in a firm. Professional firms such as solicitors and accountants are not subject to this limitation.

Like the sole trader, a partnership must also comply with the business name requirements of the *Business Names Act 1985*. The partners have unlimited liability and each partner can make the other(s) liable for his or her acts. The agreement to form a partnership is a contract, which may be oral, written, or contained in a deed. In the absence of an agreement, the *Partnership Act 1890* sets out the relationship between the partners.

The partners may dissolve the partnership by agreement at any time. The death or bankruptcy of one of the partners automatically ends the partnership, unless the partners have agreed to the contrary. A partnership can be dissolved by court order upon application by any partner on certain grounds; for example if a partner has been guilty of wilful or persistent breaches of the partnership agreement.

Details of how any assets resulting from the dissolution of the partnership are distributed after all debts and liabilities have been met are set out in the partnership agreement. In the absence of such an agreement, they are distributed according to the provisions of the *Partnership Act 1890*.

Task

Compile a list of the legal advantages and disadvantages of a partnership. Compare this with the pros and cons of the sole trader.

3.1.3 Limited Companies

Limited companies, the modern name for *joint-stock companies*, are the most important form of business organisation. Under the *Companies Act 1985* the two main categories of limited company are the *public limited company* and the *private limited company*. Limited companies are legal entities separate from their *members* (owners) and as such give them the protection of *limited liability*. The members of companies limited by shares are their *shareholders*; their liability is limited to the amount of capital they have invested in the company in the form of *shares*. Shareholders cannot be sued or prosecuted for any illegal acts committed by the company.

The main differences between a public limited company and a private limited company are:

- a public company must state in its memorandum of association that it is a public company;
- a public limited company's name must end with the words 'public limited company' or the abbreviation 'plc';
- a private limited company's name must end with the word 'limited';
- a public company must have a minimum authorised share capital of £50,000 (this amount can be varied by the Secretary of State) of which a quarter is fully paid up;
- a private company may be formed with only two shares in capital, a minimum of £2 authorised issued share capital;
- a public limited company may advertise its shares and invite the public to subscribe for shares which can then be freely bought and sold;
- a private company's shares are only available privately.

Task

What are main advantages which may result from the conversion of a sole trader's business to a limited company?

3.1.4 Forming a Company

Two documents must accompany an application to the *Registrar of Companies* by those wishing to form the company: the *memorandum and articles of association*. The memorandum of association regulates the *external affairs* of a company. Under the *Companies Act 1985* the memorandum of association must include:

- the name of the company (followed by the words 'public limited company' or 'limited' as appropriate);
- the situation of the registered office (England & Wales, Wales, or Scotland);
- the objects of the company;
- the liability of the members;
- the nominal amount of capital the company will start trading with and its division into numbers of shares and denominations;
- the signatures of at least two people who have agreed to take a minimum of one share each in the company.

The articles of association are concerned with the *internal affairs* of the company. In particular they give details of the authority which has been delegated by the company to its directors to act as its *agent*s. The law of agency is described in Section 3.4. The *Companies Act 1985* provides a set of model articles which can be adopted in whole or in part and include such matters as:

- how directors will be appointed to manage the company;
- how shares will be transferred;
- how meetings will be arranged;
- the frequency of meetings;
- the voting rights of shareholders;
- the powers of the company to borrow money.

Both the memorandum and articles of association can be *amended* at a later date if required.

The articles of association should be signed by the same two people who signed the memorandum of association. These two documents are sent to the *Registrar of Companies*, together with the *statutory declaration* duly signed by the company secretary and one of the directors, and various other forms and the relevant fee. The statutory declaration states that the requirements of the Companies Acts have been complied with. The company is incorporated when the Registrar issues a *Certificate of Incorporation*.

A company is required under the *Companies Act 1985* to hold an *annual general meeting* each year and every member is entitled to notice of this meeting. There are certain exemptions introduced by the *Companies Act 1989* relating to private companies.

In addition, the company must submit an *annual return* to the Registrar of Companies which includes:

- details of the company's share capital and share division;
- debts secured by mortgages;
- a list of members and directors.

The *Companies Act 1985* as amended by the *Companies Act 1989* contains detailed provisions concerning the preparation of company accounts, the information to be included and the submission of *audited annual accounts* to the shareholders in general meeting and to the Registrar of Companies. These requirements are less onerous for small and medium-sized companies. The company's accounting records must be kept at the *registered office* and must be open to inspection by shareholders. In addition, a register of directors' interests must be held and details of their service contracts, a register of the members and debenture holders of the company, and a register of those members holding one-tenth or more of the share capital of the company.

Task

What are the circumstances in which the memorandum and articles of association of a registered company can be altered?

3.1.5 Company Officers

A limited liability company has all the power and obligations of a legal entity, but in practice needs agents to enable it to exercise its authority. The *company secretary* and *directors* are the *registered officers* of the company; in England every company must have a secretary. The secretary is the chief administrative officer of the company and executes the instructions of the board of directors. The power of directors is normally laid down in the company's articles of association.

The term *director* is not defined in the Companies Acts but the following titles are in common use:

- *executive director* - authorised to carry out day-to-day functions;
- *non-executive director* - normally exercises no formal authority outside board meetings;
- *chairman* - may or may not have any authority other than presiding at board meetings, and can be executive or non-executive;
- *managing director* - usually the chief executive;
- *associate director* - someone who is not a registered company director and does not carry the full authority of a company director. In theory the holder should not be called a director, but this title is now widely used.

Task

Your cousin has been offered a job by a rival company. In an attempt to persuade her to stay, her present boss has offered to match the salary offered and promote her to associate director. She turns to you for advice. What are her rights and obligations as an associate director?

3.1.6 Winding up a Company

As long as there are shareholders willing to invest in a company, changes in a company's membership, including the bankruptcy or death of members, have no effect on the company. However, like a sole trader or a partnership, a registered company may become insolvent eventually leading to the company being *wound up (liquidated)*.

Details of how a registered company should be wound up are set out in the *Insolvency Act 1986*. *Compulsory* winding up usually arises as a result of a petition made by a creditor to the court. However, a company can decide to wind itself up. The most common reasons for *voluntary* winding up are because the company wishes to discontinue trading or because it wants to amalgamate with another company. If the company can meet its debts, the shareholders can wind it up; if the company cannot meet its debts, the creditors wind it up. The present members of the company are liable to contribute to the assets of the company and anyone who was a member within the year prior to the commencement of the winding-up.

A *liquidator* is appointed to take control of the company. The *Official Receiver*, an office of the Department of Trade and Industry, may act in this capacity in the case of compulsory liquidations. A *committee of inspection* is a group of creditors and/or members who assist the liquidator. When the company has been liquidated, it is struck off the register and ceases to exist.

Task

Look through the Financial Times and the business sections of other quality newspapers and collect examples of companies in the process of being wound up. Suggest ways in which these can be classified. Who would find this information of value?

3.1.7 Public Sector Organisations

Like registered companies, *public sector organisations* are also separate legal entities. They include:

- *central government departments*, such as the Department of Trade and Industry, the Department of Health and Social Security, which are administered by elected political office holders and civil servants;

- *local authorities,* such as district or county councils, whose powers are controlled by the *Local Government Act 1972* and who are administered by elected councillors and local authority officers;

- *nationalised corporations* which are set up by Act of Parliament, such as the Post Office, British Rail, the British Broadcasting Corporation.

In recent years some public sector organisations have moved over to the private sector by becoming public limited companies; for example, British Telecom plc, British Gas plc, British Petroleum plc, and the former regional water authorities and electricity boards.

Task

Find out how the flotation of a public sector organisation takes place.

Assignment 3.1: Partnership in Paradise

Bill, Richard and Jim have been working separately clearing up, replanting and repairing gardens after the winter storms. Their work has brought them in contact with each other from time to time and they are contemplating setting up a business together which they propose calling Paradise Landscape Gardening.

Bill has £20,000 and a substantial amount of equipment to put into the business. Richard has £10,000 to invest, and Jim is prepared to put £3,000 into the venture. They do not consider that they will require any additional finance.

Student activities

Bill, Richard and Jim have come to you for advice on whether it would be appropriate to form a partnership. Write notes in preparation for your meeting with them covering the following points:

(i)   a comparison of the three main forms of business organisation;

(ii) what provisions you consider would be most important to include in their partnership agreement.

3.2 Contract Law

The freedom to *contract* for goods and services is the basis of a market economy. Trading involves financial risk and it is in the mutual interest of all parties to enter legally binding agreements.

3.2.1 Types of Contract

A *contract* is an agreement intended by the parties to have legal consequences. It confers *personal rights* and *contractual obligations* upon the parties, but it does not have to be drawn up by a solicitor. A limited company or an individual can be a party to a contract. A breach of contract is a breach of civil law, just as libel, negligence, breach of confidence etc are torts (a *tort* is a general civil wrong). The two most common forms of contract are:

- *contracts by deed*, which must be signed, witnessed and attested (special rules apply to conveyances of land, etc);
- *simple contracts*.

To be valid, a simple contract must contain the following basic elements which are explained in Sections 3.2.2 to 3.2.8.

- offer
- acceptance
- form and consideration
- legality
- capacity
- legal intent
- genuine agreement

A contract which does not comply with these requirements may be *void, voidable* or *unenforceable*.

A simple contract can be written or oral, or implied by conduct. However, statute law sometimes overrides these rules. For example, the *Law of Property (Miscellaneous Provisions) Act 1989* stipulates that contracts for the sale of land must be in writing (Section 3.5.7). An oral contract for such a sale is deemed to be *unenforceable*.

> **Tasks**
>
> Which of the following examples constitute a contract?
>
> (i)   A friend agrees to take you to the station.
>
> (ii) The clerk agrees to sell you a rail ticket.
>
> (iii) A taxi driver agrees to take you to your meeting.
>
> (iv) A venture capital company agrees to invest money in your company.
>
> (v)   A waitress agrees to bring you a glass of wine.
>
> (vi) Your secretary agrees to ring your home to say you will be late.

3.2.2 Offer

Advertisements and displays of goods are not offers but *invitations to treat*. Similarly, an invitation to tender is merely an invitation to treat; only an offer or a tender can be accepted. An *offer* must be made by one party, communicated to the other party and accepted unconditionally, in that order. An offer is terminated when:

- it has been accepted;
- it has been rejected;
- it is revoked by the offeror before acceptance;
- it has lapsed;
- or if the offeree makes a counter offer which forms a new offer.

Task

You have thinking of buying yourself a Parker pen and see one on display in Smiths for £5. The assistant tells you it must be a mistake; the price tag should read £15. Can the assistant refuse to sell it to you at the advertised price?

3.2.3 Acceptance

Acceptance can be written, oral or inferred from the conduct of the parties. Only an *unconditional acceptance* of the offer results in a contract. Acceptance 'subject to contract' may imply that the matter remains in negotiation until a formal contract is settled. Generally, acceptance has to be communicated to the offeror. However, when the postal service is being used as a means of communication, there are special rules concerning the communication of the acceptance.

Task

You have been short-listed for a job as a environmental surveyor. At the interview you are offered the job and you accept. You decide to take a well-earned holiday before starting your new job. When you get back you find your new employer has written to you in your absence asking you to start a fortnight earlier than agreed. Since that date has already passed you stick to the original starting date, only to find that company has engaged someone else. What is your legal position?

3.2.4 Form and Consideration

In certain cases the contract must be made in a particular form; for example those which must be made in the form of a *deed*, such as conveyances, or those which must be in writing, such as a contract to sell land.

Consideration is the legal term for something of value which is transferred between the parties; for example, the price paid in return for the goods. However, consideration does not necessarily confer a benefit on the person making the promise, as in a contract of guarantee.

Task

You receive a note through your door offering a £20 reward for a lost cat. The next day you find the cat basking on your window sill and you are able to return it to the owners. Overjoyed to see their pet safe and well, they thank you effusively and give you £10. Can you legally claim a further £10?

3.2.5 Legality

The subject matter of the agreement must not be illegal, such as in a contract to kill. In this case the contract would be declared *void*.

Task

What other examples can you think of which may be illegal contracts?

3.2.6 Capacity

Each party must have the *capacity* (legal authority) to enter the contract. Those with limited capacity to contract include minors, corporations, the Crown, those of unsound mind, or under the influence of drink or drugs.

In general, a *registered company* is limited to achieving the objects defined in the memorandum of association. An activity that is beyond the powers of the company (ultra vires) can be declared void. The *Companies Act 1989* has greatly reduced the importance of the ultra vires rule for companies.

The same basic principles apply to *local authorities*. However, they may carry out activities that are deemed to be *reasonably incidental* to the doing of those things for which there is express or implied authority.

Task

A man sells you a car at a knock-down price. A month or so later you receive a call from the police; it turns out that your car is a stolen vehicle. You still have the receipt for the car. Can you claim that you are the rightful owner?

3.2.7 Legal Intent

The agreement must include an intention to form a legal relationship.

Task

A business contact in the City offers to take you out to lunch to discuss a company pension scheme. When you arrive at the restaurant you receive a message that your contact has been unavoidably detained. Can you sue him for breach of contract?

3.2.8 Genuine Agreement

Agreements are not binding if they are based upon duress, undue influence or misrepresentation, or where there is clearly no meeting of the minds (consensus ad idem). In such a case the contract is deemed to be *voidable*.

Task

Katey Burton asks your advice on buying a car. She has agreed to pay £1,850 for a 1983 Ford Escort she has seen. You ask her the usual questions about the condition of the car, MOT, tax etc. However, you consider that the low mileage of 10,500 in a car of that age is highly suspect and the meter may very well have been tampered with. Katey wants to know whether she is contractually bound to buy the car.

3.2.9 Breach of Contract

Remedies for loss suffered by *breach of contract* can be obtained through:

- *damages* assessed and awarded by the court to the injured party;

- an *injunction* restraining the defaulting party from continuing the breach;

- a *decree of specific performance* requiring the defaulting party to fulfil the contractual obligation.

The term *damages* means compensation awarded by a court to a plaintiff who has suffered loss as a result of an act of the defendant. Damages are awarded to place the innocent party in a situation equivalent to the contract having been fully performed. Only certain losses are recoverable.

Task

You own an interior design business. A customer who is moving into a new house orders made-to-measure curtains from you. When they are ready she refuses to take delivery, saying that her house purchase has fallen through. Can you sue her for the price of the curtains?

Assignment 3.2: The Welsh dresser

In your spare time you help out at the Citizens' Advice Bureau. One morning you receive a telephone call from Peter Simpson, the owner of Heirloom Antiques. Peter has only been trading for a year and has a problem he has not encountered before. On Friday he put a sign in the shop window which read:

Welsh dresser for sale £200 ono

John Hughes saw it and offered Peter £175. Peter said that he would accept £180, but John maintained his offer of £175. Mrs Thomas saw the advertisement later that day and offered him £185. Peter told her that he would consider her offer and let her know on Saturday. By closing time on Friday no one else had shown any interest in the dresser and he decided to post a letter of acceptance to her at 5.30 pm. Later on that evening, Mr Cox saw the sign in the window on his way to the cinema. It was just what he wanted so he put a note through the door saying: "I accept your offer to sell the Welsh dresser at £200. Please find enclosed a cheque for £200. I will call round tomorrow to pick it up."

When Peter opened up on Saturday morning he saw the note from Mr Cox and quickly sent a telemessage to Mrs Thomas revoking his acceptance of her offer. No sooner had he done so than John Hughes arrived saying that he had come to collect the dresser as he had decided to accept Peter's offer to sell it at £180. Then Mr Cox pulled up in a van he had hired.

Student activities

(i) Advise Peter. To whom has he sold the dresser?

(ii) Using a desktop publishing package write an information leaflet for use in the Citizens' Advice Bureau on the personal rights and contractual obligations of parties to a simple contract.

3.3 Employment Law

3.3.1 Employment and Self-employment

Those who work under a *contract of service (contract of employment)* are employees. An employee offers skill and labour to an employer in return for a salary or wage. The employee works under the close control of the employer and is usually employed for an indefinite but long-term period.

Those who enter a *contract for service* are self-employed. They are in business on their own account. A self-employed person (a contractor) offers skill and labour to an employer for a fee. The contractor does not work under the close control of the employer and the period of employment is usually intermittent or short-term.

It is sometimes difficult to establish the status of a worker; the *Employment Protection (Consolidation) Act 1978* merely states that an employee is somebody who works under a contract of service. However, a worker's employment status is very important since it determines many legal rights and obligations in the employment relationship.

Task

Divide the following list of workers into employed and self-employed categories (some could fall into either category):

consultants, directors, partners, civil servants, doctors, teachers, secretaries, postmen, sales representatives, lorry drivers, factory workers, shop workers, casual and part-time workers, home workers.

3.3.2 Contracts of Employment

In common with other legal contracts, a *contract of employment* must contain all the basic elements of a contract. However, many contracts of employment are informal agreements which do not clearly set out the terms that will regulate the rights and obligations of the employment relationship. Such terms that do exist commonly emanate from information given at the interview, the letter of appointment, rule books, collective agreements, and terms implied by common law and statute. It is usual for the employee to sign a written contract of employment to show his or her agreement. Apart from certain seamen and apprentices who must be given written contracts, a contract of employment can be either written or oral.

Task

Draw up a simple contract of employment containing the seven basic elements of a legal contract.

3.3.3 Forming a Contract of Employment

Advertising a job is merely an *invitation to treat;* an employer must make a *specific offer* of a job to the successful applicant on *express terms* (which may differ with those advertised). A counter offer by the applicant extinguishes the original offer and the contract is concluded on the communication of the applicant's *acceptance*. If the postal rules of acceptance apply, acceptance is complete on posting.

The contents of the contract of employment may include:

- terms *expressly agreed* by both parties which satisfy the test of reasonableness;
- terms *implied* by common law and statute, custom, work rules and collective agreements.

An *employer's duties* include the deduction of income tax under *PAYE (Schedule E)* from the employee's pay. If the employee's pay depends on piece-work, the employer must provide the opportunity to earn the expected wage. Under the *Social Security Act 1975* both employee and employer must make *Class 1 National Insurance* contributions.

Under common law and the *Health and Safety at Work Act 1974* and other statutes, an employer must maintain high standards of health and safety for employees and prepare a written statement of general policy on health and safety. The *Health and Safety Commission* issues codes of practice, which are not legally enforceable but represent good practice. Health and Safety inspectors can serve improvement notices requiring the management of the organisation to put right faults within a specified period of time. They can also issue prohibition notices which stop an activity taking place until specific remedial action has been taken.

The *Employment Protection (Consolidation) Act 1978* contains most of the employee's statutory rights, including the right to:

- certain minimum periods of notice of dismissal;
- payment of redundancy in certain circumstances;
- protection against unfair dismissal;
- protection against the employer's insolvency;
- membership of a trade union and the right to engage in trade union activities.

The Act also requires the employer to provide full-time employees, with certain exceptions, with a notice giving written particulars of employment. This is known as a *Section 1 Notice* and should be served within thirteen weeks of the commencement of employment. It is enforceable by means of complaint to an *industrial tribunal*.

Other statutes which affect with the rights of employees are the *Sex Discrimination Act 1975* and the *Race Relations Act 1976* which make it unlawful to discriminate on the grounds of sex or race. The *Equal Pay Act 1970* requires an employer to treat men and women equally in terms of pay and conditions, and is enforceable by means of complaint to an industrial tribunal.

The main legislation relating to discrimination against disabled people is the *Disabled Persons (Employment) Acts 1944 and 1958*. Although there is no direct legislation in the UK to protect job applicants from age discrimination, employers need to prove that they have acted responsibly when making selections.

The *Data Protection Act 1984* set up a data protection register. Data users are required to register with the Registrar details of computerised information held. Individuals are entitled to be given details of certain personal data held on them within 40 days of requesting it. Compensation can be claimed by individuals for distress caused by disclosure of such information to others, although an employee can authorise his or her employer to make such disclosure.

The *employee's duty* in the employment relationship is to carry out duties with reasonable care and skill, act in good faith and obey reasonable instructions.

Task

Draw up a contract of employment incorporating a statutory Section 1 Notice.

3.3.4 Terminating a Contract of Employment

Most employment relationships are *terminated* by one of the parties giving notice. The length of notice required should be contained in the Section 1 Notice given to the employee. The minimum period of notice required under the *Employment Protection (Consolidation) Act 1978* is one week for between four weeks and two years of service; and one week for each year of continuous employment up to a maximum of 12 years.

A fixed term contract expires without notice at the end of the term. It can also be terminated by agreement or by operation of law, such as the death of either of the parties.

The *Employment Protection (Consolidation) Act 1978* as amended contains provisions relating to *unfair dismissal*. For example, in cases of incompetence, the employee should have received adequate training and warnings of any shortcomings. The employer has a duty to investigate the circumstances of any offence leading to dismissal fully. The term *wrongful dismissal* refers to a dismissal in breach of contract. For example, where the employer does not give the dismissed employee the correct period of notice. A dispute concerning dismissal is settled by an industrial tribunal, with the right to appeal to the Employment Appeals Tribunal and in certain circumstances to the ordinary courts.

An employer is required to make a fixed *redundancy payment* to an employee who is made redundant. The *Employment Protection (Consolidation) Act 1978* states the conditions under which redundancy may arise. Other conditions which can lead to redundancy include those where an employee has been *laid off* or kept on *short time*.

However, not all employees are eligible for a redundancy payment. A redundant employee who unreasonably refuses an offer of alternative employment by the employer, under certain conditions loses the right to a redundancy payment provided the offer constitutes an offer of suitable employment in relation to that employee. An employee who is dismissed by reason of misconduct has no right to a redundancy payment.

The amount of the redundancy payment is calculated by the age, length of service and final remuneration of the employee. Enforcement of the right to a redundancy payment is by referral to an *industrial tribunal*, with right of appeal on a point of law to the *Employment Appeals Tribunal*.

Task

In what circumstances has an employer the right to dismiss an employee without notice?

3.3.5 Contracts for Service

The majority of statutory rights under the *Employment Protection (Consolidation) Act 1978* do not extend to those who are self-employed. A self-employed person is responsible for paying his or her own income tax under *Schedule D* on a preceding year basis. Under the *Social Security Act 1975* he or she must pay *Class 2 National Insurance* contributions, which exclude certain benefits.

Usually an employer is not liable for torts committed by a contractor and does not need to maintain such high standards of health and safety.

Task

What are the advantages and disadvantages for the self-employed person in entering into a contract for service? Compare your findings with those for an employee entering into contract of service.

Assignment 3.3: Shepherd's Needle Ltd

For the past three years your mother has been a home-worker hand-knitting sweaters for Shepherd's Needle Ltd. She works approximately 18 hours a week, knitting a set quota of garments for which she is paid a monthly salary. Today her manager rang up and told her that her services were no longer required. He said that her dismissal would take effect immediately and she would receive any salary due but not a penny more. He told her that it was because her work was unsatisfactory. Your mother is very upset; no one has complained about her work before.

As soon as you get home your mother tells you about it. You discover that she does not have a written contract of employment, nor has she ever received a statement of her main terms of employment.

Student activities

Advise your mother of her rights against Shepherd's Needle Ltd and how she might enforce them.

3.4 Agency Law

An *agent* is someone who has express or implied authority to act on behalf of a *principal* with a view to establishing a contractual relationship between the principal and a *third party*. The relationship between the agent and the principal is known as *agency*. The three main types of agent are special agents, general agents and universal agents.

3.4.1 Rights and Duties of Agents

The *rights and duties of agents* include:
- the duty to perform tasks with reasonable skill and diligence;
- the duty not to delegate authority;
- the duty to avoid a conflict of interest;
- the duty not to accept any secret profit or bribe;
- the duty of confidentiality;
- the right to remuneration from the principal;
- the right of indemnity;
- the right of lien.

3.4.2 Appointing an Agent

Any person with legal capacity to enter into a contract can appoint an agent. The agent need not possess such capacity. Authority can be:

- expressly given, orally or in writing (for example, a company gives its directors authority to act on its behalf in the articles of association);
- implied from certain relationships (for example, partners act as agents for each other);
- implied by necessity (such as in an emergency);
- ratified afterwards by the principal.

In a situation of *agency by estoppel*, the principal has not appointed the agent, but the nature of the relationship between the two parties is such that a third party is led to suppose that one is acting as the agent of the other. *Estoppel* is a rule of evidence that prevents an individual from denying a state of affairs that he or she has previously asserted to be true, either orally or through his or her actions.

Task

You own a small off-licence. A boy of about thirteen comes into the shop. He explains that his dad is in bed with 'flu and wants half bottle of whisky for medicinal purposes. Is the lad his father's agent? What other factors should be taken into consideration?

3.4.3 Liability of Agents

An agent may become *personally liable* when acting for the principal in the following ways:

- by express agreement;
- if the principal does not exist or does not have legal capacity;
- if the agent signs a contract or bill of exchange in his or her own name without indicating that he or she signs as an agent for the principal.

Task

Annie Norton makes a contract in writing with Mr Lucas without clearly showing that she is signing as an agent for Michael Golding. She enters into another contract, this time with Mr Jones, stating that she is acting as an agent, but without giving the name of her principal. Michael Golding subsequently refuses to perform the contract. Explain the position of Mr Lucas and Mr Jones in these circumstances.

3.4.4 Termination of an Agency

An agency can be terminated in the following ways:

- by mutual agreement;
- through renunciation by the agent;
- through revocation by the principal;
- through the death or mental incapacity of the agent or principal;
- through the bankruptcy of the principal;
- through the illegality of the agency (for example, because of trade sanctions);
- at the end of a fixed term (for example, power of attorney may be given during a period of absence);
- through fulfilment or frustration of purpose (for example, when an agent sells a vendor's property or the property is accidentally destroyed).

Task

Mr Fletcher authorises Rose Wallace to sell his house. Rose finds a buyer, Mr Godfrey, and completes the sale for £85,000 without knowing that elderly Mr Fletcher has died. Mr Fletcher's personal representatives repudiate the sale. Advise Rose on her legal position.

Assignment 3.4: BIT Computers Ltd

You have recently been appointed as a clerical assistant at BIT Computers Ltd. The departmental manager has asked you to chase up payment of a number of outstanding invoices. You have been very successful with all but two; one from Dataprint Ltd and the other from Computer Hardware Ltd. You investigate further and discover the following reasons:

1. Dataprint Ltd claims that the data processing manager who ordered the goods had no authority to do so. You check your records and see that the same person ordered goods six months earlier and the invoice was paid.

2. Computer Hardware Ltd states that the order was placed by a member of their staff who was receiving a commission from your company for placing the order. The member of staff has since been dismissed. After investigation you find that some small payments were made to the member of staff at Computer Hardware; unfortunately the person who made the payments left your company several months ago.

Student activities

You are anxious to impress your manager. Write him a word processed report explaining the legal position with both these cases and the action you propose the company should take.

3.5 Property Law

Land is referred to in law as *real property* (as opposed to *personal property*) and the term includes any buildings erected on the land. Technically all land is owned by the Crown. Land which is not occupied by the Crown is occupied by tenants who own an estate in that land. *Tenure* defines how the land is held and *estate* defines how long the land may be held. When an individual or corporate body purchases land they are acquiring a legal estate in land. Now there are only two kinds of legal estate: *freehold* and *leasehold*.

3.5.1 Freehold Estate

Freehold is the common term for estate which is *fee simple absolute in possession*, where the estate can be sold or bequeathed under the terms of a will. However, the rights of a holder of a fee simple estate are also subject to certain restrictions.

Task

Find some examples of restrictions which might be placed on holders of fee simple estate.

3.5.2 Leasehold Estate

Leasehold estate is held under the terms (*covenants*) of a lease for a *term of years absolute*. A lease is a formal agreement between a *lessor* and a *lessee*. A lease imposes contractual obligations, some of which are expressly agreed and some implied under common law and statute. The commercial substance of a lease is that the lessor, who owns the asset, conveys to the lessee the right of occupancy to the exclusion of all others, including the lessor, for an agreed period of time at an agreed rent.

The rights of private residential tenants are contained in the *Rent Act 1977* and the Housing Act 1988; those of council tenants in the *Housing Act 1980*; and those of business tenants in the *Landlord and Tenant Act 1954*.

Task

Rose Wallace buys a lease from Bath & West Property Services. Under the terms of the lease the property can only be used as an estate agency. After six months the business is not doing well and Rose decides to use the premises as an escort agency. Is there anything to prevent her from doing this?

3.5.3 Unregistered Land

Land in England and Wales is either *registered* or *unregistered*. Title to unregistered land can be traced through a collection of documents known as *title deeds*. The *Law of Property Act 1969* gives the purchaser of land (or his or her mortgagee) a right to have deeds produced which enable the present owner's title to be traced back to a good root of title which is at least fifteen years old.

Ownership of unregistered land is transferred by *deed of conveyance* in the case of land that is sold, or by *assent* in the case of land which has been inherited. Unregistered leasehold land is transferred by way of assignment on sale, or the lessee may grant a sub-lease. The *Land Charges Register* contains the names of the proprietors of unregistered land and details of any mortgages, charges, leases etc on the land.

3.5.4 Registered Land

Registered land is governed by the *Land Registration Act 1925* and its amendments. Registered land is identified at the *Land Registry* by a title number. A *land certificate* is issued as evidence of the state guaranteed title, in place of the title deeds.

In December 1990 the Land Registry made its records available to the public. This enables prospective buyers and others to verify ownership of registered land without recourse to the title deeds. In addition any restrictions that might affect it will be disclosed; for example, whether business use is prohibited. Other information available includes the number of mortgages taken out by the owner and, sometimes, the price at which the land has changed hands.

Ownership of registered land is transferred by *deed of transfer*. The vendor exchanges the *land certificate* for the agreed purchase price on completion of the sale. The purchaser can then have his or her name substituted for the vendor's on the Land Register.

Task

A couple bought an old farm house because they wanted to bring up their children in the country. However, when they moved in they discovered that lorries passed their house every two minutes on their way to and from a nearby mineral extraction site. The estate agents who sold them the house had described it as "away from it all"; their solicitors had carried out a land search on their behalf; no mention had been made of the extraction site. What advice would you offer the couple?

3.5.5 Mortgages

Whether freehold or leasehold, registered or unregistered, a legal estate in land can be purchased by an individual or corporate body for cash or, more often, on a *mortgage*. A mortgage is a transaction whereby as security for a loan of money, the borrower transfers to the lender an interest in some property of the borrower, real or personal, on the condition that the lender's interest in the property will be terminated on repayment of the loan. The borrower is called the *mortgagor* and the lender the *mortgagee*.

Task

Obtain leaflets on mortgage agreements from different banks and building societies and compare their terms.

3.5.6 Occupier's Liability

Occupiers of land and buildings hold legal responsibility for the safety of those who come onto their land or enter their premises. Lawful entrants are protected by the *Occupiers Liability Act 1957*. The liability of an occupier towards trespassers is contained in the *Occupiers Liability Act 1984*.

Task

Compile a list of lawful entrants and divide them into three categories:
- those with express permission of entry;
- those with implied permission of entry;
- those with statutory right of entry.

3.5.7 Buying a Business

In common with other legal contracts, an agreement to purchase a business contains all the basic elements of a contract. As already noted, the *Law of Property (Miscellaneous Provisions) Act 1989* stipulates that a contract for the sale of land must be in writing and signed by each party. The *conveyance* of the land must be by way of a deed.

The purchase price of a business may include both *tangible property*, such as stock, and *intangible property (choses)*. Examples of *choses in action* are patents, copyright and goodwill. *Choses in possession* are such items as office furniture, vehicles, equipment etc. As with private property, a business can be bought by cash, loan or mortgage.

> ## Task
> You are thinking of purchasing a business. How would you set about obtaining a valuation of an existing business? What professional help would you enlist?

Assignment 3.5: A shining example

Ron Greenham has recently set up in business restoring and selling furniture from leasehold premises in the town centre. One morning a regular customer, Mrs Goldberg, slipped on the polished floor, bumping her head and spraining her wrist. Ron helped her up, apologised profusely and arranged a taxi to take her home.

His apprentice was working in the back room. When Ron went through to tell him about the accident he was very upset. He told Ron that the previous evening he had spilt some polish as he was locking up and had meant to clear it up first thing in the morning.

As they were talking Ron noticed through the window that a gap had appeared in the somewhat dilapidated fence round the back yard and that the empty tins which were normally stacked in the yard had been knocked over. When he reported the matter to the police he was told that they were questioning a 14-year old boy who was treated in Casualty during the night for caustic soda burns to his hands. Some of the tins stacked in Ron's yard had originally contained caustic soda.

Student activities

Ron Greenham has contacted you for advice. Write him a letter clearly explaining his liability, if any, to his customer, Mrs Goldberg, and to the boy, if indeed his injuries were found to have been caused by handling tins on Ron's premises.

3.6 Banking Law

3.6.1 Banking Services

The *Bills of Exchange Act 1882* defines a *banker* as a body of persons, whether incorporated or not, who carry on the business of banking. The *Banking Act 1987* abolished the distinction between recognised banks and licensed deposit-takers established in the Banking Act 1979. There is now a single category of authorised deposit-takers. Such institutions must not describe themselves as bankers unless they have paid-up capital of at least £5m, or are exempt.

A banker provides the following key *services*:

- accepting *cash* from customers;
- collecting *cheques* on behalf of customers and crediting the proceeds to the customer's account;

- honouring *payment orders* drawn on them by customers;
- maintaining *current accounts* into which the *debits* and *credits* are entered.

> **Task**
>
> Obtain details of the range of accounts offered to business customers by local banks and draw up a table comparing the services available.

3.6.2 Banking Agreements

A customer of a bank has a *contractual relationship* with the bank which should include the maintenance of an account. In common with other legal contracts, a contract between a banker and a customer must contain all the basic elements of a contract.

The terms of the contract are implied and generally there is no written contract. However, it is usual for a bank to enter into written agreements with customers on certain matters such as cheque card and credit card agreements, borrowing agreements under the *Consumer Credit Act 1974*, and mandates covering signing instructions on accounts.

> **Task**
>
> Most people use the services of a bank to help administer their financial transactions. Examine any written agreements you may have made with a bank on such matters as cash withdrawal cards, cheque guarantee cards, overdraft facilities or personal loans. Identify the key contractual elements.

3.6.3 Rights and Duties of a Banker

The *rights and duties of a banker* include:

- the duty to honour the customer's cheques and other payment instructions if the account is in credit or up to an agreed overdraft limit;
- a duty not to disclose information about the customer's affairs without the customer's express or implied consent;
- the duty to disclose such information if required to do so under court order or by statute;
- the right of lien (the bank's right to certain securities deposited with them, such as stocks and shares, when the customer owes money to the bank);
- the right to combine (set-off) accounts of a customer under certain rules to arrive at a figure of net indebtedness to the bank;
- the right to appropriate payments under certain rules.

In addition, a banker may be liable to *non-customers* for:

- breach of trust (for example, if it allows misappropriation of trust funds);
- tort (for example, if the bank gives some form of free advice which results in a loss to the enquirer);
- negligently or fraudulently given replies to an enquirer on the creditworthiness of a customer which cause a loss to the enquirer.

Task

For what could a bank be sued if it fails to keep one of its implied duties to a customer?

3.6.4 Negotiable Instruments

Certain contractual rights to receive sums of money can be transferred from one person to another because they are contained in *negotiable instruments*. These written documents are recognised in law as having the characteristic of negotiability through commercial custom or statute. They include *bills of exchange, cheques, promissory notes* and *bank notes*

The key features of negotiability are:

- the instrument is transferred simply by delivery of the document, with or without endorsement according to the circumstances;
- notice of the transfer does not have to be given to the person(s) due to pay;
- the holder has the right to sue in his or her own name to enforce payment;
- the title of the holder does not depend on the title of the previous holder (the transferee) providing certain conditions are met;
- the title of the holder passes free from defects in title providing it is received in good faith for value and without notice of any defect in title. This means that a new holder of a negotiable instrument must be paid the full amount; the normal right to set-off amounts owed cannot be exercised.

Task

Compare the characteristics of a postal order with those listed above. Is it a negotiable instrument?

3.6.5 Bills of Exchange

A *bill of exchange* is a payment instrument and is defined by the *Bills of Exchange Act 1882*. It is an unconditional order in writing, addressed by one person (the *drawer*) to another (the *drawee*). It is signed by the drawer, requiring the drawee to pay on demand or at a fixed or determinable future date, a specified sum of money to, or to the order of, a specified person or to bearer.

No person can be held liable on a bill of exchange unless he or she has signed it. The signature need not be by hand but must be authorised. The payee presents the bill to the drawee who *accepts* it by signing the face of the bill, usually adding the date. If the bill is presented to the drawee and the drawee refuses to accept it, the bill is said to be *dishonoured by non-acceptance*. Presentation of bills of exchange for acceptance and payment must conform to certain rules.

Task

Obtain a blank bill of exchange and identify the sections to be filled in by each of the three parties.

3.6.6 Cheques

A *cheque* is a payment instrument. It is a *bill of exchange* drawn on a banker and payable on demand within a reasonable time, usually six months. Acceptance is not necessary. Since it is a bill of exchange, there are three parties to a cheque: the *drawer* (the bank customer), the *drawee* (the bank) and the *payee* (the person or persons named).

A cheque can be hand-written, typed or printed. Large organisations may print their cheques, including the signature; many retailers now print the transaction details on customers' cheques at the point of sale.

The cheque should be dated. A post-dated cheque is not a cheque since it is not payable on demand, but it can be presented for payment on or after the stated date. A debt may be legally enforced at any time within six years of the issue of a cheque under the *Limitation Act 1980*.

The payee is usually named and can be an individual, joint individuals or a corporate body. An open cheque can be cashed at the branch of the bank on which it has been drawn, but if it has been crossed it must be paid into a bank account. Endorsement (the payee's signature on the reverse) of an order cheque is required unless it is paid directly into the payee's own account. By endorsing a cheque, a payee renounces his or her interest in it and can use it to pay a debt to another person. However, a cheque crossed with the words *'not negotiable'* is not a negotiable instrument and cannot be used in this way.

The drawer may be an individual, joint individuals or a corporate body. The drawer must sign the face of the cheque. Under the *Bills of Exchange Act 1882* a forged or unauthorised signature renders the cheque void.

The *Cheques Act 1957* abolishes the need to endorse an order cheque if it is paid directly into the payee's own account. It also stated that a cheque is proof of payment of a debt. This obviates the need to issue receipts for payments made by cheque, although a receipt should always be given if requested.

In recent years it has become common practice to accept cheque payments of sums up to £50 or £100 only if supported by an appropriate *cheque card*. This contains a specimen signature of the card holder and the issuing banker guarantees to meet the cheque up to the specified maximum amount. In addition, a cheque card permits the holder to cash personal cheques for amounts up to the specified sum at any branch of a specified bank or group of banks.

Task

Richard Hardwick has an account with the Midland Bank. He pays £200 to his accountant, William Collis, whose account is with the Royal Bank of Scotland. Name the drawer, drawee and payee in this transaction.

3.6.7 Promissory Notes

Promissory notes are also payment instruments. However, there are only two parties: the *drawer* and the *payee*. In a promissory note (for example, a bank note) the drawer *promises* to pay.

Task

Study a five or ten pound note and identify the characteristics which define it as a promissory note.

3.6.8 Banker's Drafts

Banker's drafts are payment instruments with only two parties: the bank draws the draft on itself and is therefore *both drawer and drawee*. The holder of a banker's draft has the right to treat it as if it were a *bill of exchange* or a *promissory note*.

Task

You have advertised your computer for sale at £499 to include a selection of software. Someone rings you and offers £400. You tell him that you would like to accept his offer. He says it is too big a sum to pay in cash and wants to pay by cheque when he picks the computer up. However, his cheque card only guarantees his cheques up to £50. Drop him a line explaining the difference between a banker's draft and a cheque and why you would prefer a banker's draft.

Assignment 3.6: At crossed purposes

You are a graduate trainee with the Capel Bank Ltd. The manager asks you to attend to the following letter.

The Manager   3 September 1991
Capel Bank Ltd
High Street
Stockton

Dear Sir

Ref: Account No. 13752846

I have just received my bank statement and was shocked to see that cheque number 402586 for £50 has been cleared. This cheque was made out to my daughter, Julia Cunningham, who endorsed it and gave it to her boyfriend. I understand that he used it to buy some sports equipment, endorsing the cheque in favour of the shop. I did not intend the money to be used in this way as it was meant to be a present to Julia for passing her exams. Please reclaim the money from the shop and credit my account accordingly.

Yours faithfully

John Cunningham

John Cunningham

Student activities

Answer Mr Cunningham's letter explaining the legal position and giving him guidance on how to prevent such an incident occurring again.

3.7 Consumer Law

3.7.1 A Consumer Sale

A *consumer sale* contains the following key elements:

- The seller of the goods must sell them in the course of business.
- The purchaser of the goods must not buy them or hold himself as buying them in the course of business.
- The goods must be of a type ordinarily supplied for private use or consumption.

In a *private sale*, where goods are not bought from a person or organisation in business, the principle is caveat emptor, let the buyer take care.

Tasks

Which of the following transactions meets the description of a consumer sale?

(i) Matthew Kingston sells his motor scooter to Thames Motorcycles Ltd.

(ii) He then buys a Vauxhall Cavalier from Derek Brown.

(iii) Next he buys a tankful of unleaded petrol from the garage.

(iv) Finally, he purchases a set of adjustable spanners from Halfords.

3.7.2 A Contract of Sale

A consumer buys goods by means of a contract with the seller. As in any other simple contract, a *contract of sale* confers personal rights and contractual obligations on the parties providing all the essential elements of a contract are present.

Contracts of sale are a very common type of transaction. The *Sale of Goods Act 1979,* which must be read in conjunction with the *Unfair Contract Terms Act 1977*, regulates the rights and obligations of the parties to a consumer sale. A contract of sale of goods is defined as one in which the seller transfers, or agrees to transfer, the property in goods to the buyer, for a money consideration called the price.

The term *property in goods* means ownership. The term *goods* includes all movable personal property (except money), but excludes immovable possessions such as a house or land. It also excludes intangible property such as a copyright or patent.

Task

From your own experience of buying clothes, analyse a typical sale and describe the essential elements of contract in each sale which define the transaction as a contract of sale.

3.7.3 Conditions and Warranties

A contract of sale contains *express* terms, which are stated orally or in writing, and *implied* terms, which are implied by statute, custom or by the courts. Major terms in a contract, whether express or implied, are referred to as *conditions*; minor terms are known as *warranties*.

The *Sale of Goods Act 1979* lays down a stringent trading code which benefits all consumers. It provides that a contract of sale contains certain implied conditions including the following:

- an implied condition that the seller has the right to sell the goods;

- an implied warranty that the goods are free from any charge of encumbrance not disclosed or known to the buyer before or at the time of the contract of sale;

- an implied warranty that the buyer shall have and enjoy quiet possession of the goods;

- in a sale of goods by description there is an implied condition that goods shall correspond with the description (including weight, size, quantity and ingredients); if the goods are sold by sample as well as by description, the goods must correspond with the description and not just with the sample alone;

- an implied condition that goods are of merchantable quality.

- an implied condition that where the seller sells goods in the course of a business and the buyer, expressly or by implication, makes known to the seller any particular purpose for which the goods are being bought, the goods supplied are reasonably fit for that purpose.

Task

Examine any warranties or guarantees you may have for consumer goods bought recently. Which clauses refer to the terms of the Sale of Goods Act 1979 and which are additional to your statutory rights?

3.7.4 Breach of Contract

The *seller's duty* is to deliver the goods; the *buyer's duty* is to accept and pay for them in accordance with the terms of the contract of sale. An unpaid seller has certain rights against the goods, even though the property in the goods has passed to the buyer:

- a lien on the goods for the price while the seller is in possession of them;

- a right to stop the goods in transit after the seller has parted with possession if the buyer becomes insolvent;

- a right of resale as limited by the *Sale of Goods Act 1979*.

In addition to these remedies against the goods, the seller can also sue the buyer for the price if the property has passed to the buyer, or if the buyer has failed to pay for the goods by a specified date. If the buyer refuses to accept and pay for the goods, the seller can sue for damages arising from the *breach of contract*.

The buyer's remedies include the right to sue the seller for damages for non-delivery. In addition, the buyer can claim specific performance of the seller's promise to deliver if, in the opinion of the court, monetary damages would not be sufficient remedy. For example, if the goods comprised something unique, such as an original manuscript, the seller could be required to fulfil his or her contractual obligation. The buyer can also sue the seller for damages for breach of warranty, or claim for damages in diminution or extinction of the price as a result of the seller's *breach of warranty*.

Task

Tom Chapman asks Fastframe to reframe a large oil painting which his wife has recently inherited. He wants it to be ready for his wife's birthday. Fastframe orders the frame from the manufacturer who promises delivery the week before Tom's wife's birthday. However, the manufacturer delays delivery and Tom cancels the order and takes the picture to another framer. Can Fastframe claim damages from the manufacturer for the loss of profit the business has sustained?

3.7.5 Contracts for Goods and Services

A contract for *goods and services* is not a contract of sale, but such contracts are provided for by the *Supply of Goods and Services Act 1982*. These include:

- contracts for exchange or barter, such as a voucher on a cereal packet with an invitation to send off for a free gift, or contracts for work and materials where there is a transfer of property in the goods, such as in a maintenance contract;
- contracts for the hire of goods;
- contracts for the supply of services.

With regard to *goods* supplied under such contracts, the Act implies similar conditions to those contained in the *Sale of Goods Act 1979*. With regard to *services*, the Act implies terms relating to the use of reasonable care and skill, performing within a reasonable time and charging a reasonable fee.

A *hire purchase agreement* (Section 3.7.6) is not a contract of sale. It is an option to buy rather than an obligation to buy. Goods supplied under such an agreement are covered by the *Supply of Goods (Implied Terms) Act 1973* which implies similar conditions to those contained in the *Sale of Goods Act 1979*.

Task

Compile a list of examples of contracts for goods and services.

3.7.6 Consumer Credit Agreements

Hire purchase agreements and other forms of *consumer credit* are provided for by the *Consumer Credit Act 1974*. A *consumer credit agreement* is defined as a personal agreement where the borrower is an individual or partnership, not a company, and the amount loaned does not exceed £15,000. Agreements falling within this definition are known as *regulated agreements*. The Act regulates the loan of money or the supply of goods on credit by:

- giving the consumer adequate and accurate information on which to make an informed choice;
- imposing a level of trading standards;
- providing consumer protection.

Under provisions contained in the *Fair Trading Act 1973*, the Director General of Fair Trading is responsible for supervising the working of the *Consumer Credit Act 1974*. The Director General's duties include:

- administering the licensing system set up by the Act;
- exercising adjudicating functions relating to the issue, renewal, variation, suspension and revocation of licences and other matters;
- generally supervising the working and enforcement of the regulations;
- where necessary, taking steps to enforce the regulations.

Tasks

(i)   Collect a variety of examples of consumer credit agreements ranging from high street shops to credit companies advertising in newspapers. Now compare these with a hire purchase agreement. What are the additional rights a hire purchase agreement offers?

(ii)   At what stage in a credit sale agreement does ownership of the goods pass to the purchaser?

(iii)   At what stage in a hire purchase agreement does ownership of the goods pass to the purchaser?

3.7.7 Unsolicited Goods and Services

Under the *Unsolicited Goods and Services Act 1971* goods and services need not be paid for, and unordered goods may be kept by the recipient if not collected by the sender within six months of delivery or within 30 days of receiving notice from the recipient as to where the goods can be collected. The Act imposes criminal and civil sanctions on traders indulging in *inertia selling*, which involves demanding payment for unsolicited goods and services.

Task

Every year you receive a packet of Christmas cards and labels in the post from a well known charity. You support the aims of the charity, but never get round to sending off a cheque. The accompanying letter asks you to return the goods if you do not intend to buy them. Are you obliged to send any money? Are you obliged to return the goods?

3.7.8 Trade Descriptions

A *trade description* can apply to goods or services and may be oral or written. Oral descriptions can be made by the seller or the consumer. Written descriptions include any markings on the goods or packaging relating to such matters as quantity, size, list of ingredients, fitness for purpose etc.

Under the *Trade Descriptions Acts 1968* and *1972* it is an offence to:

- apply a false trade description to goods;
- supply goods to which a false trade description has been applied;
- make a false statement knowingly or recklessly as to the provision of service accommodation or facilities.

The Acts only apply to sales which are made as an integral part of a person's trade or business. A purchaser in a private sale must seek remedies available under civil law.

The legislation is enforced by local authority *trading standards officers* who are empowered to purchase goods or services, enter premises to make checks and require suppliers to produce documents. Before a local authority brings a prosecution, the Department of Trade and Industry is informed to prevent numerous prosecutions of the same false trade description.

Tasks

(i) Orchard Fruit agrees to sell ten boxes of Cox's apples to Mr Greengage, the grocer. When the boxes are delivered, two are found to contain Golden Delicious apples. What legal advice would you offer Mr Greengage?

(ii) Liz and Roger Bristowe book a self-catering seaside holiday in Spain through Joe Anderson, the owner of the villa. When they arrive they find that the villa is 20 km from the sea, any glimpse of which is obscured by new hotels under construction. What is their legal position?

3.7.9 Consumer Protection and Safety

The *Consumer Protection Act 1987* introduced the concept of *product liability*. This means that if a defect in a product causes injury to a person, whether or not that person is the purchaser, the producer is liable without the injured party having to show fault. This is known as strict liability. The Act makes it an offence not to comply with a general safety requirement and various powers are provided to:

- make safety regulations;
- make an order for forfeiture;
- serve a prohibition notice;
- serve a suspension notice;
- serve a notice to warn.

A supplier who breaches the regulations commits an offence and is also liable under civil law for any injuries caused as a result. In defence, the seller may be able to show that all reasonable steps were taken and all due diligence was exercised to avoid committing the offence. The legislation is communicated to traders and enforced by local authority trading standards officers who have the power of entry, search, seizure and testing.

The *Consumer Protection Act 1987* also makes it an offence for any person in the course of business to give a consumer any misleading indication as to the price of goods, services, accommodation or facilities available. A Code of Practice on Price Indications was published in 1988 which provides traders with guidelines on acceptable pricing practices.

Task

See if you can find any examples of legal cases brought under the Consumer Protection Act 1987 reported in the local press.

3.7.10 The Preparation and Sale of Food

The Food Safety Act 1990 regulates the standard and quality of food and drink sold for human consumption. The act contains a number of offences relating to the sale of food which is injurious to health, unfit for human consumption or so contaminated that it is not reasonable to expect it to be eaten. The Act also covers the sale of sub-standard food, that is food which is fit for consumption but is not the quality requested, and the sale of food which is falsely labelled or labelled in such a way that it is likely to mislead a consumer.

Local authority trading standards officers and environmental health officers are empowered to enforce the Act. A successful prosecution can result in a substantial fine or imprisonment. A prohibition order can be made which will curtail the activities of the offending trader.

Task

Mrs Edwards buys a dozen eggs whilst out for the day with her cousin in the country. When she gets home she makes herself an omelette for supper with four of the eggs. During the night she becomes very ill and calls the doctor, who suspects salmonella food poisoning. The remaining eggs are sent to the Public Health Laboratory for analysis and the doctor's suspicions are confirmed. Fortunately Mrs Edwards has a strong constitution and recovers after a week. What legal action would you advise her to take? What would be the position if her cousin kept chickens and had given her the eggs?

Assignment 3.7: Keeping the customers satisfied

You have recently joined the training department of a large fashion retailer. One of the problems your company is encountering is that of customers returning purchases claiming that they are faulty. The company has a high turnover of staff and they are responding in different ways to customers' complaints. Some give a refund or credit note; some offer to exchange the goods; others refuse to take any action until the supplier has commented on the complaint. The company now wants to formulate a complaints policy.

Student activities

The training manager asks you to design a simple instruction leaflet, which can be given to all the sales staff, setting out the procedure to be followed in cases of returned goods. You should bear in mind the legal position of the company and the customer. Use a desktop publishing package to produce your leaflet.

3.8 Fair Trading Law

3.8.1 Monopolies and Mergers

In a market economy it is possible for unfair trading practices to develop which may be detrimental to both competitors and consumers. The structure of the market in the UK is controlled through provisions in the *Fair Trading Act 1973* which:

- define a *monopoly* situation and a *merger* situation;
- empower the *Monopolies and Mergers Commission* to investigate such situations;
- empower the Secretary of State for Trade and Industry to take action to remedy such situations.

A monopoly share occurs if a business organisation has or is likely to have control of 25 per cent of a particular market, or if the total assets of the merged organisation exceed £5m.

The Secretary of State is empowered to order:
- the transfer of property from one organisation to another;
- the adjustment of contracts;
- the reallocation of shares in an organisation;
- the prohibition of a merger.

Task

Find examples of mergers which have been rejected by the government and identify the grounds on which the companies involved have defended their attempted actions.

3.8.2 Restrictive Trade Practices in the UK

It is in the consumer's best interests that *restrictive trade practices* are controlled. These include agreements between suppliers, agreements between suppliers and distributors or retailers, and other anti-competitive practices. The *Restrictive Trade Practices Acts 1976 and 1977* provide for the registration and judicial investigation of certain restrictive trading agreements, and for the prohibition of agreements which are found to be contrary to the resale price of goods. Registration is with the Director General of Fair Trading.

The *Resale Price Act 1976* aims to abolish *resale price maintenance* in the UK, except where it can be shown to be in the public interest; certain goods are exempt. Civil action may be brought by any person affected by breach of the provisions in the Act, or by the Crown.

The *Competition Act 1980* seeks to control anti-competitive practices in the supply of goods and services in the UK. Contraventions are referred to the Monopolies and Mergers Commission after preliminary investigation by the Director General of Fair Trading.

Task

In groups, debate the motion: The monopoly of the Post Office is not in the consumer's best interest.

3.8.3 Restrictive Trade Practices in the EEC

In addition to UK law, *Article 85 of the Treaty of Rome* prohibits all agreements which prevent, restrict or distort competition within the Common Market and which may affect trade between member states of the EEC. Monopolies in the EEC are controlled by *Article 86 of the Treaty of Rome*. This states that abuse by one or more undertakings of a *dominant position* within the Common Market or a substantial part of it is prohibited in so far as it may affect trade between member states.

Mergers are controlled by Regulation 4064/89 which came into force in 1990. This regulation does not affect purely domestic mergers.

Task

Is a sales agreement relating only to trade within England covered under the provisions of the Treaty of Rome?

Assignment 3.8: Mighty Cat plc

You are an assistant in the marketing department of Mighty Cat plc, a pet food manufacturer, which has about 30 per cent of the cat food market in the UK. In a drive to secure a greater share of the European market, the company is contemplating entering into the following agreements:

- to supply its products solely to Speedy Distribution Ltd in the UK, Vitesse SRL in France and Schnelligkeit AG in Germany;
- that the distribution companies will not supply outside their own countries;
- that the distribution companies will not sell below a price recommended by Mighty Cat plc;
- Mighty Cat plc will ensure that any distributors appointed in other countries will not supply in the UK, France or Germany.

Student activities

The marketing director has asked to you write a word processed report on the legal implications of these agreements in the context of EEC and UK competition law.

3.9 Insurance Law

3.9.1 Insurance Contracts

The purpose of an *insurance contract* is the indemnification against loss, or the payment of a specified sum or the equivalent in the provision of services, upon the happening of an uncertain event. The parties to the contract are the *insurer* and the *insured*. The insured agrees pays a *premium* for the consideration that the insurer agrees to compensate the insured in the event of him or her suffering a loss on the occurrence of a specified event.

The main principle underlying insurance is the *pooling of risk*. This simply involves a large number of people contributing to a fund, out of which compensation can be paid if or when the loss insured against occurs. By maintaining records, insurance companies are able to calculate the probability of the many risks insured against with great accuracy.

In common with other legal contracts, an insurance contract must contain all the basic elements of a contract. The main events insured against by businesses are:

- the death, disability or sickness of key members of staff;
- the destruction of buildings and contents by fire;
- the loss of goods and property by theft;
- the loss of motor vehicles through accidents;
- third party claims arising from accidents;
- marine losses.

A contract of insurance is a written agreement, details of which are contained in the *policy document*.

Task

If you have life cover, a buildings, contents or personal possessions policy, or motor insurance, look up your policy document and identify the key elements of a legal contract.

3.9.2 Characteristics of an Insurance Contract

In addition to possessing the essential elements of a contract, all insurance agreements must be based on the following principles:

- insurable interest;
- utmost good faith;
- indemnity.

The first condition requires that the insured must suffer an equivalent loss before he or she is entitled to compensation by insurance. Therefore he or she must have an *insurable interest* in whatever risk is being insured against.

The principle of *utmost good faith* in insurance contracts requires that all parties must disclose all relevant particulars which might influence any party's willingness to make the contract. The contract is voidable whether non-disclosure of a material fact is innocent or fraudulent.

Task

What is the difference between an insurance contract and a bet on a horse?

3.9.3 Life Assurance

The difference between *insurance* and *assurance* is that with insurance it is uncertain that the event insured against will take place. With assurance the event is assured (it is certain to take place); the only uncertainty is *when* it will take place.

In a contract of life assurance the insurer agrees to pay the person for whose benefit the contract is entered into a sum of money or an *annuity* upon the death of the assured; premiums are paid until the death of the assured. An *endowment* policy is a combination of life assurance and investment. If the assured survives the specified period during which his or her life is assured, he or she receives a sum of money (with or without profits). Premiums are paid only for the specified period.

It is generally only possible to take out life assurance on your own life or another person's in whom you have a financial interest, such as a spouse or business partner. A person who criminally causes the death of the assured is precluded from receiving any monies due under the contract. Although under the *Suicide Act 1961* suicide is no longer a crime, life assurance monies cannot be claimed if the assured commits suicide whilst sane.

Task

Application forms for life cover ask a number of personal questions. One such question asks whether the applicant has been tested for HIV and, if so, was the result positive or negative. Debate whether the applicant is in breach of the principle of utmost good faith if he or she fails to reveal a negative result on the form.

3.9.4 Fire Insurance

Fire was probably one of the earliest risks to be insured against, since wood used to be the main building material. The first insurance companies ran their own fire brigades in order to try and minimise losses. A contract of fire insurance is purely one of indemnity. The insurer agrees to indemnify the insured against loss by fire of the subject of the policy, for a consideration consisting of a premium paid by the insured.

Under the *Law of Property Act 1925* money payable in respect of damage to property, which is the subject of a contract of sale under a policy of insurance maintained by the vendor, is to be paid by the vendor to the purchaser on completion. The same Act requires that all monies received by a mortgagor in respect of an insurance claim for loss or damage by fire to a mortgaged property be used to *make good* that damage or loss; in the absence of such an agreement or obligation, the monies should be used in or towards the *discharge* of the mortgage.

After the insurance company has paid out in full what is due under a policy, the insurer is entitled under the principle of *subrogation* to every legal and equitable right of the insured, whether the right arises out of contract or tort.

Task

You usually park your car outside your house. One night your car is hit by a third party and catches fire on impact. Your car is a write-off and your insurers make you a payment based on total loss. However, the expensive cassette/radio is almost unscathed and on the night of the accident you decide to remove it before it is stolen. Shortly afterwards you read a report in the local paper that the third party has been successfully sued by your insurers and damages have been awarded. You write to your insurers asking them why they have not kept you informed of this development. They do not answer this point, but instead ask you for information on the whereabouts of the cassette/radio. What are the respective legal obligations in this instance?

3.9.5 Marine Insurance

Under the *Marine Insurance Act 1906* a contract of marine insurance is defined as a contract whereby the insurer undertakes to indemnify the insured, in the manner and to the extent thereby agreed, against the losses incident to marine adventure. A contract of marine insurance may be extended by its express terms or by usage of trade, so as to protect the insured against losses on inland waters or against any land risk incidental to a sea voyage.

Marine insurance policies can be classified as follows:

- *voyage policies* where the contract is to insure the marine property from one place to another (or others);
- *time policies* where the contract is to insure the marine property for a defined period of time;
- *mixed policies* which combine voyage and time policies;
- *valued policies* which specify the agreed value of the marine property;
- *unvalued policies* which leave the insurable value of the marine property to be ascertained subsequently, subject to the limit of the sum insured;
- *floating policies* which describe the insurance in general terms but leave the name of the ship(s) and other details to be defined by subsequent declaration, usually by endorsement on the policy.

The best known centre for marine insurance is Lloyd's, an association of London underwriters which was incorporated by Act of Parliament in 1871. Today all kinds of insurance are accepted and marine insurance comprises less than half of Lloyd's total business.

Task

What is an insurer's liability if a ship deviates from the voyage contemplated by the policy, but regains her route before any loss occurs?

3.9.6 Liability Insurance

This type of insurance indemnifies the insured against his or her liability to third parties. Householders can insure against their liability to visitors and neighbours; professionals can insure against liability for professional negligence.

Under the *Employers' Liability (Compulsory Insurance) Act 1969* employers, with certain exceptions, must insure against liability for bodily injury or disease sustained by their employees and arising out of and in the course of their employment in Great Britain or on oil rigs in designated areas.

The *Road Traffic Act 1972* requires every driver to insure against liability in respect of the death or bodily injury of any person caused by the use of the motor vehicle on the road. Failure to do so constitutes a criminal offence. If the driver is not adequately insured, the third party can obtain compensation from the Motor Insurers' Bureau.

Under the *Third Parties (Rights against Insurers) Act 1930* if a person who is insured against liability to third parties becomes bankrupt or makes a composition or arrangement with his or her creditors, the rights of the insured against the insurance company in respect of any claim are transferred and vested in the third party.

Task

If you have motor insurance, look up terms of the policy relating to cover of third party liability.

Assignment 3.9: Billy the braggart

One evening in the pub you overhear a conversation between Billy, a married friend of yours, and John the barman:

Billy: ....so I've decided this insurance is a good idea. I'm going to insure my house for £80,000 and the contents for £5,000. And I thought I'd take out a policy on my life, the wife's life and my mate Gareth's life. Then I'll be safe as houses! Get it? Ha ha ha!

John: Hold on a minute Billy, my old son, your house is worth more than that. You've got that continental fitted kitchen - I bet that's worth £10,000 for a start, all that double glazing, fitted carpets, not to mention your Linda's jewellery and your hi-fi equipment.

Billy: Oh, don't worry, I've thought about that, but its okay; I'm going to take out a new for old policy - they won't know I'm underestimating things a little.

John: Well, I don't know. You ought to be careful. Remember that bit of trouble you had when you first came here. I remember you and your Linda were pretty badly hurt in the smash up you had in that car you, er..... borrowed. I thought you were going to do things by the book now.

Billy: Yeah, well that was before I settled down. I was a bit dumb then. No need to mention that to the insurance people; it's all water under the bridge now. Anyway, the wife's fully recovered - you can't see the scars where they operated. And we've got the kids to think of now. That's why I decided to take out a policy on Gareth. It would give me and Linda more security.

John: Well, I suppose so. Excuse me, there's a customer....

You are very perturbed by this conversation and feel that Billy is about to make some very big mistakes. However, you realise by his bragging tone that he has had a few pints and it would be better not to approach him now.

Student activities

Write a letter to Billy setting out clearly the principles of an insurance agreement and compare these with what Billy proposes. Give examples of the likely outcome in the event of a claim if he goes ahead with his ideas too hastily. Advise him on what steps he and Linda might take if they want to use insurance to protect themselves against loss.

Section 4
Business Policy

by Judith Jordan

MA, BTEC Co-ordinator and Lecturer in Business Policy at Bristol Polytechnic

Business policy is concerned with organisations' approaches to formulating strategies and the range, nature and likely outcomes of common strategic actions.

Recommended Reading

Argenti, C., *Practical Corporate Planning,* Unwin, 1989

Howe, Stewart, *Corporate Strategy,* Macmillan, 1986

Johnson, G., & Scholes, K., *Exploring Corporate Strategy,* Prentice Hall, 1989

Luffman, G., *Business Policy,* Blackwell, 1987

Porter, M. E., *Competitive Strategy: Techniques for Analysing Industries and Competitors,* Tree Press, 1980

Porter, M. E., *Competitive Advantage: Creating and Sustaining Superior Performance,* Tree Press, 1985

Thompson, J. L., *Strategic Management – Awareness and Change,* Chapman & Hall, 1990

The M.D. had really outflanked the competition this time... Sprogett & Son were consolidating their position.

Contents

4.1 External Strategic Analysis

The purpose of *external strategic analysis* is to provide a basis for managers to consider the opportunities and threats which face their businesses. The structural features of the market (the industry's underlying economic characteristics) influence the nature and intensity of competition. The formulation of a successful strategy requires that such factors are taken into account. When a thorough analysis of the general and specific environment of the organisation has taken place, the potential opportunities and threats facing the firm can be identified.

4.1.1 The General Environment

Strategists first need to assess what is likely to happen to the business if present policies remain unchanged. An *environmental audit* is a useful starting point; it involves identifying those factors which have critical impact on the firm.

Environmental influences can be classified as:

- economic
- social and cultural
- political and legal
- technological

External influences do not always fit neatly into a particular category since they may be the result of a complex amalgamation of many forces.

The object of the audit is not to list all possible influences, but to identify those factors which are of key importance to the success of the business. For example, defence companies such as British Aerospace and Marconi need to pay particular attention to the political environment: the end of the Cold War in Europe; the Gulf War. Other companies may need to focus attention on social and demographic variables. Cow and Gate, the baby food company, needs to be aware of changes in the birth rate, changing attitudes to packaged baby food, food scares, etc.

Task

Identify the environmental forces which have critical impact on either the organisation for which you work or the college where you are studying. Which of them are currently the most important? Which will be the most important in the next few years?

4.1.2 Assessing Uncertainty

The nature of the external environment varies between firms. Some organisations operate in static, predictable environments; others in fast-moving, unpredictable ones. To understand the environment, the strategist must be aware of the degree of *uncertainty* facing the organisation.

G Johnson and K Scholes argue that uncertainty increases as environmental influences become more dynamic and more complex. *Dynamism* refers to the rate and frequency of change. In a static environment the past usually acts as a good guide to the future. In a dynamic environment firms need to explore a variety of possible future states of the environment. A range of 'what if' situations can be analysed by generating *scenarios* or by using structured expert opinion such as the *Delphi technique*.

Complexity increases when:

- there is a great diversity of environmental influences;

- the amount of knowledge required to handle the environment increases;
- environmental influences are highly interconnected.

High levels of complexity require organisations to develop sophisticated information-processing and modelling techniques in order to understand their environment. Techniques such as *multiple regression, factor analysis* and *input-output modelling* can be used to structure large quantities of interrelated data.

Example: Scenario planning

Companies operating in the oil industry face an environment that is both dynamic and complex. Decisions made by managers have long-term but very uncertain consequences. Many of the major oil companies engage in scenario planning in order to analyse and assess possible strategic outcomes. Four possible scenarios are outlined below.

Scenario A: More of the same

The national economy remains dependent on fossil fuels. OPEC regains dominance or wars in the Middle East restrict supply. Demand and price remain high. A seller's market prevails.

Scenario B: The optimistic view

Structural changes in the world economy lead to the resolution of budget and trade deficit problems. World trade flourishes. The developed economies improve energy efficiency, but demand for fossil fuels increases in developing nations. Energy prices remain buoyant and a seller's market prevails.

Scenario C: The pessimistic view

Failure to resolve economic problems lead to deepening world recession and a rise in protectionism. Oil prices are low due to a slump in demand, but there is still dependence on fossil fuels.

Scenario D: The technological breakthrough

New technological discoveries radically reduce dependence on oil. Energy prices are low and a buyer's market prevails.

Each scenario must be internally consistent and sufficiently detailed for planners to make valid inferences about the likely impact of the environment on the organisation.

Task

Assess the degree of uncertainty facing the following retailers:
- Marks & Spencer;
- your local greengrocer.

4.1.3 The Industry Environment

Having analysed the current and possible future state of the general environment, the next step is to look in more depth at the firm's specific *industry environment*. The impact of the general environment on the business organisation is broad; there is a wide variety of influences of different intensities. In contrast, the industrial environment is much closer to the firm and its effects are continuous and direct.

An *industry* can be defined as a collection of firms with a common interest. The common interest may be derived from demand or supply conditions. On the demand side, firms may produce products which are considered by consumers to be substitutes for each other. For example, the soft drinks industry consists of a group of firms producing carbonated drinks and cordials which are considered as substitutes for each other by the consumer. On the supply side, firms produce products which use similar technologies. For example, the plastics industry may consist of a group of firms making dissimilar products, but using the same kind of production method.

Industries are composed of players whose actions may pose a direct threat to the organisation. Strategists need to examine the *industry environment* in a systematic way if their policies are to be successful A useful approach is provided by *M E Porter*. It is argued that *competition* within an industry is dependent on its underlying economic structure. In Porter's model there are five main forces which influence the intensity of competition:

- Rivalry between existing competitors (Section 4.1.4)
- The threat of new entry (Section 4.1.5)
- Buyer power (Section 4.1.6)
- Supplier power (Section 4.1.7)
- The threat of substitute products (Section 4.1.8)

These in turn are influenced by the structural characteristics of the industry. In the brewing industry, for example, the structural conditions of the market suggest that competition will be intense, but will largely take place under terms which are set by the national brewers.

Task

Draw up a list of the firms which comprise the soft drinks industry and identify the products which may be considered as substitutes.

4.1.4 Rivalry Between Existing Competitors

Rivalry between business organisations takes many forms; for example, price cutting, advertising battles, and product innovation. In some industries rivalry can be cut-throat and bitter; in others there are collusive agreements. The nature and intensity of such rivalry is determined by:

- market concentration (the more concentrated the market the greater the likelihood of collusion);
- the diversity of competitors (the more diverse the competitors the more intense the rivalry);
- the cost structure (the greater the fixity and indivisibility of the cost structure, the more intense the competition, particularly in times of low demand);
- the degree of product differentiation (the more homogeneous the product, the greater the rivalry);
- barriers to exit (the more difficult it is for a firm to leave the market, the more intense the competition, particularly when demand falls).

Example

In 1987 there were some 220 brewers in the UK; three were brewers without tied estate, six were national producers, 11 were regional producers, and 41 operated on a local basis. The remainder were mainly very small producers supplying beer through a single outlet or a small number of owned outlets.

Despite the relatively large number of brewers, production was concentrated in the hands of the six national producers who accounted for 75 per cent of all beer production in the UK. Competitors ranged from large diversified companies, such as Grand Metropolitan plc, to independent specialist producers, such as Wadworth & Co Ltd. Economies of scale are available in brewing. Research suggests that the minimum efficient brewery size is four million barrels per annum. However, demand for a wide variety of beers, together with the decline in overall demand, has restricted brewers' ability to achieve such economies.

Beer is a differentiated product. Differentiation is achieved through differences in taste, strength, branding and advertising, and differences in the location and nature of public houses. Barriers to exit are not particularly high, although there are some sunk costs associated with advertising expenditure and highly specific capital equipment.

Task

Identify the main competitors in the personal savings market and collect illustrations of their rivalry.

4.1.5 The Threat of New Entry

Competition depends not only on rivalry between established competitors, but also on the *threat of new competition* from potential entrants. The likelihood of entry depends on the height of entry barriers, the height of exit barriers and the potential entrant's assessment of the market.

The height of *entry barriers* is measured by the extent to which an established firm can raise its price above average cost without attracting entry. The main sources of entry barriers are:

- economies of scale;
- product differentiation;
- absolute cost advantages;
- large capital requirement;
- switching costs;
- government policy;
- restricted access to customers or suppliers.

Recently emphasis has been placed not only on entry conditions but also on *exit barriers*. It is argued that entry barriers, such as large capital requirements, are only effective if such outlays are not recoverable on exit. The main sources of exit barriers are:

- sunk costs and the existence of specialised assets;
- fixed costs of exit;
- government and social barriers;
- strategic barriers;
- emotional barriers.

If exit barriers are low, new firms are more likely to enter the market. The new entrant's *assessment of the market* depends on its view of the prospects of the industry in general; also on its view of the established firms' reaction to its entry. The threat of new entry is likely to be reduced if established firms can offer a credible threat of *retaliation*. Retaliation appears more likely when:

- established firms have excess capacity;
- the industry has a past history of retaliation;
- established firms are large and diversified.

Example

Entry to the brewing industry was limited during the 1980s. The little entry that did take place took the form of:

- ownership changes (for example, Courage was acquired by Hanson and later by Elders IXL);
- licensing arrangements (for example, foreign brewers of well known brands such as Budweiser and Miller Lite entered into agreements with established UK producers);
- newcomers, who entered the market on a very small scale.

The major barrier to entry is vertical integration by the brewers. This restricts the access of potential entrants to customers and increases the cost of entry.

Task

You are considering setting up a small business offering a student loan service. What problems would you face in trying to enter this market?

4.1.6 Buyer Power

If buyers possess bargaining strength, generally they depress industry profitability and increase industry competition. Buyer power depends on:

- the level of buyer concentration;
- the degree of product differentiation;
- the degree of backward vertical integration;
- the level of buyer information.

Example

Most brewers are also wholesalers: they sell beer to retail outlets and to each other. Forward vertical integration has reduced buyer power in the on-licence sector, but in the off-licence sector supermarkets and independent chains have some buying power.

4.1.7 Supplier Power

Suppliers can threaten to increase costs or alter the quality of inputs into the production process and thus influence industry profitability and competition. *Supplier power* depends on such things as:

- the degree of supplier concentration;
- the importance of the industry to the supplier;
- the degree of production differentiation (Section 4.3.6);
- the degree of forward vertical integration.

Example

The basic ingredients for brewing beer are cereal (usually malted barley), hops, yeast and water. They are all readily available and there is little supplier power in the brewing market.

Tasks

In groups, consider the implications for food manufacturers of the introduction of own label brands by the major supermarkets. Identify the buyer and the supplier in this context and then consider:

(i) the impact on buyer power;

(ii) the impact on supplier power.

4.1.8 The Threat of Substitute Products

Competition comes not only from within the industry itself but also from outside the industry in terms of *substitute products*. Identifying substitute products is a matter of searching for other products which can perform the same function as the product of the industry. Reducing the threat from substitutes may require collective industry action.

Example

Substitute products include both alcoholic and non-alcoholic drinks. In recent years expenditure on spirits and cider has risen more rapidly than on beer. In addition, non-alcoholic drinks have increased in popularity. Most national brewers have interests in other parts of the drinks market which reduces the threat of substitute products.

Tasks

You have inherited £1,000 which you want to invest on the stock market. However, you are aware that environmental pressures may threaten the future performance of industries. What substitute products might threaten the following industries?

(i)   the tobacco industry;

(ii) the sugar industry;

(iii) the processed food industry.

Assignment 4.1: Times are changing

You have been working for nine months for a small family-owned company. The founder of the firm has recently died and his daughter has taken over as managing director. She has just finished a degree in Zoology and has no business experience. However, she is aware that the company has been declining steadily over the last five years due to her father's poor health. As a start, she has asked you to prepare a report analysing the external environment of the company.

Student activities

(i)   Select a firm of your choice, perhaps one you or a relative has worked for, to represent the company in the assignment.

(ii) Conduct an analysis of the company's external environment, outlining the main opportunities and threats facing it.

(iii) Submit a word-processed report to the managing director with any recommendations you consider are appropriate.

4.2 Internal Strategic Analysis

The purpose of *internal strategic analysis* is to assess the strategic capabilities of the organisation. By identifying the firm's strengths and weaknesses, strategy can be formulated to match competences with future environmental opportunities.

4.2.1 Objectives

A strategy is a plan of action. A strategy can only be successful if it enables the organisation to reach its *objectives*. The first step in internal strategic analysis, therefore, is to identify the firm's objectives. It is common to refer to *mission statements*, *objectives* and *targets*.

The *mission* of an organisation is a visionary statement concerning its essential purpose or reason for being. Mission statements are general. They are often implicit and unwritten.

Objectives are desired states or results. Typical objectives derived from economic theory include:

- profit maximisation
- sales revenue maximisation
- growth maximisation
- managerial utility maximisation

If objectives can be measured and relate to a particular time scale they become targets.

Example

Extracts from the 1988 annual report of the Beecham Group plc.

Mission statement

'Beecham seeks to enhance shareholder value by superior performance, and is committed to supplying customers with quality products, providing employees with a challenging environment which encourages excellence, and to fulfilling its responsibilities to the communities in which it operates.'

Statement of objectives

'Beecham's business objective is to achieve a competitive advantage in the field of health and personal care and to build on these core businesses for the long-term by investing in research and marketing.'

Statement of targets

Beecham seeks 'to generate a return on equity of at least 20% and a return on operating assets of between 35% and 40%.'

R M Cyert and J G March argue that the goals of a firm emerge from a process of negotiation between groups or coalitions within the organisation. Coalitions are of groups of individuals with shared expectations. These groups can be formally identified as *stakeholders* (Section 4.4.4) in the firm; that is any group or individual who can affect or is affected by the performance of the organisation. A list of the principal stakeholders and their likely interest in performance targets, adapted from *J L Thompson*, is given below.

Stakeholder	*Interest*
Shareholders	Market value of their investment
	Stability in dividends
	Size of dividend
Managers	Sales growth
	Asset growth
	Profitability
Employees	Wage increase
	Numbers employed
	Job security
Society	Productivity gains
	Exports
	Profitability
	Social welfare

The various stakeholders have different goals, so the objectives of the firm represent a compromise between interest groups. As the expectations of the various groups can differ widely, it is normal for *conflict* to exist in organisations. Objectives tend to emerge as the wishes of the dominant group after a bargaining process between coalitions; hence the *power structure* of the organisation is important. Stakeholders are not affected in the same way by every strategic decision. Thus, the composition of coalitions is fluid and can transcend formal structures.

Organisations are likely to have *multiple objectives* and seek *satisficing* rather than maximising solutions; that is to say, they seek satisfactory solutions rather than optimal ones. For example, a firm may be happy with a satisfactory profit or a reasonable growth rate, rather than the maximum attainable profit and the fastest possible growth rate.

In recent years increasing attention has been paid to social *responsibility* as an objective which refers to the acceptance by the organisation of social responsibilities which are wider than the legal minimum. Social responsibility can involve, amongst other things, product safety, improved working conditions, avoidance of pollution and the use of non-sustainable resources, and avoidance of discrimination.

Task

Compare the objectives of a public and a private enterprise. In what ways are they different? In what ways are they similar?

4.2.2 Resources

Having ascertained the objectives of the firm, it is then necessary to establish what the firm does well and what it does badly. Carrying out a *resource audit* is a good starting point. The aim of a resource audit is to identify the links between the firm's various activities. A thorough resource audit provides a useful insight into ways of creating or sustaining *competitive advantage*.

One approach to resource auditing is provided by *value chain analysis* developed by *M E Porter*. Value chain analysis groups the organisation's primary activities into five main areas:

- inbound logistics (such as warehousing and receipt of inputs into the production process);
- operations (such as production systems);
- outbound logistics (such as distribution to retailers);
- market and sales (such as advertising);
- service (such as repairs).

Primary activities are supported by:

- procurement (such as purchasing);
- technology development (such as automation);
- human resource management (such as recruitment and training);
- the organisation's infrastructure (such as financial control systems).

Example: Comparison of two retail organisations, Argos and Harrods, using Porter's value chain analysis.

Argos offers a no-frills service to its customers and focuses on low price offers which must be sustained over the life of the Argos catalogue. The activities associated with receiving, storing and distributing goods to Argos stores (inbound logistics) and the retail operation itself must be tightly controlled to keep costs down. Computerised control systems are an important feature of the Argos system and illustrate the link between a support system (technology development) and primary activities (inbound logistics and operations) which Argos has managed to exploit. Argos offers little to its customers in terms of advice or after-sales service and staff need little product knowledge, since specifications are outlined in the catalogue.

By contrast, Harrods appeals to a customer group that is service rather than price-sensitive. Buyers and merchandisers focus on exclusive products and range; links with suppliers and the procurement function are important. Customer contact is high. This has implications for staff training and recruitment (human resource management). Information technology is used to improve communications with customers; for example Harrods' Wardrobe Service provides a database of individual customers' sizes and requirements, hence support activity (technology development) and primary activity (service) are linked to create competitive advantage.

As already mentioned, the resource audit also involves measuring how effectively current resources are being utilised. *Resource utilisation* can be measured in terms of *efficiency* and *effectiveness*. Efficiency refers to how well resources have been utilised regardless of the purpose for which they are employed.

Efficiency measures include profitability, capacity utilisation and yield. Effectiveness refers to how well resources are being allocated to those activities which are most important for the organisation as a whole. Measures of effectiveness involve monitoring:

- the use of capital;
- the use of people;
- the use of research and development;
- goodwill.

For example, efficiency in a library might be measured in terms of the ratio of librarians to the number of books issued. This would measure the efficiency of staff in issuing books, but would not indicate how effectively staff were dealing with enquiries; library users may be borrowing books which do not meet their requirements.

The value chain framework is chosen as the basis for resource auditing because it lends itself to the analysis of links between different parts of a firm's activities and allows the strategist insight into the sources of competitive advantage. Alternative models such as the *7S framework*, developed by *Waterman, Peters and Phillips*, or the analysis of *functional* areas of the organisation, such as marketing, production and finance, can also form a sound basis for a systematic internal analysis.

> **Task**
>
> Draw up a value chain for a book shop.

4.2.3 Finance

The financial resources of a firm are particularly important. The role of *finance* is not only to provide funding for the organisation, but also to monitor the use of those funds. Section 1.2.13 gives details of sources of funds. The *cost* and *availability* of such funds influence the ability of the company to pursue certain strategies and give rise to the possibility of competitive advantage. For example, a firm with access to a cheap source of capital will be in a good position to make the most of environmental opportunities.

The *monitoring of performance* using financial ratios can act as a guide to strategic capability. Details of financial ratios are given in Section 1.5.2. However, financial ratios can be misleading if used in isolation; there needs to be some sensible basis for comparison. Not all financial ratios are of equal strategic importance to the organisation and they should be used in association with the identification of distinctive competences through value chain analysis.

> **Task**
>
> Obtain copies of the published accounts of a limited company for the last three years. Analyse how their financial performance has varied over the period. What do you consider to be their financial strengths and weaknesses?

4.2.4 SWOT Analysis

SWOT is an acronym for strengths, weaknesses, opportunities, and threats. Internal analysis enables the organisation to identify its strengths and weaknesses; external analysis identifies opportunities and threats. SWOT analysis pulls the two elements together. The summary SWOT statements may also include a scoring system. For example, the larger the score, the more significant the issue. *Positive scores* may be used to indicate positive opportunities and strengths, *negative scores* may be used to indicate threats and weaknesses. A SWOT grid can be adapted to suit a variety of purposes and preferences, but its main role is to focus attention on key issues.

Example

F W Woolworth & Co Ltd was acquired by the Paternoster consortium from its American parent company in 1982. At the time of the take-over Woolworth was considered to be in very poor shape. A SWOT analysis undertaken at the time of the change of ownership might have identified the following points. The strengths and weaknesses would have been identified as a result of value chain analysis or a functional audit of the firm. Opportunities and threats would been identified through external analysis.

Weaknesses

- excessive numbers of suppliers (some 8,000), some providing inferior quality merchandise;
- imbalances in store locations: small shops in growth areas and large shops in declining areas;
- low average spend per customer;
- outmoded image;
- poor management information systems;
- staff promotion through length of service;
- autocratic management style;
- declining profitability.

Strengths

- a large number of stores in prime high street locations;
- a strong identity (Woolworth is a household name);
- an established position in certain market segments (for example, sweets, garden items, records);
- a loyal workforce;
- B & Q, a subsidiary, flourishing in the growing DIY market.

Opportunities

- increased affluence of shoppers;
- changes in consumer attitudes and tastes;
- demographic changes favouring the elderly and the young, but with little change in the 22 – 44 age group;
- growth in out-of-town shopping.

Threats

- consumer requirements moving away from low prices to quality, convenience and service;
- increased competition in the retail market;
- possibility of a take-over bid;
- growth in out-of-town shopping (can be an opportunity or a threat).

Task

Using the SWOT framework, analyse any organisation with which you are familiar.

Assignment 4.2: Declaring a penalty

At a meeting of the supporters of the local football club you have a heated argument with the manager over the club's lack of performance during the season. At the end of the meeting you apologise to him. He tells you that he agrees with many of your comments, but does not have the time or skills to sit back and make an objective assessment of the club's strengths and weaknesses. A few days later you receive a letter from him asking whether you would be willing to undertake such an analysis.

Student activities

(i)   Select any club or society with which you are familiar to represent the club in the assignment.

(ii)   Conduct an internal analysis, identifying the club's strengths and weaknesses.

(iii) Write a brief report on your findings.

4.3 Identifying Alternatives

Having completed an assessment of the organisation's internal and external position, the next step is to generate strategic options which will consider where the business should go. It is common to assume that the major objective of business organisations is growth and to identify alternative ways of achieving growth. However, there are circumstances where growth is not the main goal and therefore this section focuses on identifying *alternative development strategies* rather than growth strategies. The organisation needs to identify:

- how it is going to develop (generic strategy);
- the areas in which it is going to develop (strategic direction);
- the method by which such development is to be achieved (strategic method).

4.3.1 Generic Strategies

Generic strategies are the ways in which an organisation might seek to create or to sustain competitive advantage; in other words, outperform its rivals. *M E Porter* identifies three main generic strategies:

- cost leadership
- differentiation
- focus

The organisation needs to make a conscious choice about the type of competitive advantage it seeks to develop so that the means of achieving this advantage can be clearly addressed. Businesses attempting to mix generic strategies run the risk of achieving mediocre performances because they are trying to be all things to all people.

Cost leadership occurs when the company achieves lower costs than its competitors across a broad range of market segments. Cost leadership may be achieved through the various elements in the value chain; for example, by obtaining a low cost source of raw materials, by obtaining the benefits of experience or economies of scale, or by obtaining low cost means of distribution. Japanese companies have been particularly successful in developing cost leadership strategies in consumer durable markets such as cars, microwave ovens and video recorders.

Differentiation occurs when the company has a range of clearly differentiated products which it promotes to different segments of the market. Differentiation can be achieved in a variety of ways: by differentiating the physical nature of the product, its packaging, the service or distribution system associated with it. For example, Kelloggs have been successful in differentiating its breakfast cereals from those of competitors.

Focus occurs when the company concentrates its activity on a single market segment or a narrow range of market segments. Focus can be achieved in a number of different ways, such as by concentrating on a particular buyer group or geographical area. For example, in the bicycle industry Muddy Fox has found a specialist niche market supplying mountain bikes.

Task

Identify the generic strategies of the following food retailers:

- a national supermarket chain;
- a petrol forecourt shop;
- a local delicatessen shop.

4.3.2 Alternative Directions for Strategic Development

The following matrix, adapted from *H J Ansoff*, identifies some of the alternative directions in which development can take place.

	Existing products	*New products*
Existing markets	Do nothing Withdrawal Consolidation/retrenchment Market penetration	Product development
New markets	Market development	Diversification

4.3.3 Existing Markets/Existing Products

The *'do nothing'* strategy implies the continuation of an existing strategy. This may be appropriate in the short-term when the environment is static or when the firm is waiting to see how situations develop. However, in the long-term such tactics are unlikely to be realistic or beneficial. They may reflect a lack of strategic awareness on the part of the management team.

Withdrawal may take place through the sale of the business or through divestment, the sale of part of the business. Withdrawal may be an appropriate strategy if:

- there is an irreversible decline in demand;
- the firm is over extended;

- the firm is adversely affected by competitive pressure and environmental change;

- the opportunity cost is such that a better return can be earned if the resources used in the particular line of business are engaged elsewhere.

Large conglomerate groups sometimes find themselves too thinly spread and may choose to withdraw from selected markets. For example, by the 1980s the Thorn Group had diversified into a wide variety of businesses, including music, engineering, domestic appliances, video distribution, film studios and cinemas. Thorn decided to refocus on four core businesses: rental and retail, music, lighting and technology. It subsequently withdrew from film production and cinema.

Consolidation takes place when a firm concentrates its activities on those areas where it has established a competitive advantage and focuses its attention on maintaining its market share. When this strategy has been prompted by falling profits, the situation is often referred to as *retrenchment*. Both cases may involve the firm in improvements to cost structure, increased emphasis on quality and increased marketing activity. In the case of retrenchment, the cost reductions may involve redundancies or the sale of assets.

Example

British Steel went through a substantial programme of retrenchment in the 1980s. More recently car manufacturers, faced with falling demand, have announced substantial cutbacks in production and employment.

Market penetration involves gaining market share as opposed to maintaining it (consolidation). When the overall market is growing, penetration may be relatively easy to achieve, because the absolute volume of sales of all firms in the market is growing and some firms may not be able to satisfy demand. In a static or declining market, a firm pursuing a market penetration strategy is likely to face intense competition.

Example

The Japanese manufacturer of bicycle components, Shimano, has been highly successful in penetrating the European market, despite facing competition from established French and Italian manufacturers. Shimano is now estimated to hold some 55 per cent of the world market in derailleur-type gears.

Task

Identify the different risks which may be associated with each of the above strategies.

4.3.4 Existing Markets/New Products

Product development involves the firm in substantial modifications, additions or changes to its present product range, but it operates from the security of its established customer base. In research and development-intensive industries, product development may be the main direction of strategy because product life cycles are short, and because new products may be a natural spin-off from the research and development process. New product development can be risky and expensive.

Examples of product development in the detergent market are apparent to most consumers. Shoppers are now faced with choices between biological and non-biological, liquid and powder, concentrated (and ultra concentrated) and standard versions of the product.

Task

Select a make and model of car and identify the product development that has taken place over the last five years.

4.3.5 New Markets/Existing products

Market development can include entering new geographical areas, promoting new uses for an existing product and entering new market segments. It is an appropriate strategy to pursue when the organisation's distinct competence rests with product rather than the market.

Example

In 1991 United Biscuits undertook market development on a geographical basis when it purchased a majority shareholding in Oxford Biscuits, Scandinavia's largest biscuit manufacturer. Market development through new market segments is illustrated by the attempt to promote Johnson's Baby Lotion as a moisturising cream for adults.

Task

Identify the main factors a major retailer would have to consider before opening a store in a new area.

4.3.6 New Markets/New Products

Diversification can be classified as horizontal, vertical or conglomerate:

Horizontal diversification refers to the development of activities which are complementary to or competitive with the organisation's existing activities. It is often difficult to distinguish between horizontal diversification and market penetration because classification depends on how narrowly product boundaries are drawn.

Nestlé's takeover of Rowntree Mackintosh in 1988 is an example of horizontal diversification. Nestlé is one of the world's largest food companies, but its share of the UK chocolate confectionery market only amounted to some 3 per cent in 1987; Rowntree held around 26 per cent and had a particularly strong range of countline products such as KitKat. Nestlé's acquisition enhanced its UK market position and reduced its reliance on sales of solid chocolate bars, demand for which is growing more slowly than demand for chocolate-coated products such as Mars Bars. Nestlé's acquisition could be viewed either as horizontal diversification into a broader range of confectionery products or increased penetration of the UK confectionery market depending on where the industry boundary is drawn.

Vertical integration refers to the development of activities which involve the preceding or succeeding stages in the organisation's production process. Backward or upstream vertical integration takes place when the organisation engages in an activity related to the preceding stage in its production process. Forward or downstream vertical integration takes place when the organisation engages in an activity related to a succeeding stage in its production process.

Obvious examples of vertical diversification include the brewers' control of public houses and the oil industry's combination of exploration, refining, and distribution.

Conglomerate diversification refers to the situation where at face value the new activity of the organisation seems to bear little or no relation to its existing products or markets. For example, Hanson Trust's interests include engineering, batteries, building products and cigarettes.

The *advantages* of diversification include:

- cost savings due to the effects of *synergy* (where the combined effect exceeds the sum of the individual effects);
- spreading of risk;
- control of supplies (mainly related to vertical integration);
- control of markets (mainly related to vertical integration);
- improved access to information;
- escape from declining markets;
- exploitation of under-utilised assets.

The possible *disadvantages* of diversification include:

- inefficiency due to loss of synergy;
- inefficiency due to loss of managerial control.

Task

Go to your local library and find examples of the three types of diversification outlined above in Who Owns Whom.

4.3.7 Methods of Strategic Development

Organisations need to select not only the direction in which they might develop but also the *method* by which any particular direction of development might be achieved. The three main methods of development are:

- internal development (Section 4.3.8)
- external development (Section 4.3.9)
- joint ventures (Section 4.3.10)

The choice between strategic methods is a trade-off between costs, risk and speed.

4.3.8 Internal Development

Internal development (organic growth) may be pursued when:

- the product is in the early stages of its life cycle;
- the products are highly technical in their design or method of manufacture and the organisation wishes to move along its experience curve;
- costs need to be spread over time;
- there is sufficient time available to develop organically;
- the new products or markets are close to the firm's existing portfolio;
- there are no suitable acquisitions available;
- there are no under-utilised resources.

Companies such as IBM favour organic growth.

137

Task

Draw up a list of the advantages and disadvantages of pursuing internal development.

4.3.9 External Development

External development (acquisition) may be pursued when:

- the product is in the later stages of its life cycle;
- the company lacks the knowledge or resources to develop internally;
- costs of acquisition are advantageous compared with internal development;
- speed is of the essence;
- the acquirer wishes to eliminate spare capacity in the industry or wishes to avoid competitive retaliation.

Examples of acquisitions include the now infamous bid by Guinness for Distillers, Trustee Savings Bank's acquisition of Swan National, the car rental business, and Anglia Building Society's merger with Nationwide Building Society.

Task

Scrutinise the financial press for examples of acquisitions and analyse the possible reasons using the above list as a guide.

4.3.10 Joint Ventures

Joint ventures can take a variety of forms. *Consortia* are formal agreements between two or more firms to collaborate in a particular venture. Such collaboration may take the form of a temporary agreement in circumstances where the product or service is on a one-off basis and where the pooling of several specialist skills is necessary. Alternatively, the agreement may involve the joint ownership of a business. Many multinational companies operate through joint ventures and such collaborative ventures are common when the costs of a particular development are very high and beyond the reach of a single company.

In recent years many Japanese companies have entered into joint ventures with UK firms. For example, Fujitsu entered into joint ventures with ICL, JVC with Thorn EMI; the Channel Tunnel project is another example.

A *franchise* is an agreement between two or more parties in which the franchisor allows the franchisee to undertake part of the business. In return for a lump sum initial investment and on-going royalties, the typical franchisor provides exclusive rights to supply a product under the franchisor's name in a prescribed area. In addition, the franchisor may provide the franchisee with training and information support, national advertising, materials and equipment. Well known franchises include Wimpy and McDonalds fast food chains, Dyno-Rod and the Sock Shop.

Licensing is an arrangement whereby an organisation is permitted to produce a product or service which has been designed by another and is protected by patent law. It is common in science-based industries. An example of licensing in the brewing industry is given in Section 4.1.3.

Agencies (Section 3.4) are perhaps the simplest form of joint development. The business organisation (the principal) enters an agreement with an individual or firm to act as its agent in selling its products. This enables the principal to establish an extensive sales network cheaply, but poses problems of monitoring and control of sales effort. Agency is frequently used in the mail order catalogue market.

Task

Write a letter to a friend who is contemplating entering into a franchise agreement explaining the advantages and disadvantages.

Assignment 4.3: A fund-raising strategy

The president of the students' union has decided to raise funds for various sports activities by seeking donations from local industry. She believes that approaches to companies would be more successful if the students' union was seen to have an interest and knowledge of industry. To demonstrate this, she has asked you to write an article of approximately 2,000 words on any company of your choice, preferably a generous one, for the students' journal.

Student activities

(i)   Select a local company and collect as much information on it as possible.

(ii) Trace the changes of strategy and strategic direction of the company over a number of years.

(iii) Relate these changes to those which have taken place in the organisation's external and internal environment.

(iv) Prepare an article suitable for publication in the students' journal using a desktop publishing package if possible. Include tables and diagrams where appropriate.

4.4 Techniques of Appraisal and Evaluation

Having generated a set of potential strategic options, it is necessary to choose between them. There is no single evaluation technique to provide a definitive answer to the question of which strategy a firm should select. However, all options should be judged against the criteria of *appropriateness, feasibility* and *desirability*.

Appropriateness is a measure of the extent to which the strategy fits the situation identified in the strategic analysis (that is, the extent to which the strategy is logical and makes the most of available opportunities and strengths, and minimises threats and weaknesses). Feasibility assesses the extent to which the strategy will work in practice. Desirability measures the extent to which the strategy is acceptable to stakeholders.

4.4.1 Assessing the Appropriateness of Strategies

A strategy is *appropriate* if it provides a good strategic fit; that is, the strategy provides a suitable match between the organisation's objectives, its environment and its capabilities. Approaches which emphasise strategic logic include:

- SWOT analysis (Section 4.2.4);

- product portfolio analysis (Section 4.4.2);

- life cycle analysis (Section 4.4.3);

- competitive advantage analysis (Section 4.4.4).

In all these approaches the organisation identifies where its activities are currently positioned in terms of a matrix and uses this information to gain insight into its present portfolio and guide its future strategy. Firms may seek to achieve a more balanced portfolio of activities. The approaches differ in their identification of the critical variables.

4.4.2 Product Portfolio Analysis

Product portfolio analysis emphasises the nature of markets and an organisation's competitive standing. The Boston Consulting Group matrix, which is typical of this approach, is illustrated below

	Existing products	*New products*
Existing markets	Stars	Question marks
New markets	Cash cows	Dogs

Stars are market leaders in growth markets. They need to defend their market position and require on-going investment; consequently they do not generate as much profit for the organisation as cash cows. Examples include products in the hi-tech market.

Cash cows are well established products in mature markets which generate funds for other parts of the business. Examples include Rank Xerox's 914 copier and British Telecom's UK telephone network.

Question marks are products with low market share competing in rapidly expanding markets. If they are successful they become stars, but in the question mark stage they are risky and require on-going investment. This makes them, at best, only marginally profitable in the short-term. IBM's new family of personal computers, the PS2 range, is an example of a question mark product, perhaps destined to become a star.

Dogs are cash cows past their best. They are products which have lost market share to competitors and are operating in static or at best slow growing markets. Their profitability is declining and eventually they may be withdrawn. Examples include electromechanical typewriters and cash registers which have been superseded by word processors and sophisticated electronic tills.

The theory suggests that portfolios should be reasonably balanced between stars, cash cows and question marks. Some writers have cast doubts on the practical application of this approach and in recent years there have been a number of modifications and extensions to the model.

Task

Prepare speech notes for a debate where you are to support the motion: *The Boston Consulting Group matrix is now a dog.*

4.4.3 Life Cycle Analysis

Life cycle analysis is similar to the product portfolio approach, but considers an organisation's positioning with respect to industry maturity and competitive position. Based on the model developed by *Arthur D Little*, the position within the life cycle is determined in relation to eight descriptors of evolution:

- market growth rate;
- growth potential;
- breadth of product lines;
- number of competitors;
- spread of market share between competitors;
- customer loyalty;
- entry barriers;
- technology.

The position in relation to competition can be classified as:

- dominant
- strong
- favourable
- tenable
- weak

Use of this approach narrows the range of strategic options open to the organisation and identifies those which are worthy of further consideration. The Shell Directional Policy matrix is another similar approach.

For example, the Post Office may find most of its products located in mature or aging markets in which its competitive position is strong; Mercury, in the telecommunications market, may find a number of its products in embryonic markets in a weak competitive position. The current positioning of the firm's portfolio of products has a strong bearing on its future strategy.

Task

What problems do you think there are in attempting to apply Arthur D. Little's eight descriptors of evolution to a recently formed high-tech company?

4.4.4 Competitive Advantage Analysis

Competitive advantage analysis is an extension of the portfolio approach. In this case the dimensions are the development stages of the industry (growth, maturity or decline) and strategic position of the organisation (leader or follower). As in the other approaches, the analysis seeks to narrow the set of strategies worthy of consideration by identifying those which are not appropriate to the firm's current circumstances.

IBM, for example, might be classified as a leader in a growth market, using a strategy of product innovation to keep ahead, whereas the Rover Group might be classified as a follower in a mature market, needing to adopt policies of differentiation or focus.

Research evidence can also be used to establish a *strategic logic* or to explain why some strategies are more appropriate than others. One of the most important sources of such evidence are the on-going *profit impact of market strategy (PIMS)* studies. PIMS is a sophisticated computed model based on data submitted by around 3,000 businesses which provide information on factors such as the business environment, competitive position, research and development and sales and marketing strategies. Some of the major findings of PIMS include:

- high relative market share has a strong influence on profitability;
- high relative product quality is related to high return on investment;
- high investment intensity is associated with low profitability;
- high productivity is associated with high return on capital.

Task

What are the limitations of PIMS for the purpose of strategic evaluation?

4.4.5 Selecting Alternatives

Since more than one strategy is likely to be appropriate, the strategist needs to screen the alternatives before looking at feasibility and desirability in more detail. Alternative options need to be assessed in relation to each other or in relation to a 'do nothing' situation. *Planning gap analysis* uses the 'do nothing' situation as the basis for comparison. It enables managers to consider the degree of change and risk involved in closing the gap between projected future performance with present policies unchanged and desired targets. Other techniques for screening options include the following.

In *ranking methods* strategies are scored against a predetermined set of criteria.

Example

A small hypothetical company in the carpet industry is considering the following strategic options:

Strategy A   Establish a strong brand identity for own carpets using extensive marketing and promotional activity.

Strategy B   Focus on the contract market, supplying solely to commercial and industrial buyers.

Strategy C   Withdraw from carpet manufacture, import carpets and capitalise on contacts with the retail trade by acting as a wholesaler.

These strategies could be ranked against a set of criteria such as:

1. The desire to remain a small, independent company.
2. The desire to capitalise on the firm's established reputation for quality.
3. The need to achieve a higher rate of return on capital employed.

The criteria would obviously relate to the objectives of the firm.

Strategy A might rank highly in terms of criteria 1 and 2, but only attract a low score for criteria 3. Strategy B might attract a reasonable score for criteria 3, but a lower score in terms of criteria 1. Scores could be aggregated to give some overall ranking of alternatives.

In *scenario techniques* (Section 4.1.2) options are assessed in relation to a range of possible future states of the environment.

In *decision tree techniques* (Section 9.4.8) options are identified and simultaneously ranked, and some alternatives are progressively eliminated.

> **Task**
>
> Use a decision tree approach to describe the following options available to Burpitt Brewery:
>
> Strategy A: Develop 20 fast food counters in the public houses. If this strategy is successful, the company could decide to install 30 more counters in two years' time or could hold and develop another line of business at a later stage. If the fast food market does not take off, the fast food activity could be franchised or closed down.
>
> Strategy B: Diversify into the hotel business. If demand is high, a high return from this project is forecast and the company could consider building an annex to the premises in three years' time. If demand is poor, the project could still be profitable, but it might be worth finding a hotel chain willing to acquire this particular hotel at the end of the second year.

4.4.6 Assessing the Feasibility of Strategies

Even if an option is suitable in terms of its strategic logic, it may not be capable of being successfully implemented by the firm. In particular, the strategy may not be *financially feasible,* so managers may use *funds flow forecasts* (Section 1.4.7) and *break-even analysis* (Section 1.7.5) to establish whether an option is a feasible alternative.

Funds flow forecasts seek to establish what funds will be required for any strategy and the likely source of those funds. The statistics indicate that most funds used by established organisations are generated internally through retained profit. However, funds can also be raised through the issue of equity or by borrowing. The analysis should highlight whether the proposed strategy is financially feasible.

Break-even analysis considers the sales volume required to cover all the fixed costs associated with a product or service. The technique can be used to assess the risk inherent in a particular option, particularly if demand is uncertain and alternative options have markedly different cost structures.

Strategies need to be feasible in terms of their *financial* requirements and their *resource* requirements, their timing and the organisation's ability to sustain competitive advantage. *Resource planning* is necessary to identify whether the lack of any key resource will place a constraint on development. For example, institutions of higher education might decide that offering short course to up-date managers' skills is an appropriate response to changes in the educational environment. However, if staff are not available to run such courses, the strategy is appropriate but not feasible.

It may be important for an organisation to act quickly once an opportunity has been spotted. This is not always feasible or advisable, particularly if speed prevents the organisation from making a proper assessment of the resource and other implications of the strategy. Finally, the likely response of competitors to a strategic move needs to be considered or the strategy may be rendered unworkable by retaliatory responses. In the newspaper industry, Eddie Shah launched the *Today* newspaper using information technology to gain competitive advantage. Other newspapers soon followed suit and *Today* lost market share.

Task

You have decided to purchase a new compact disc player. Prepare a funds flow forecast for yourself on the basis of this decision. Is this option feasible?

4.4.7 Assessing the Desirability of Strategies

A strategy's *desirability* depends on its ability to meet the objectives of the organisation. The appropriate measure of desirability therefore varies according to the firm's goals. Typically desirability is judged in terms of:

- profitability;
- risk profile;
- social costs and benefits;
- the needs and expectations of shareholders.

Profitability measures (Section 1.7.6) relate anticipated earnings to the amount of capital investment needed to generate those earnings. All other things being equal, the higher the profit the more acceptable the option. The most common measures of profitability are:

- accounting rate of return (ARR);
- payback technique;
- discounted cash flow, including net present value and internal rate of return (IRR).

Risk occurs whenever a choice is made and the potential outcome is uncertain. All other things being equal, the lower the risk the more acceptable the option. According to *J Johnson* and *K Scholes* the main methods of assessing risk are:

- *Sensitivity analysis*: For example, assessing how sensitive outcomes are to changes in assumptions. What happens if demand is less favourable than anticipated or competitors more successful in a new product launch?

- *Financial ratios*: For example, what is the company's break-even point? Is it highly geared?

- *Decision matrices*: In some cases the strategist may be able to establish a matrix of possible outcomes and then establish criteria for decision-making. For example, the maxi-min approach is to assume the worst and select the strategy which produces the best outcome in such unfavourable circumstances.

- *Simulation modelling:* Attempts are sometimes made to construct quantitative models which encompass the relationships between strategic variables (Section 7.4.1). The models can then be used to test a number of 'what if' situations.

- *Heuristic (rule of thumb) techniques*: For example, a satisfactory outcome must create at least 10 per cent rate of return or must leave 15 per cent spare capacity.

Social costs and benefits may diverge from private costs and benefits and can be an important consideration, particularly for public sector organisations' evaluation of alternative options. *Cost benefit analysis* is similar to investment appraisal, but attempts to place a monetary value on intangible as well as tangible costs and benefits. All other things being equal, the greater the net benefit, the more desirable the option.

For example, PowerGen is considering an investment in flue gas desulphurisation plant. The main benefits of such investment accrue to society through a reduction in acid rain pollution, rather than to PowerGen's shareholders in the form of increased profits. The investment would therefore need to be justified in terms of social benefit and social responsibility, rather than private financial gain.

The needs and expectations of *stakeholders* influence the desirability of a particular strategy. Stakeholders include the following groups:

- shareholders
- employees
- consumers
- distributors
- suppliers
- financiers
- the government
- society

Strategies may be pursued because they are regarded as desirable by those who exercise power or influence. Such strategies are not always the most appropriate or feasible, but ignoring stakeholders' desires can jeopardise a strategy's chance of success.

Task

Make a list of the stakeholders involved in a national charity of your choice. Which of the evaluation techniques featured in this section would you consider to be most appropriate for a charitable organisation?

Assignment 4.4: The Burton Group

The students' debating society has managed to get a speaker from the Burton Group plc for the next meeting. The title of the debate is *We have always served the customer successfully* and you have been asked to oppose the motion.

The speaker is enthusiastic about the debate and says that he will propose the motion with vigour and will not resent any criticisms you make as long as they are well researched.

Student activities

(i) Research and evaluate the strategic changes and relative successes of the Burton group during the 1980s.

(ii) Which strategies were effective and why?

(iii) Which strategies were ill-conceived and why?

(iv) Prepare notes for your speech, concentrating on what you consider to be the six most important arguments against the motion.

4.5 Strategic Implementation

Having evaluated the alternatives and selected a particular course of action, the strategist can then put the plan into action. Certain features of the business can facilitate or detract from successful *implementation*. These features are considered below.

4.5.1 Strategic Implementation and Resource Planning

Strategic change necessitates change in resources. Successful implementation requires careful *planning of resource requirements* and allocations at both the corporate and functional level.

The allocation of resources at a corporate level between business units or divisions depends on the speed and extent of change within the organisation. It also depends on the degree of instability in the environment. In times of rapid change, the centre of the organisation may act as an investment bank judging the claims of competing units; constrained bidding may take place where various divisions bid for resources within defined conditions. In more static situations, where only small resource changes are required, allocation may proceed on the basis of historically determined formulae.

At a functional level, resource allocation normally takes place through the setting of *budgets* (Section 1.8.1). Budgets are one outcome of the resource planning process which involves:

- identifying resource requirements;
- analysing links between different functional areas and the fit between both existing and required resources;
- identifying key priorities;
- constructing a plan of action;
- translating the resource implications of the plan into budgets.

A budget is a financial plan setting targets for the revenues, expenditures and resources required to put a formulated strategy into action. There are a number of different kinds of budget:

- *capital budgets* concern the allocation of resources for buildings, plant and equipment;
- *sales budgets* reflect the anticipated cash flow into the organisation on the basis of forecast sales;
- *consolidated budgets* project the implications of a strategic decision on the overall performance of the business.

Budgeting normally takes place on an annual basis and previous experience is carried forward and used as a base. *Zero-based budgets* assume no previous experience and every proposed activity has to be justified anew. Budgets are one of the key elements in monitoring performance.

Tasks

Interview a manager in a local business and try to ascertain:

(i)   how the budgetary process operates in their organisation;

(ii) what measures of performance, if any, are utilised;

(iii) what feedback the manager gets and how he or she responds to it.

4.5.2 Strategic Implementation and Cultural Change

In some cases the implementation of a new strategy involves a *change in the culture* of the organisation (Section 6.4.2). Changing the culture involves breaking down current beliefs and assumptions (the unfreezing process) and promoting the adoption of a new set of beliefs. The unfreezing process needs some kind of trigger to set it in motion which will lead to a challenge to the existing ways of doing things. Inevitably the dismantling of the old sets of assumptions involves some changes in the *power structure* of the organisation. Some groups may have a vested interest in the organisation remaining unchanged.

Change is often facilitated by the intervention of an outsider. Establishing a new culture recipe is aided by developing active participation in the strategy process, showing the concrete benefits of change through action, and by using symbolic action to reinforce cultural change.

In recent years the banking industry has undergone rapid change as a result of deregulation, technological change and globalisation of financial markets. Traditionally bank employees were viewed as staid and conservative; accuracy, attention to detail and aversion to risk were deemed to be virtues, and promotion was based on time served and loyalty. Such a culture does not fit well in the new, more competitive environment to which banks are adapting.

Implementing a more market-orientated approach involves changes in recruitment, training, payment systems, organisational structure, branch design, corporate image and product range. A change in culture often requires significant changes in all aspects of the organisation's activities. The Bank of Ireland, for example, appointed Mark Hely Hutchinson to spearhead strategic change, triggered by deteriorating performance in a changing market.

Task

Consider what kind of cultural change was required within Abbey National when it changed its status from building society to public limited company.

4.5.3 Strategic Implementation and Change in Organisational Structure

Organisational structure is the framework through which strategy is implemented. It determines the authority, communication systems and allocation of tasks within the business. Therefore it is a critical factor in success. Organisational structures can be classified as follows:

- *Entrepreneurial structures* are organised around the owner/manager and totally centralised, with no division of responsibility. It is appropriate for small companies in early stages of development.

- *Functional structures* are organised around the functional tasks carried out in the organisation, such as marketing, production, finance. It is appropriate for small/medium-sized companies with few plants operating in a static environment.

- *Multi-divisional structures* are organised into units which are responsible for a defined market, service or product area. Divisions are decentralised profit centres which are seen as strategic business units for planning and control purposes. It is appropriate for large organisations which have grown through acquisition or where appropriate divisional splits exist. It is also a common structure in complex and dynamic market environments.

- *Holding companies* are organised as a set of separate, independent operating companies, but with a headquarters which is principally an investment company. A holding company is an appropriate structure for conglomerates with highly diverse holdings, or for companies pursuing a strategy of buying and selling businesses.

- *A matrix* is a combination of structures. It requires dual reporting of managers, for example to a mix of functional and business unit heads. It is an appropriate structure for large multi-product or multinational companies with significant interrelationships and interdependencies.

When deciding an appropriate structure, strategists need to consider the rate of change in the environment of the firm, the complexity of the production process and associated technology, and the nature of the strategy to be pursued. A functional structure, for example, may be inappropriate for a strategy of extensive diversification.

Task

Draw an organisational chart for an organisation with which you are familiar. How does it fit into the above classifications? What are the advantages and disadvantages of this structure?

4.5.4 Strategic Implementation and Regulatory Systems

Regulatory systems are procedures which promote changes in individuals' behaviour and assist in bringing about strategic change. They include:

- *Incentive and reward systems* which encourage compliance with required changes. Rewards may be monetary, for example bonus schemes, profit sharing schemes, or non-monetary such as promotion or enhanced status.

- *Training schemes* which ensure that personnel are able to undertake the new tasks required of them.

- *Management style* determines the way in which regulatory systems are put into effect. Management styles can be classified as:

    ◦ entrepreneurial/conservative
    ◦ autocratic/democratic
    ◦ mechanistic/organic

The most appropriate style of management depends on a variety of circumstances, including such factors as the size and complexity of the organisation, the prevailing culture and attitudes, the extent of environmental change, the evolutionary stage of the business, as well as managers' personalities and preferences.

Example

When F W Woolworth was acquired by the Paternoster consortium in 1982, the new management team set about implementing strategic change, including changing the regulatory systems. Don Rose, writing in Long Range Planning (February 1989) points out that 'Woolworth recruited via the Job Centres. Recruitment interviews lasted about 10 minutes. Induction took 20 minutes. Training consisted of on-the-job learning.' The management styles was autocratic and mechanistic. The new company instigated an *Excellence Programme* setting up both management and staff training programmes; a tailor-made course was introduced for store and head office managers with an emphasis on two-way communication with staff. Staff now receive on-going training and there are cash rewards associated with achievement.

Task

Investigate the reward system that operates in the college where you are studying.

Assignment 4.5: All in the implementation

You have been asked to host a visiting speaker to your college. He is a successful self-made businessman and after his speech he offers to take the students' committee out to a lavish dinner. During dinner he tells you that in his experience business problems are not caused by lack of entrepreneurship. He explains that his own company has grown rapidly during the last decade and he is now able to leave its running entirely in hands of a manager. Other changes have been forced on the company through rapid growth. He complains to you that there is no book to tell you how to make changes successfully. Out of personal interest and gratitude for the dinner you decide to send him a report explaining how strategic change can be implemented.

Student activities

Write a word-processed report for the businessman discussing:

(i)   the significant strategic changes made by business organisations;

(ii)   those features which appear to assist successful implementation;

(iii) those features which appear to detract from successful implementation.

Wherever possible, use actual examples from companies which have undergone significant strategic changes in recent years to illustrate your report.

4.6 Strategic Formulation

The preceding sections have considered the stages in the business policy process in a logical sequence from *analysis* to *choice* and *implementation*. In practice, strategies are not always formulated in a neat, rational way but are the result of a tangled set of social, political and cultural processes. Strategic change does not normally occur as a major one-off event, but as a series of gradual or incremental developments, with only occasional global shifts.

4.6.1 Strategic Formulation in Practice

It has been argued that managers do not necessarily seek to control strategy, but that strategy emerges in response to awareness of a problem. It is useful to distinguish between *intended* and *emergent* strategies and between *intended* and *realised* strategies. The various stages in the strategic decision-making process are shown in the following diagram.

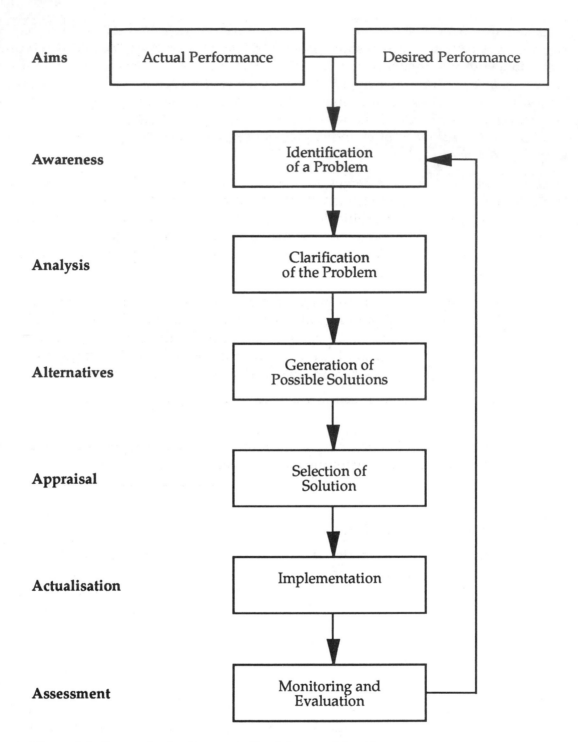

Figure 4.1 *Stages in the Strategic Decision-making Process*

The awareness of a problem is likely to come from the subjective *interpretation of signals* which indicate some deviation of performance from the expected norm. The search for information and solutions is likely to be governed by *bounded rationality*. Since individuals are limited in their ability to retrieve, process and store information, their rationality is constrained. The search rests heavily on managers' past experience and their perceptions of the views of powerful members of the organisation. Therefore, the systematic, planned approach to strategy implicit in business policy analysis is not always adopted.

Three distinct approaches or modes of strategy formulation have been identified by *J L Thompson:*

In the *entrepreneurial mode* a visionary strategic leader formulates strategy. The selection is made in an informal way which permits creativity and flair. The strategy is then presented by the strategic leader to other managers. This is a top-down approach in which it is difficult to separate the stages of analysis and choice but implementation is a later stage in the process. The advantage of this mode is that the strategic awareness and strength of the leader can be fully utilised. The disadvantage is that it is heavily dependent on the abilities of an individual and does not involve members of the team in the strategy formulation process.

In the *adaptive mode* a strategy emerges as managers throughout the organisation learn from experience and adapt to change in the environment. This is a bottom-up approach in which there may be little formal analysis and it may be difficult to distinguish between choice and implementation. The advantage of this mode is that it involves limited change, little risk and ensures that implementation is an integral part of strategy formulation. The disadvantage is that the strategy can be fragmented and disjointed decisions may be common.

In a *planning mode* planning is carried out in advance of taking action and the analyst plays a major role. The focus is on a systematic appraisal of alternatives. Analysis precedes choice, which precedes implementation. The advantage of this mode is that it is systematic and structured, thus facilitating the integration and co-ordination of decision in complex organisations. The disadvantage is that it may inhibit creativity and be inappropriate where speed of action and timing are critical.

Task

Identify examples of organisations which have adopted entrepreneurial, adaptive and planning modes of strategy formulation at different times.

4.6.2 Strategic Formulation and Culture

Strategist themselves have a major influence on strategy. They both influence and are influenced by the *corporate culture*. The term *culture* refers to the basic assumptions and beliefs that are shared by members of the organisation. Culture is deep-seated. It affects behaviour unconsciously and is slow to change. *R E Miles and C C Snow* suggest the following classification of corporate cultures:

- *defenders*: conservative, low risk strategies, secure market;
- *prospectors*: innovative, risk taking strategies, breaking new ground;
- *analysers*: stable: concerned with the search for efficiency, have formal structures; changing: followers rather than leaders, adapt to change;
- *reactors*: unable to respond effectively to changing pressures; confronted by crisis which forces change.

The type of culture in an organisation influences the appropriate mode of strategy formulation. For example, defenders place emphasis on planning modes, whereas prospectors favour a more entrepreneurial approach. Faced with the same environments, organisations with different cultures produce different strategic responses.

The strategists' perceptions of the internal and external environment are filtered through the cultural recipe, which is embedded in a cultural web of routines, central systems, structures, symbols and rituals.

Faced with signals of declining performance, managers will seek solutions within the existing recipe; it is only when these solutions fail that the recipe itself will be challenged.

Task

Find examples of each different type of organisational culture. What kind of culture do you think exists within the following organisations?

- British Rail
- Amstrad

Assignment 4.6: Conducting interviews

A university has advertised a post for a researcher in strategic formulation. You have applied for the job and have been shortlisted. To prepare yourself for the interview, you have revised your lecture notes on strategy formulation. You decide it would be useful to construct the sort of questions a researcher might ask if conducting a survey of different modes of strategy formulation adopted by organisations.

Student activities

(i) Prepare a list of questions you might ask senior managers in organisations to ascertain the mode of strategy formulation employed.

(ii) Compare your questions with theory to ensure that you have covered all aspects.

(iii) Consider how you might analyse the responses you receive from different managers.

(iv) Identify which journals might publish an article on your findings.

(v) If possible, test your questions by interviewing a senior manager of an organisation to which you have access.

4.7 Outcome Evaluations

Successful implementation of strategy involves change. It is necessary to have some way of monitoring change and assessing whether objectives have been achieved. *Monitoring and evaluation systems* need to be established to provide feedback which can, if necessary, lead to modification and improvements in strategy.

4.7.1 Performance Indicators

It is necessary to decide on the indicators which will effectively monitor performance and to set specific measurements for each *performance indicator*. Performance indicators can take a variety of forms. *Financial performance* is monitored through ratio analysis, capital budgeting and cash flow budgeting. *Market performance* is monitored through market share analysis and demand analysis. The efficiency and effectiveness of physical resources is monitored through capacity utilisation, yield and quality control. The *efficiency and effectiveness of human resources* is monitored through work measurement, output measurement, labour turnover and staff appraisal.

Task

What kind of performance indicators are appropriate for the following organisations?
- a factory
- a hospital
- a newsagent
- a polytechnic

4.7.2 Control and Feedback

If an organisation is failing to achieve its desired objectives, corrective action should be taken by modifying the strategy itself, or by taking action at management or operational level. Effective *control and feedback* require:

- effective monitoring of performance;
- delegation of responsibilities to appropriate subdivisions of the organisation;
- agreement on the targets against which performance is to be measured; this may involve participation in the objective setting process;
- highlighting both successful and unsuccessful outcomes.

In order to remain successful, organisations need to master the *management of change*. The CBI Report (1985) suggests that key aspects of successful strategic management are:

- sound financial control;
- decentralised decision-making;
- attention to customers and products;
- motivation of employees.

Task

Assess the monitoring and feedback mechanisms that exist for your Business Policy course.

Assignment 4.7: A question of confirmation

You have been appointed as a research assistant by the CBI which has decided to carry out a follow-up survey to the 1985 report on strategic management. On the strength of a pilot survey based on one company, the CBI has asked you to draw up proposals for a more extensive survey.

Student activities

(i)   Review the CBI report and any subsequent research andpublications on strategic management.

(ii) Compile a list of the criteria you consider are important indicators of success.

(iii) Select a company you consider to be successful and to which you have access. Does the company exhibit the four key characteristics highlighted by the CBI report?

(iv) Are there any other factors you can identify which may be contributing to its success?

(v)   Write a proposal to the CBI outlining the results of your review of the literature and research within the company and suggesting ways in which the study might be extended. Use a desktop publishing package if possible and include some quantitative performance indicators in graphical form to illustrate your findings.

Section 5
Employee Relations

by Sally Howe

BA (Hons), MIPM, Senior Lecturer in Personnel Management at Bristol Business School

The study of employee relations is concerned with the rules, regulations and practices surrounding the recruitment, selection, development and retention of employees.

Recommended Reading

Armstrong, M., *A Handbook of Personnel Management Practice,* Kogan Page, 1984

Salamon, Michael, *Industrial Relations Theory and Practice,* Prentice Hall, 1987

Torrington, D., & Hall, L., *Personnel Management,* Prentice Hall, 1987

Theory's fine, but...

Contents

5.1 A Framework for the Management of People

5.1.1 Employee Management

All business organisations need to plan for and manage the people they employ to achieve the best use of the skills and experience they possess. The organisation also needs to consider its social and legal responsibilities to the workforce. A business's objectives for its staff must be established and policies and procedures set. Policies are normally defined for the following areas:

- social responsibility;
- employment;
- pay and conditions of employment;
- promotion;
- training and development;
- employee relations;
- health and safety.

The management of people involves two levels of management, *line management* and *employee relations*. All line managers are responsible for the employees under them and in addition there may be a specialist *personnel manager* who is also responsible for those same employees.

The need for a personnel specialist is influenced by a variety of factors:

- the size of the organisation;
- the need for standardisation between departments;
- the need for specialist knowledge of employment legislation;
- the need for other specialist skills such as job analysis and recruitment;
- the need for co-ordinated personnel information.

The traditional view of personnel management is that it provides an advisory service, reacting to and interpreting corporate plans to determine the human requirements. Personnel managers are often considered as playing a welfare role, looking after employees' well-being and arguing their case to management.

Recently the concept of *human resource management* has become more widespread. This places more emphasis on the proactive role of the management of people: the planning, monitoring and control of employees, who are considered as a resource in the same way as money or other raw materials. The principal roles of a personnel manager are:

- to innovate, devise and propose new policies and procedures;
- to administer and manage the activities for which the personnel department is responsible;
- to solve problems.

The practical application of these roles depends on the management style of the organisation.

Task

Outline the main functions of personnel management and draft a policy statement for each of the areas of personnel practice.

5.1.2 The Context of Personnel Management

Personnel management does not occur in isolation; it is greatly affected by the environment in which the organisation operates. Both the internal and external environment of the organisation should be considered.

External factors include:

- competition;
- changes in markets;
- economic forces;
- government policies;
- public opinion;
- trade unions.

Internal factors include:

- the size of the business organisation;
- its structure;
- its current performance;
- the type of employees;
- the business's management style;
- the organisational climate.

The relationship between personnel managers and other managers is also important. Personnel management sometimes suffers from low status which can limit its contribution to the business.

Task

Analyse any organisation known to you and evaluate the influence of internal and external factors in the determination of personnel policy.

5.1.3 The Personnel Audit

In order to assess the effectiveness of the management of people in an organisation, it may be useful to carry out a *personnel audit*. This aims to identify the major external and internal factors affecting the management of people and ensures that the correct policies and procedures are in place. Major areas of investigation for a personnel audit include:

- personnel policy;
- organisation analysis;
- communications procedures;
- manpower administration;
- training and development;
- employee relations;
- pay and benefits.

Task

Design a suitable questionnaire to carry out a personnel audit which will investigate the areas outlined above.

5.1.4 Personnel Record Systems

Personnel records provide the basic information for manpower policies, plans and procedures. They allow management to keep details of the knowledge and skills of their workforce on file and they reduce reliance on unsupported, personal views. Thus they contribute to the more effective operation of the organisation.

Typical records on *individual* employees might include:

- personal details such as name, sex, date of birth, address, education, qualifications, previous experience. tax code, national insurance number, next of kin, disabilities etc;
- employment details such as the date employment began, the date the present job started, job title;
- details of terms and conditions;
- absence details;
- details of any accidents;
- details of any disciplinary action taken;
- training records.

Personnel records should also provide *collective* information, for example:

- the numbers and occupations of employees required by the manpower plan;
- analyses of employees by age, sex, grade and length of service;
- time-keeping, absence and labour turnover statistics;
- records of total wage and salary costs.

Personnel records should contain only relevant information and this should be safeguarded effectively. If computerised, the requirements of the *DataProtection Act 1984* (Section 3.3) will apply.

Task

Design a form for collecting personnel information for the individual, and on a departmental basis.

Assignment 5.1: Sprocket & Sons Ltd

You have recently been appointed as personnel manager at Sprocket & Sons Ltd, a medium-sized company which has expanded rapidly in recent years and now employs 200 people. Prior to your appointment there was no personnel specialist and the line managers carried out any personnel activities necessary in the manner they thought fit. This has led to considerable inconsistency and a complete absence of planning.

Student activities

Prepare a word processed report for the managing director, Derek Gray, making recommendations on how best to implement the following:

(i) a personnel audit of the company;

(ii) the establishment of an effective centralised personnel record system;

(iii) policy statements for each of the areas of personnel practice identified.

5.2 Recruitment And Selection

5.2.1 Manpower Planning

This is concerned with assessing the *quantity* and *quality* of labour. The purpose of *manpower planning* is to have the right number of people of the right type in the right place at the right time. Successful manpower planning ensures that:

- corporate plans are examined in terms of their manpower implications;
- adequate staffing levels are maintained;
- career development and training is carried out in a systematic way;
- productivity is increased as a result of efficient manpower utilisation.

In order to construct a manpower plan, the *demand* for labour must be balanced with the *supply* of labour for each category of worker. Manpower plans are normally made on a five-year rolling basis, with perhaps two years planned in detail and three years in outline. Computerised systems allow the sophisticated processing of information collected on employees to determine patterns of promotion, resignation etc. Analyses include:

Annual labour turnover index

$$\frac{\text{Leavers in the year}}{\text{Average number of staff employed in the year}} \times 100$$

Stability index

$$\frac{\text{Number of staff with one year's service or more}}{\text{Number of staff employed one year ago}} \times 100$$

Cohort analysis

A group of employees in similar jobs are identified who joined the organisation at the same time. A detailed record is kept in order to give some indication of the general trends in the organisation. The analysis may take a considerable period of time. Sometimes the *half-life* is used which is the time it takes half the original group to leave.

Census

This is a detailed survey of leavers over a fixed period of time, usually one year.

Retention profiles

Staff are placed in groups according to the year of joining. At the end of year the number remaining in each year group is calculated as a percentage of the total number joining that year.

Task

The following data has been collected from one head office department.

Name	Age	Length of service (years)	Name	Age	Length of service (years)
Adams F C	58	20	Chambers S C	30	10
Asprey A	20	´	Denby N	59	10
Barker J	49	20	Gibbons S	49	17
Clark A	55	17	Jenkins P	50	16
Coles C	21	´	Kieran B	24	1
Craddock F	54	17	Lawson S	23	2
Dart S R	26	2	Lesley L	53	15
Derek D	60	20	Lewis D	65	17
Fraser L	49	10	Ludlow M	61	35
Martin J	32	12	Matthews M	55	20
Morgan N	29	7	Morris C	39	12
Nottall J	50	17	Paton P	44	7
Porch B	60	17	Pritchard L	22	´
Reed C	54	17	Reid A M	45	5

(i) Construct a graph showing the number of employees in each of the following age groups:

20-25   26-30   31-35   36-40   41-45   46-50   51-55   56-60   Over 60

Analyse the age profile and suggest implications this may have for resourcing the department in future.

(ii) During the past year, five members of staff have left. However, there were only four job vacancies as one of the posts was filled twice in the year. Calculate the annual labour turnover index (take the total number as the average), and the stability index (assume no change in the total number of employees).

5.2.2 Demand Forecasting Techniques

There are three main techniques:

- *statistical methods*: ratio/trend analyses which involve taking historical data and projecting it into the future;
- *work study*: organisation and methods analyses;
- *managerial judgement*: using the knowledge of experienced staff.

Task

Consider the following ratios for a department of an insurance company. How many underwriters would you employ next year?

Year	Underwriters	Proposals	Ratio
-3	9	2,000	1:222
-2	10	2,500	1:250
-1	12	3,600	1:300
current	14	4,200	1:300
next	?	4,800*	

* Estimate

5.2.3 Supply Forecasting Techniques

Factors to consider include:

- demographic trends affecting the numbers of workers in each age group;
- changes in the proportion of male/females in the workforce etc;
- skills shortages in particular employment categories;
- closures/openings of other places of work in the area;
- housing developments;
- national/local unemployment levels;
- numbers of local school-leavers;
- transport developments and travel-to-work patterns.

Task

Compile a list of statistics which determine the supply of labour in various categories in your area.

5.2.4 Balancing Supply and Demand

When *demand exceeds supply,* tactics include:

- increasing recruitment;
- improving salaries/benefits;
- accelerating training programmes;
- retraining or transferring staff from areas of oversupply;
- amending business plans.

When *supply exceeds demand,* tactics include:

- creating voluntary/compulsory redundancies;
- offering early retirement;
- making use of natural wastage;
- transferring staff to areas of undersupply;
- restricting overtime, introducing job sharing, part-time jobs etc.

Task

If a company is experiencing difficulties in recruiting staff for a particular job, what measures could be introduced which might help the situation?

5.2.5 Job Analysis

This is the systematic process of collecting and analysing information about jobs. It can then be used for a variety of purposes, including the preparation of a *job description* and *person specification.*

A job description might include:

- job title, company, department, reporting relationships etc;
- overall purpose of the job or a statement of the general context of the work;
- key areas of the job;
- working conditions;
- performance standards and consequences of error;
- contacts made.

A person specification might include:

- educational qualifications;
- previous work experience;
- appearance and manner;
- personality factors;
- age, status, mobility etc;
- general intelligence and special aptitudes.

Methods of collecting data for a job description include:

- structured/unstructured interviews;
- questionnaires;
- work diaries;
- observation;
- participant observation;
- checklists/inventories which can be computer-scored to describe the level of operation;
- secondary data such as previous job descriptions, performance appraisals, training manuals etc;
- expert conference with managers, trainers, organisation and methods specialists etc.

Tasks

(i) Draw up lists of the advantages and disadvantages of the above methods.

(ii) How would you collect job information about the following jobs?

- a hospital nurse;

- an insurance company clerical worker;

- the general manager of a small business.

5.2.6 Equal Opportunities

The recruitment and selection process is designed to *discriminate* between candidates. However, it is unlawful for an employer to discriminate on the grounds of sex or race. Discrimination can be *direct* or *indirect*. In addition, the law requires an employer to treat men and women equally in terms of pay and conditions, although certain jobs can require genuine occupational qualifications which allow the selection of candidates of only one sex. Section 3.3 gives details of the legislation relating to these issues.

Although there is no direct legislation to protect job applicants from age discrimination in the UK, employers need to prove that they have acted responsibly when making selections.

Task

Draw up a list of the positive measures which can be taken to reduce discrimination in the workforce.

5.2.7 Recruitment and Advertising

The first issue an organisation needs to consider once a position becomes vacant is whether to re-employ. The manpower plan should be examined and the following points considered:

- Could the work be re-organised?
- Could the work be mechanised/computerised?
- Could the job become part-time, worked in shifts etc?
- Could the work be sub-contracted more economically?

Only if the answer to all these questions is 'no', should recruitment take place.

The second stage is to determine the key requirements of the job from the job description and person specification. After this the *source(s) of recruitment* should be considered. These include:

- advertising in the national Press;
- advertising in the local Press;
- advertising in technical/specialist Press;
- internal advertisements;
- vacancy lists outside premises;
- job centres;
- commercial employment agencies;

- management selection consultants;
- executive search consultants (head-hunters);
- universities and colleges (the milk round);
- schools and the careers service;
- youth training schemes.

The third stage is to design the ***advertisement*** or appoint an advertising or recruitment agency to carry out the task. The decision to use an agency or not may depend on the level of the job, its specialist nature and the expertise available within the employing organisation. The advertisement should include:

- the name and brief details of the employing organisation;
- the job title and main duties;
- key points of the person specification;
- details of salary;
- action to be taken (for example, 'Write with full details to ....').

Tasks

(i) Draw up a list of the advantages and disadvantages of each source of recruitment.

(ii) Which source(s) would you use for the following?

- a labourer on a building site;
- a wordprocessing operator;
- a computer analyst;
- a marketing director;
- a sales assistant.

5.2.8 Selection Methods

If the recruitment drive is successful it should result in a number of well qualified applicants. They should either have been asked to submit a ***curriculum vitae*** or complete an ***application form***. Most organisations favour the completion of an application form which allows easy comparison between candidates and minimises discrimination.

The next stage is to draw up a ***shortlist*** of candidates and set up a control system to ensure that all respondents know the outcome of their application and the stage it has reached. To minimise discrimination more than one individual should be involved in drawing up the shortlist.

Shortlisted applicants are then asked to participate in further selection procedures. These include:

- individual/group interviews;
- achievement tests;
- aptitude tests;
- personality profiles;
- assessment centres.

The choice of ***selection method*** depends on the level of the job, the expertise available and the budget. An ***interview*** is the most common form of selection. This gives the candidate and the employer an opportunity to ask questions and expand upon the information already given. The candidate is able to meet representatives of the organisation and may be able to view the working area. The employer can assess the candidate's communication skills and suitability. The interview may be conducted by a member of the personnel department, the line manager or both. Often a pre-selection interview takes place and appropriate candidates invited to attend a second interview.

A *report form* is completed to record the results of the interview. This should encourage objective information collection, rather than opinions, and should concentrate on the key criteria identified as essential to the job.

The correlation between the results of an interview and the candidate's eventual ability to perform the job (known as its *validity*) is often very low. The *reliability* of the interview is also suspect. If a candidate is interviewed again after a period of time, different judgements are often made.

Many organisations use a range of *selection tests* such as the following:

- achievement tests to measure a skill held, such as numeracy. typing, driving;

- general intelligence tests, often referred to as IQ tests;

- aptitude tests to measure a candidate's ability to work with words and figures, manual dexterity etc;

- trainability tests which usually involve some form of simulation exercise.

Personality profiling aims to assess personality (Section 8.1). The two main concepts which have led to the development of assessment methods are:

- that personality can be divided into types and individuals can be compared with types;

- that personality can be profiled by identifying *behavioural factors* which are opposed to one another (such as outgoing/shy) and plotting where the candidate's personality fits between the two extremes.

Some organisations use *assessment centres* where a combination of selection methods are used over a longer period of time. Candidates are brought together so that assessment can be made of how individuals interact with others as well as how they perform alone.

After the candidate has been selected, *references* may be taken up from the current employer, school or college to check the accuracy of the information given and ask for a general comment on suitability for the appointment.

Tasks

(i) Design an application form for a clerical vacancy. Decide what information is necessary to allow you to compare the candidate with the key criteria for the job.

(ii) Which selection method(s) would you use for each of the following categories of staff?

- clerk/typists;
- graduate trainees;
- accounts managers.

5.2.9 Contract of Employment

This should include:

- the names of the employer and employee;
- the job title;
- the date on which employment began;
- the normal hours of work and related conditions;
- the scale and rate of remuneration and method of payment;
- holiday entitlement and pay;
- terms and conditions relating to sickness, injury and pay;
- length of notice due to and from employee;
- disciplinary rules and procedure;
- employee grievance arrangements;
- conditions of employment relating to any trade union membership.

The legal implications of contracts of employment are detailed in Section 3.3.

Task

Construct a contract of employment for an organisation known to you.

Assignment 5.2: Situations vacant

You have recently been appointed as a personnel officer in a well-known retail company. There are several vacancies which need to be filled and you are anxious to appoint staff who are good performers and fit in well with the company. You report to the personnel manager, Chris Roberts, who is experienced and has been with the company for a number of years.

Student activities

(i) Select one job in the organisation that needs to be filled and write a memo the personnel manager explaining why you feel it is necessary to recruit someone for this position. Support your memo with a job description and a person description. Include a draft recruitment advertisement for the position, plus proposals for timing, frequency and media to be used. Recommend any other sources of recruitment you think might be appropriate. Justify your proposals.

(ii) Design a word processed draft programme outlining how you could organise a day devoted to the selection of a final candidate from a shortlist. Details should include arrangements for the reception of candidates, a programme of events, and should include at least three methods of assessment. Support your selection programme with a rationale.

5.3 Interview Techniques

5.3.1 Sources of Bias

The interpersonal factors which determine the way people react to each other are complex. *Sources of bias* include:

- the effect of first and last impressions;
- the interviewer's frame of reference which includes his or her own ideas, beliefs and values;
- physical appearances;
- stereotyping;
- the 'halo and horns' effect whereby only the favourable or unfavourable aspects of the interview are perceived in order to confirm the original impression made;
- speech and jargon;
- non-verbal communication (Section 8.2.4).

Task

Watch a television programme with the volume off and concentrate on the non-verbal communication going on. Draw up a list of expressions and gestures which indicate people's moods. How do individuals relate to one another non-verbally?

5.3.2 Improving Interview Techniques

An *interview* (Section 8.2.7) can be described as a conversation with a purpose. The employer should arrange a comfortable location for the interview, away from distractions, and allow an appropriate amount of time. It is useful to have more than one opinion. This can be achieved by having more than one interviewer present or sequential interviews. Interviewers should be trained to recognise and eliminate bias and structure the interview logically.

The interviewees should be aware of the *impression* (Section 8.2.3) they make. They should dress carefully and arrive punctually. Questions should be answered fully with examples given of relevant experience. Candidates should consider what questions they may wish to ask about the organisation and the job vacancy.

Task

Write an article for your local newspaper under the headline: *Interview technique - how to make a good impression.*

5.3.3 Preparation and Interview Structure

Before conducting an interview the interviewer should collect and read all the relevant documents. The interview should be structured logically with sequential questions. Highlighting key issues or using checklists may assist with this. Both the interviewer and interviewee should have the opportunity to ask questions. Questions (Section 8.2.7) should be *open-ended* to allow the candidate to expand on the information requested. Probing questions asking for actual illustrations or factual details ensure that in-depth information is collected. The interviewer should avoid asking *leading* questions which indicate the answer expected.

The interviewee should prepare for the interview by researching the organisation and reading carefully any literature provided. A list of questions he or she may wish to ask should be prepared in advance. The candidate should also check his or her travel arrangements and plan a suitable mode of dress.

Task

Design an interview report form which can be used afterwards by an interviewer to record the basic information given by the candidate and the opinions of the interviewer.

5.3.4 Interview Strategies

Depending on the purpose of the interview, different *strategies* may be adopted. The most common is the *friendly strategy* where the interviewer aims to relax the interviewee. Another possibility is the *problem-solving* strategy where a theoretical problem is posed and the interviewee is asked to comment on it. Occasionally a *stress strategy* is used which puts the interviewee under pressure to see how he or she reacts. Whichever strategy is adopted, the whole interview process should be reviewed regularly to ensure that it remains effective.

Task

Give examples of situations in which the three different interview strategies might be used appropriately.

Assignment 5.3: Smartscene Stores

You are the training manager for Smartscene Stores and have been asked to construct a training programme to help the store managers develop their interview skills when selecting staff.

Student activities

Prepare a training brief for this course using a desktop publishing package.

5.4 Development And Retention

5.4.1 Job Evaluation

Job evaluation is concerned with assessing the relative demands of jobs within the organisation in order to provide a fair basis for a payment system. Judgements about *job values* should be made on objective rather than subjective grounds and should be based on job content rather than the job holder. An up-to-date *job description* is an essential requirement for this process. Techniques used in job evaluation include:

• *ranking* where jobs are compared with each other and arranged in order of importance;

- *job classification* where descriptions of the qualities and skills required in each grade are made, and jobs are then compared with these outlines and slotted into the appropriate place;

- *points rating* where a job is broken down into a number of factors and these are then scored for each job;

- *factor comparison* where jobs are broken down into factors as before, but each factor is given a monetary value.

Where large numbers of jobs are involved, **bench-mark jobs** may be selected at various levels in the organisation and placed in order. These provide a framework for placing other jobs. Job evaluation depends heavily on judgements made and an evaluation committee with representatives from both management and unions may be set up to minimise bias.

Task

Draw up a list of the advantages and disadvantages of each job evaluation technique listed above in terms of cost, time needed and fairness. Which of the methods do you think would be most useful?

5.4.2 Pay Structures and Benefits

In order to decide *levels of pay*, various issues need to be considered:

- national and local market rates;
- equity: a fair relationship between effort, skills and rewards should be demonstrated;
- manpower requirements;
- budget;
- employee expectations which often depend on the strength of union power;
- legislation, particularly the requirements of the **Equal Pay Act 1970** (Section 3.3).

Pay is linked directly to the type of employment concerned. Variations include:

- full-time regular hours per week;
- shift work;
- part-time work;
- flexible working hours;
- annual hours.

Payments may be made weekly or monthly, in cash or directly into a bank or building society account.

In addition to basic pay, many organisations have evolved more sophisticated systems which link reward and effort. These include:

- fringe benefits;
- bonus schemes and commission payments;
- profit sharing;
- performance related pay.

Tasks

(i) What type of employment and method of payment would be appropriate for the following organisations?

   • a fire service;

   • clerical company;

   • a petrol station.

(ii) How can fringe benefits, bonus schemes and commission payments, profit sharing and performance-related pay contribute to the motivation and retention of staff?

5.4.3 Performance Appraisal

The objectives of *performance appraisal* are:

- to improve current performance by identifying and communicating individual strengths and weaknesses, and setting performance standards where appropriate;

- to identify potential for the future thereby allowing succession planning and effective manpower planning;

- to contribute to management development;

- to identify current talents within the organisation by identifying and responding to training needs for the individual and the organisation;

- to provide a basis for determining salary reviews;

- to provide a means of establishing a written record of performance and of the substance of an appraisal interview;

- to act as a means of formal communication.

Methods used to achieve these objectives and styles of performance appraisal vary according to the nature of the job and the management style. Four main methods of appraisal in regular use are:

- *linear scales* where factors relevant to effective job performance are identified and a scale designed so that the appraiser can rate the employee;

- *management by objectives* where targets are agreed between the appraiser and the appraised for a fixed period, and performance is measured by the success in reaching these targets;

- *comparative methods* where members of a department are compared with each other;

- *behavioural systems* where practical examples of behaviour are used.

Where appraisal information is recorded in written form, care is needed in the design of the appraisal form. Appraisal can be *open*, where the individual can read and comment on their assessment, or *closed*, where the appraised does not see the report. Appraisers should receive training to maximise the benefits of this system.

Most appraisal is accompanied by an *appraisal interview*. To be effective the individual being appraised should be told in advance and allowed to carry out *self-appraisal* before the interview. This can be very useful in comparing employee and manager perceptions. The interview should be conducted in a friendly, open atmosphere. Information about performance targets and factual data should be collected in advance. The emphasis should be on positive development rather than criticism. Appraisal should be seen as an on-going process, not just an annual formality.

Task

Design an appraisal system for a college lecturer, stating whether it is an open or closed system.

5.4.4 Training and Development

Training is the systematic development of the knowledge, skills and attitudes required by an individual to perform adequately a given task or job. The process requires:

- the identification of training needs at organisational, departmental and individual levels;
- these needs then need to be met by an effective training programme which considers the budget, training location, method and instructors available.

The choice of *method* includes:

- programmed learning/distance learning;
- lectures;
- videos/films;
- group methods such as syndicate exercises, discussions,
- seminars;
- simulations such as business games, role play and case studies;
- manuals.

The training programme should be *evaluated* to determine whether it has produced the desired changes in employees' behaviour and whether the results make a worthwhile contribution to the overall aims of the organisation. Possible evaluation methods include:

- the use of properly designed and applied tests used before and after training;
- the use of course assessments;
- performance appraisal and other performance measurement techniques;
- the use of interviews before and after training;
- the use of untrained control groups for comparison;
- the use of cost-benefit analysis to quantify benefits as far as possible.

Management development is a systematic process which aims to ensure that the business has the effective managers it needs to meet its present and future requirements. It is concerned with improving the performance of existing managers, giving them the opportunity for growth and development, and ensuring as far as possible that management succession within the organisation is planned for.

The objectives of a typical management development programme are to improve the financial performance and long-term growth of the company by:

- improving the performance of managers;
- identifying managers with further potential;
- assisting chief executives and managers throughout the organisation to provide adequate succession and to create a system whereby this is kept under regular review.

Methods of management development include:

- *appraisal and self-development* to identify training needs;
- *action learning*: a problem solving approach involving moving staff so that they experience different situations and get involved with different projects;
- *coaching*: an informal system between a developing manager and a more senior manager;
- *peer relationships*: sharing knowledge and experience with a group of similar employees;
- *management by objectives*.

Task

List the benefits and problems of internal training conducted in the workplace, internal training conducted away from the workplace and training carried out by external consultants. Which would be the most appropriate for the following?

- visual display unit (VDU) operator training;
- sales training;
- management training.

5.4.5 Health and Safety

Health and safety procedures and programmes are concerned with protecting employees and others against the hazards arising from their employment or links with the organisation. The major legislation covering this area is the *Health and Safety at Work Act 1974* (Section 3.3).

Task

Draft a model health and safety policy for a business organisation.

Assignment 5.4: Forbright Brothers Ltd

You are the personnel manager for Forbright Brothers Ltd, a small manufacturing company in the West Midlands. You have become concerned recently at the high level of employee turnover and absenteeism. Your investigations indicate that staff are dissatisfied with the systems for paying, appraising and training staff. At present the shop floor staff are paid a basic wage plus bonuses for extra production. There is no formal system of appraisal and they receive only minimal on-site training. The clerical and managerial staff do not have a bonus system and are paid a fixed rate for the job. There is a very basic system of appraisal for these employees which only succeeds in identifying the really poor performers. Training for these grades also takes place at the workplace. Absenteeism is highest amongst the clerical workers who do not lose pay for short-term absence. The high turnover of staff takes place in all grades. Comments by ex-employees include: "It was like the blind leading the blind there." "Nobody knew what they were doing."

Student activities

Prepare a word processed report for your managing director, Richard Keys, outlining the steps you intend to take to reduce wastage and raise employee morale.

5.5 Industrial Relations

5.5.1 Structure and Types of Trade Unions

The term *industrial relations* refers broadly to relations between employers and their workers. It is a specialist area of organisational management and study. *Industrial relations* and *employee relations* are seen often as interchangeable. However, industrial relations emerged from the unionised manual workers in manufacturing, whereas the term *employee relations* came into greater use with the development of less unionised white collar employment and the service and commercial sectors of the economy.

A *trade union* is described by the *Trade Union and Labour Relations Act 1974* as an organisation which either consists wholly or mainly of workers of one or more descriptions, whose principal purposes include the regulation of relations between workers of that or those descriptions and employers or employer's associations; or consists of such organisations or their representatives.

There are some basic similarities in the structure of trade unions. The headquarters have full-time officials headed by an executive and a president or general secretary. The holders of these posts are normally elected for a fixed term. They provide advisory, legal and welfare services, and professional negotiators to take part in national level negotiations with employers. They are responsible for implementing union policy which is determined by delegates at the union's annual national conference. These delegates are elected by the members through the branch structure, and vote on issues of general importance.

The next level is generally the district or regional level with full-time paid officials, and a committee of delegates from local branches. The local branch may consist of the union members at one place of work or bring together employees from a number of different employers in the locality.

At the workplace level the role of the shop steward is the most important. The shop steward is in daily contact with the members; he or she acts as a spokesperson to management. Shop stewards are elected by the members.

There are four widely recognised types of trade union:

- *craft unions* which are made up of skilled workers who carry out the same craft;
- *general unions* which bring together all categories of worker across a range of industries, such as the Transport and General Workers' Union;
- *industrial unions* which organise all the employees, whatever their craft, for a specific industry, such as shipbuilding, railways etc;
- *occupational* or *non-manual unions* which organise technical, clerical, professional, supervisory and managerial staff separately from other employees.

> **Task**
>
> Obtain recruitment literature from a range of different unions. Compare and contrast the structure and functions of the various unions.

5.5.2 Rights of Trade Unions

An *independent trade union* is one that is not dominated or controlled by an employer. A union can apply to the certification officer appointed by the Secretary of State for a certificate of independence.

This grants the union certain rights and privileges under the *Trade Union and Labour Relations Act 1974*, the *Employment Acts 1980, 1982 and 1988*, and the *Trade Union Act 1984*. These include:

- the right to belong to a trade union and to take part in its activities and not be penalised for doing so;
- the right to be consulted on redundancy or the transfer of the employer's undertaking;
- the right to receive information from the employer to assist in the bargaining process;
- the right to reasonable time off for union business;
- the right to appoint safety representatives;
- the right not to be unfairly treated by your own union.

In some industries there is a *union membership agreement* which requires employees to join a particular trade union. This is often referred to as a *closed shop agreement*. Under the *Employment Act 1988*, however, it is illegal to dismiss an employee who refuses to join a trade union and the employer may engage a worker who is not a member of the trade union. This has dramatically weakened the closed shop arrangement.

Task

Obtain leaflets from the Department of Employment and from the Arbitration, Conciliation and Advisory Service (ACAS) on employment legislation. Review the contents to familiarise yourself with the main details of current legislation.

5.5.3 Trade Union Action

Trade unions derive their power from their *members*. They can exert pressure on an employer by taking *collective action*. Provided they act in accordance with the law, they cannot be sued; they enjoy *immunity*.

A *trade dispute* is defined by the *Trade Union and Labour Relations Act 1974* as disputes over:

- terms and conditions of employment or the physical conditions in which any workers are required to work;
- engagement or non-engagement, termination or suspension of one or more workers;
- allocation of work between workers (demarcation disputes);
- matters of discipline;
- membership or non-membership of an independent trade union;
- facilities for officials of trades unions;
- machinery for negotiation or consultation and other procedures relating to any of the above.

The ultimate sanction in a trade dispute is the right to strike. Under the *Trade Union Act 1984* the strike must have been approved in a secret ballot of the union members involved. The *Employment Act 1988* further defines how the ballot should be conducted.

When a strike has been called the union members may engage in *peaceful picketing* to deter other employees from entering the workplace. It is only lawful if carried out at or near the place of work. *The Advisory, Conciliation and Arbitration Service (ACAS)* (Section 5.5.4) Code of Practice indicates that no more than six pickets should stand at any entrance to the workplace.

Secondary action occurs when attempts are made to persuade the employees of another employer not involved in the dispute to break their contracts of employment. If an organisation associated with an employer in dispute takes over work from him, the employees may lawfully refuse to deal with *(black)* that work. Other sanctions include *working to rule* and *sit-ins*.

Task

Research the reasons for the breakdown between employer and union(s) in any recent industrial dispute that has received national publicity, the position each has taken and the progress of the dispute. Pay particular attention to any ballots which have taken place and how they are conducted. Was strike action or picketing part of the industrial action? If so, was it lawful?

5.5.4 The National Structures

The major *national organisations* involved in this area are:

- The *Trades Union Congress (TUC)* which acts as the collective voice of British trade unionism by providing a forum for debate and involving the majority of the major trade unions. Unions become affiliated to the TUC.

- *Trades councils* are the local counterparts of the TUC. They are voluntary groups of trade unions on a regional basis.

- *Employers' associations* are collective organisations representing the employers in a particular industry or industry sector.

- The *Confederation of British Industry (CBI)* is the employers' equivalent of the TUC and is composed of employers' associations, trade associations and individual business organisations.

State institutions include:

- The *Advisory, Conciliation and Arbitration Service (ACAS)* which is an independent organisation able to intervene at the request of one or more of the parties in a dispute. In addition to providing negotiating and arbitration services, it gives direct advice to employers and issues codes of practice.

- *Industrial tribunals* hear claims brought under any of the Acts relevant to employment. A tribunal consists of three people: a chairman, who must be legally qualified, and two lay members drawn from employers, trades unions and others.

- *Employment appeal tribunals* hear appeals against decisions made at industrial tribunals.

Task

Obtain details of the above organisations' roles and functions.

5.5.5 Negotiation and Collective Bargaining

Negotiation (Section 8.2.9) is the process of resolving differences between unions and management through face-to-face discussions. If conflict is to be prevented, an effective negotiation process should be designed which allows issues to be debated and resolved at an early stage. The results of successful negotiation are a set of *collective rules and procedures* which regulate the employment process.

There are two main categories of agreement: *substantive agreements* which lay down the terms and conditions of employment to be reflected in each employee's contract of employment; and *procedural agreements* which set out the procedures that should be adhered to in specific situations.

The following main items are the products of successful negotiation:

- A *company rule book* which aims to protect and clarify company policy for employees. It includes matters concerned with the contract of employment, disciplinary offences, health and safety issues and work performance. The rules cannot cover every eventuality in employment, but should aim to establish general guidelines to be followed.

- A *disciplinary procedure* which should be set out in writing and identify the stages of the procedure and the penalties imposed. Individuals should have the right to be accompanied by a representative and the right of appeal. The code should specify what action is taken by what level of management.

- A *grievance procedure* which should provide an effective mechanism for employees to raise a grievance with management. The procedure should be set out in writing and state to whom the complaint should be made. The employee should be allowed a representative and have the right of appeal to more senior management. The time scale for action should be stated and meetings should be properly minuted.

- A *disputes procedure* which should be a method of allowing collective grievances to be heard. The structure should largely follow that of the grievance procedure.

Collective bargaining involves the determination of pay and conditions of employment between the union and the employer. The main methods are:

- *distributive bargaining* where each side takes a stand and bargains to achieve the best result for their side at the expense of the other;

- *integrative bargaining/productivity* deals where both parties can negotiate a gain by linking pay to productivity;

- *no-strike deals* and *pendulum arbitration* which is a new aspect of union/employer bargaining where the union agrees a no-strike deal in return for sole bargaining rights with the employer. Linked to this participative style where employer and union work more closely together, is the concept of pendulum arbitration. This involves a straight choice between the position of management or the union by an independent arbitrator (usually ACAS). The results of arbitration are binding on both sides.

Task

Design disciplinary and grievance procedures for an organisation known to you.

5.5.6 Employee Participation and Consultation

In addition to the collective bargaining activities of the organisation, many employers are developing systems of communication which allow employees a wider say in how the company is run. This more democratic style of management is increasingly common in service and high-technology industries, sometimes obviating the need for formal trade union representation. The current picture is of declining membership of trade unions and growing interest in alternative ways of involving employees in the management process. Potential methods of increasing participation and involvement include:

- *share ownership schemes* which encourage employees to become shareholders in their company;

- *suggestion schemes;*
- *quality circles;*
- *autonomous work groups;*
- *employee communications* such as annual employee reports and videos, briefing sessions, meetings, handbooks etc.

The idea of legislating for involvement, particularly by requiring employee representation on the board of directors, has been the subject of an EC draft, the *Fifth Directive,* and was the subject of the *1977 Bullock Report.* The EC would also like to formalise procedures for informing and consulting with employees of larger organisations. Various methods of achieving this have been put forward in the *Vredling Initiative.*

Task

Write a short word processed report suggesting ways of increasing employee participation in business organisations.

5.5.7 Dismissal

Dismissal takes place when an employer terminates a contract of employment with or without *notice.* Termination without notice is known as *instant* or *summary dismissal.* If it takes place in breach of the terms of the contract of employment it is known as *unfair dismissal.* Dismissal can also take place when an employer acts in breach of the contract of employment in such a way as to force the employee to terminate the contract. This is known as *forced resignation* or *constructive dismissal.*

There are two basic reasons for dismissal: *redundancy,* where the job has ceased to exist, and *incompetence,* where the services provided by the employee are unsatisfactory.

The *Employment Protection (Consolidation) Act 1978* (Section 3.3) states the conditions under which redundancy may arise. The employer must communicate with recognised trade unions and allow the employee time off for re-training and to attend job interviews. The same Act also contains provisions relating to unfair dismissal. There is a considerable amount of legislation protecting the rights of the individual in employment; an employer must demonstrate he has acted fairly when dismissing an employee.

Task

Outline the main areas for which a business organisation should have written rules and state how the rules should be communicated to employees.

Assignment 5.5: The goodwill visit

As a member of the local Chamber of Commerce you have been asked to participate in a programme of events being planned for a goodwill visit of industrialists from Japan. The visitors are particularly interested in British trade unionism.

Student activities

(i) Prepare a hand-out using a desktop publishing package for the visitors on the following issues: What are the major trade unions in Britain, how many unions are there, and how are they structured? What proportion of British employees belong to a trade union and how do they decide which trade union to join? How do unions which recruit the same types of worker co-exist and is there any conflict over membership?

(ii) Prepare notes for a ten-minute presentation on the history, structure, membership and current policies of a particular trade union.

5.6 Organisational Change

5.6.1 Management of Organisational and Technological Change

Business organisations are subject to change and as a result must be restructured periodically. *External pressure* to change may be the result of market pressures or economic policies. *Internal pressure* may be the result of the introduction of new technology or innovative systems.

Employees often resist change (Section 8.1.13) because it is seen as a threat to familiar patterns of behaviour, status and/or financial rewards. If not properly managed, change can decrease morale, motivation and commitment and create conflict within an organisation. The *management of change* involves the following processes:

- full *communication and involvement* of employees with the changes planned and reasons given for them;

- *negotiation and consultation* with employee representatives about the way in which the changes will take place;

- *training* staff to meet the new requirements;

- *counselling and appraisal* to identify concerns and areas of future development;

- *reassurance* that status and benefits will be maintained.

The more participation and involvement the employees have in the process, the more smoothly change will be implemented.

Task

Prepare a brief word processed report outlining how the introduction of the computerisation of a particular aspect of work currently handled manually should be implemented.

5.6.2 New Patterns of Work/Labour Flexibility

The traditional view of employment is of a full-time, permanent contract with one employer. Although this arrangement still applies to the majority of employment situations, an increasing number of employees now work to *new patterns* which aim to give greater *labour flexibility*. The major types of flexible work pattern are:

- *Shift work*: Some organisations operate for periods longer than a normal working day, sometimes operating continuously. This requires that employees work in shifts which can involve patterns of day and/or night working.

- *Part-time work*: In practice anyone working less than full-time hours may be considered a part-time worker. Legally, employees who work less than 16 hours per week do not enjoy the same employment rights as full-time employees.

- *Flexible work hours*: Standard core times are set for the working day when all employees are expected to be present. On either side of the core period are flexible hours when employees can start and finish work to suit themselves as long as they fulfil their total contractual hours.

- *Task-based systems*: These require that a certain amount of work is completed before the employee is free to leave. This motivates the employee to work quickly and efficiently.

- *Annual hours*: The employee contracts to provide the employer with a certain number of hours each year. The employee works when the job requires it, which may involve considerable variation in the pattern of work.

- *Job share*: This is where two or more employees share a full-time job. It can result in greater flexibility and cover for absence.

- *Short-term contracts*: The worker is self-employed (Section 3.3) and is contracted for a fixed period. The contract is either renewed or terminated at the end of the period.

- *Consultancy*: The worker is self-employed (Section 3.3) and is contracted to carry out a specific task.

Task

Give examples of what type of employment would be most suited to each of the methods of working listed above.

5.6.3 Job Design and Restructuring

Organisational change often requires that jobs are *redesigned* and overall work *restructured*. *Job design* aims to develop work tasks which motivate and provide satisfaction for the employee. Factors which influence *job satisfaction* include:

- variety of tasks, location, machinery and people;
- autonomy in deciding methods and ways of working;
- responsibility;
- interaction with others;
- task significance;
- goals and feedback.

Where practical these items should be considered when designing or redesigning jobs. There may be limitations in the design of the job, however, due to the requirements of technology, union and employee attitudes, inter-job demarcations, management values and style. Common elements of job design include *job rotation, job enlargement* and *job enrichment*.

Organisational restructuring aims to analyse roles and relationships so that tasks are organised, divided and co-ordinated in order to maximise the effectiveness of the organisation. The design process leads to the establishment of a *formal* organisational structure. There may also be an *informal* structure which needs to be considered. An analysis of the organisational structure should cover how activities are grouped together, the span of control of managers and supervisors, and the number of levels in the hierarchy. Relationships, decision-making, management style, and the organisational climate should also be assessed.

Task

Select a job with which you are familiar and for which you can obtain a job description. What potential is there to increase job satisfaction by redesigning the work? Prepare a proposal for redesigning this job.

Assignment 5.6: Thrifty Finance plc

You are the personnel manager for Thrifty Finance plc. Competition in the financial services sector has led the company to make major investments in new technology in order to provide an efficient service for customers. At the same time the company wants to extend the branch opening hours to provide a service until 8pm on weekdays and all day on Saturdays.

Student activities

The board of directors has asked you to present a paper at the next board meeting considering the following questions:

(i) How should the new technology be introduced to maximise the benefits to the customer, whilst ensuring staff are trained and competent to use it?

(ii) How should the branch offices be staffed to ensure a full quota of competent staff are available throughout the new opening hours?

Prepare a word processed report and suitable notes for your presentation.

Section 6
Marketing

by Monica Hall

Senior Lecturer in Marketing at Bristol Business School

Marketing involves the analysis of existing and potential markets, the identification of customer needs and wants, and the establishment of policy within the current social and economic environment whilst anticipating future trends.

Recommended Reading

Giles, G. B., *Marketing*, M & E Handbooks, 1989

Kotler, P., *Principles of Marketing*, Prentice Hall, 1989

Morden, A. R., *Elements of Marketing*, 2nd Edition, DP Publications, 1991

Oliver, G., *Marketing Today*, Prentice Hall, 1985

Tull, Donald, & Kahle, Lynn, *Marketing Management*, Maxwell Macmillan International, 1990

Nobody had told William that the pin had fallen from the string chart only that afternoon.

Contents

6.1 The Role of Marketing

The *role of marketing* within an organisation, whether trading or non-profit making, is concerned with:

- facilitating the *exchange* process through marketing activities directed at the consumer;
- *collecting and analysing* relevant information on the market and the consumer;
- acting as the *integrative* function within the organisation.

6.1.1 The Exchange Process

The *exchange process* involves putting a value on goods and services. Several features then evolve:

- the commodity gains a *price* which becomes known to buyers;
- the price becomes subject to *market forces* engendered by the existence of many buyers and usually several sellers;
- unless the seller has a monopoly, market forces tend to lower the price as sellers *compete* to sell the highest volume.

Sellers respond to this competitive situation in many ways, but basically they respond by:

- differentiating their products in order to introduce *marketable* features not found in their competitors' products, and/or
- differentiating products to appeal to buyers whose requirements can be distinguished as different from those of other buyers.

Tasks

(i) Identify a commodity market and research the mechanisms by which buyers and sellers effect transactions in this market.

(ii) Identify two products where sellers have differentiated their products from those of the competition by appealing to different types of buyer.

6.1.2 The Information Role of Marketing

Buyers need *information* on products and services such as the difference between one product and another, where and how they can be bought and their prices. This encourages sellers to promote products, a process which is linked to two factors:

- the *brand name* of the product or service;
- the *corporate image* of the organisation.

The provision of information to the buyer facilitates the exchange process and falls into three parts:

- information about the market such as its size and value, its structure, the competition;
- information about the buyer or consumer such as their needs and wants, attitudes and motivations, lifestyle and aspirations;
- an analysis of this information to satisfy those needs and wants profitably.

The Chartered Institute of Marketing summarises this aspect of marketing thus: "Marketing is the management process responsible for identifying, anticipating and satisfying customer requirements profitably."

Task

Compile a list of brand names and conduct a survey to ascertain how many respondents can identify the product associated with each brand.

6.1.3 The Integrative Role of Marketing

Marketing *integrates* the consumer's requirements with the activities of the other organisational functions such as finance, human resources and production. Thus, the role of marketing includes the collection and analysis of relevant information, and its dissemination throughout the organisation. This allows the principles of consumer sovereignty to be practised. The principle of *consumer sovereignty* is that meeting the consumer's requirements is the primary function of an organisation.

The *marketing concept* provides that the most important managerial task in any organisation is to understand the needs and wants of the consumer, and to ensure that the operations of the organisation are adapted to deliver the required goods and services to the consumer more efficiently and profitably than its competitors.

Tasks

(i)   In groups, research and list the five major tasks/objectives of the following organisational functions:

  • finance
  • human resources
  • production
  • sales and distribution

(ii) List five reasons why a knowledge of the consumer's needs and wants, behaviour and attitudes might assist the better operation of these functions. Why might the dissemination of marketing information improve job satisfaction in an organisation?

Assignment 6.1: The marketing-oriented organisation

You are contemplating starting a business with two friends. You are all agreed that it will be a marketing-oriented organisation, although your friends do not know what this means.

You have decided to give them a good and bad example of a marketing-oriented organisation to help them understand the essential principles and practices.

Student activities

(i)   Select an organisation that you think is successfully marketing-orientated. Justify your choice. Your reasons may cover such areas as communication with the consumer, distribution of the product or service, price, after-sales service and corporate image.

(ii) Now do the same for an organisation you believe is inadequately marketing-orientated, justifying your choice

---

6.2 Market Appraisal

Market appraisal is concerned with the collection and analysis of information that is relevant to a market or its consumers. This data is both internal and external to the organisation. The purpose of information-gathering and analysis is to gain knowledge of the *overall environment* in which marketing strategies will operate. The overall environment can be broken down into specific environments or cultures:

- the organisation itself;
- the industry of which the organisation is a part;
- the technology affecting the products or services;
- the national and/or international economy;
- the consumer market;
- the political climate, the legal system and ethical codes prevailing.

6.2.1 The Marketing Information System

The *marketing information system (MIS)* is described in detail in Section 6.8. The characteristics of a good information system are that it is:

- reliable and accurate
- up-to-date
- complete and precise
- intelligible
- relevant
- timely
- cost-effective

The information to be yielded by the MIS can be categorised in two basic ways:

- *uncontrollable (external)*: environmental, competitive, institutional and legal;
- *controllable (internal)*: functional and aesthetic aspects of the product branding and packaging.

Tasks

(i) Choose an organisation marketing its products to the housewife. Discover as many sources as you can of information in the following categories which might contribute to the marketing information system of the organisation:

- the industry of which the organisation is a part;
- the technology affecting its services;
- national economic indicators;
- the consumer market.

(ii) List the political, legal and ethical forces which you feel might affect the organisation's current operations.

6.2.2 Internal Information

All organisational functions yield information of value to marketing managers. The function most closely allied to that of marketing is the sales and distribution department, which may provide the following information:

- sales invoices;
- customer records and analysis;
- sales costs;
- trade promotional expenditure and evaluation.

If the producer is selling directly to the end-user, the *customer* is also the *consumer*. However, usually there are other organisations in the distribution chain such as agents, wholesalers and retailers who are the organisation's customers and sell on to the consumer. Thus, the producer's sales function is primarily concerned with the organisation's customers, whilst the marketing function is concerned with their consumers.

It is the basic sales function to *push* product through the distribution system aided by the basic marketing function of generating consumer demand to *pull* products off the shelves at the end of the distribution chain.

See Section 6.7.1 for further details of internal information sources.

Tasks

Obtain some examples of sales invoices and customer guarantee cards.

(i) How much information of value to marketing can be obtained from a typical invoice?

(ii) How much consumer information can be obtained from a guarantee card? To what use might it be put?

6.2.3 External Information

External information sources include:

- *primary information* which has been commissioned for a specific purpose;

189

• *secondary information* which has been gathered and analysed for a different but related purpose. This is sometimes known as desk research.

See Section 6.7.2 for further details of external information sources.

Task

As a group, organise your class to research and categorise the sources of business information available to you within your college. Why should secondary information be treated with caution?

6.2.4 Researching the Market

It is essential to know as much as possible about the market in which products and services are sold. Organisations can subscribe to *market research* specialists who provide information on:

• major competitors in a defined market;
• the size of the market in terms of turnover;
• the size of the market in units sold;
• sales of competing products in total;
• sales of competing products by sales area;
• sales of competing products by television area;
• promotional activity among competing products;
• a profile of retail outlets in a particular market;
• marketing/sales data broken down by retail profile;

Other sources of information include government statistics and specially commissioned market research on such areas as consumer behaviour and attitudes, brand attributes, pricing and buying intentions.

Task

Define the following terms and give examples:
   • quantitative research;
   • qualitative research.

6.2.5 Researching the Consumer

Providers of goods and services want to know two basic things:

• Who is buying our product and why?
• Who is not buying our product and why?

Information from surveys carried out by *consumer research* specialists on consumers' attitudes and behaviour can be bought by interested organisations. This is a considerable growth industry with analysed data held on databases which can be searched and cross-referenced. Determinants of consumer behaviour include:

• economic determinants of consumer demand;
• behavioural determinants of consumer demand such as individual personality (Section 8.1) and motivation, lifestyle and culture, family and peer group influence.

Task

The development of consumer research as a social science has been greatly advanced by refinements of statistical techniques and by the use of sophisticated data processing methods. In groups, research, consider and summarise the purposes of the following techniques in the light of this statement:

- sampling (in broad terms)
- questionnaires
- psychographics
- ACORN
- JICNAR
- TGI

6.2.6 Market Segmentation

In modern mass markets most categories of product cater for a wide range of consumers whose individual needs, wants, motivations and attitudes vary. Markets can rarely cater for individual needs, so consumers are categorised by the commonality of their interests, attitudes or behaviour. The marketing effort is targeted on these groups, which is the most cost-effective method of communicating with mass consumers. The provision of such variety rests on the principle of *market segmentation*. This principle seeks to identify subsections of main markets, known as *segments*, in which:

- the characteristics of products within a segment differ as much as possible from products in other segments of the same market;
- the consumers in a particular segment have identifiable characteristics which differentiate them from consumers in other segments of the same market.

To be *viable* in terms of logistics and profit, segments must be:

- identifiable
- measurable
- accessible

Segments can be defined in terms of *consumer characteristics* and/or *product characteristics*. Consumer characteristics include such variables as:

- age
- sex
- socio-demographic profile
- geographical location
- psychographic profile

Product characteristics include:

- benefit segmentation;
- vendor segmentation, for example business-to-business markets;
- segmentation by retail criteria such as shelf footage.

Complex modern mass markets are divided into segments and subsegments, according to many criteria. It is the task of every competitor in a market to analyse and decide how segmentation occurs in its market, and to utilise such analysis in the following decision-making processes:

- *positioning* its products within the segment;
- *targeting* the consumers for each segment.

This involves:

- communicating with consumers in each segment;
- developing existing products to better supply the needs of consumers in market segments;
- defining and assessing the business potential of gaps in the market;
- developing new products to fill gaps in market segments which are viable and show profit potential.

The only markets in which segmentation does not occur are commodity markets or those where the product is unique.

Task

Using your fellow students as a sample, identify the segments they can be placed in on the basis of consumer characteristics.

Assignment 6.2: A positive marketing strategy

You have been appointed as an administrative assistant in a new marketing company. To help you understand the business, the managing director has asked you to identify the market segments for their main clients and the research requirements for marketing decision-making. The three main clients are:

a double glazing manufacturer ;

a health and fitness club;

a car polish manufacturer.

Student activities

Write a word processed report to the managing director which:

(i)   explains how the market is segmented for each client;

(ii) examines the research requirements necessary for marketing decision-making and explain what information the research will provide and what form the research will take.

6.3 Product Strategy And Tactics

6.3.1 The Marketing Mix

The marketing process begins with the establishment of *marketing objectives*. *Marketing strategies* are then devised in the form of short, medium or long-term plans for the achievement of these objectives. The final stage is tactical: the creation of *marketing programmes* of activities in support of the marketing strategies.

Although the *marketing mix* is broadly tactical, it contains elements of strategy and planning. It is concerned with the practicalities of how objectives and strategies can be brought to fruition and includes operational and financial details. It is usually analysed on the basis of the *four 'P's*:

- *the product*: its life cycle, planning and development, and brand management (Section 6.3);
- *the price*: pricing determinants, the behaviour of costs and pricing policy (Section 6.4);
- *promotion*: the promotional mix, advertising media and methods, sales promotion, personal selling, sales force motivation and management (Section 6.5);
- *the place*: distribution channels, operational management, customer service and direct marketing methods (Section 6.6).

The four 'P's are interdependent. The emphasis laid on each element is the result of analysis through the marketing information system and consumer research. The main vehicle for systematic analysis of marketing information and research is the *marketing audit* (Section 6.7).

Task

Select a well known product and a well known service and research the activities used to promote them. Identify any differences and explain what the reasons may be.

6.3.2 The Product

A product exists merely to satisfy a consumer need or want. It is actually a service, packaged. Products include:

- fast-moving consumer goods;
- consumer durables;
- industrial or business-to-business products;
- government services;
- individual services;
- charities;
- political parties.

The categorisation of market offerings into products and services takes place along a continuum which can be defined in terms of time. For example:

- Product: a compact disc by Madonna
- Service: hiring a video of a Madonna concert
- Service: attending a Madonna concert

The compact disc is the most durable and the concert the least durable.

Task

Using examples, analyse other ways of distinguishing the characteristics of products and services. Is it valid to treat them differently in marketing terms?

6.3.3 The Product Life Cycle

The concept of the *product life cycle* (Section 7.2.2) is important when planning marketing activity. Products have a finite life cycle which has four clearly distinguishable stages:

- introduction
- growth
- maturity (incorporating saturation)
- decline

The marketing strategy and tactics vary according to which stage a product is at. This affects the following activities:

- sales and profit forecasting;
- cash flow forecasting;
- research and development costs;
- consumer characteristics;
- response to competitive activity;
- branding strategies;
- market development strategies;
- marketing expenditure;
- distribution policy;
- pricing policy;
- product development policy.

Task

In groups, consider the following products and decide how the theory of the product life cycle affects the marketing decisions and activities listed above:

- Coca-Cola
- Poppy Day
- Mars ice-cream
- Teenage Mutant Ninja Turtles

6.3.4 The Product Mix

In an organisation marketing only one product, it might be quite easy to formulate strategy and tactics using such marketing theories as segmentation and the product life cycle. However, most organisations market more than one product and these are often very similar to each other. Therefore, organisations must be aware of the effect of each product's marketing strategies on its other products. Ideally, marketing activity should increase sales only at the expense of competitors' products.

Managing this problem introduces the concept of the *product mix*. This is the range of an organisation's products and brands. It should be positioned according to the pattern of demand in the various target market segments. There are five elements involved:

- The *product mix* is the total range of products and services in all markets and segments.
- The *product line* comprises the products or range of products aimed at any one segment/consumer type.

- The *mix width* is the number of product lines in the mix.
- The *mix depth* is the number of products in any one product line.
- The *mix consistency* is the composition of the product lines in the mix: alike or dissimilar.

Task

Visit a local manufacturing firm to discuss and analyse their product mix and the value of the product life cycle in their marketing planning.

6.3.5 Product Planning

Product planning can be divided into the development of existing products and markets, and the development of new products and markets. Strategies for product development can be either *proactive*, carrying the greatest risk of failure but also the possibility of the highest profit, or *reactive* where risks are lower. In addition, development costs may be less but the potential profit is generally lower.

For continued growth and profitability, an organisation's product mix should include products at various stages in the product life cycle.

Development of existing products includes:

- the analysis of product mix/life cycles;
- strategies to maximise growth potential in young products;
- strategies to prolong the profitability of the mature stage and stave off decline;
- strategies to manage the decline of products in the most profitable and least damaging way.

The failure rate among new product ideas is high. Therefore, it is necessary to adopt policies which encourage *innovation* and *invention* from various sources.

Internal sources include:

- market research;
- market feedback from sales and trade;
- market gap analysis;
- analysis of demographic trends;
- economic/technological research;
- modifying existing products;
- company understanding of consumer/markets;
- research and development;
- brainstorming.

External sources include:

- product development agencies;
- foreign products;
- franchising/licensing;
- takeovers, acquisitions, mergers;
- sponsoring research;
- patents research (unused or expired);
- technological breakthrough in processes;

- technological breakthrough in materials;
- inventors.

New product planning is complex and necessitates the setting of *targets* and *timetables* in the following areas:

- technological research and development;
- market and consumer research;
- plant and equipment purchase/modification;
- staff development;
- financial planning;
- marketing and sales activity planning.

New product ideas must be *screened* to eliminate potential failures. Initial or wide mesh screening eliminates those which not viable for such reasons as lack of organisational experience/skill or lack of funding. Subsequent screening involves:

- market/segment potential demand identification;
- potential life cycle/development for profit;
- pattern of demand;
- growth prospects of total market;
- substitution effects;
- competitive capabilities;
- likely competitive market reaction;
- product mix compatibility;
- compatibility with long-term objectives;
- labour skills availability;
- financial planning;
- technological planning;
- distribution planning.

Diligent screening can save a great deal of time and money, and can prevent some failure in the market-place.

When new product ideas have passed through the screening, development and design stages, full-scale production risks are reduced by using prototypes and/or pilot plants to provide products for *test-marketing*. The purpose of test marketing is to evaluate the new product idea and its marketing support and activity in conditions as similar as possible to the market in which it will ultimately be launched.

At all stages of new product development, negative feedback indicates a need to rethink the proposal. The selection of a test market depends on the following factors:

- a good match with the total market in terms of distribution outlets, population profile, income profile and media;
- viability in logistical terms such as promotional test capability, co-operation in distribution channels and relative isolation from the rest of the market.

All test market choices are a compromise. Control areas, consumer research before and after testing, and evaluation criteria are equally important. Alternatives to test marketing include consumer panels and rolling launches.

Tasks

(i) How can strategies such as line extensions, product improvements and technological innovation prolong the profitable life of a mature product? What role does on-going consumer research play in this process?

(ii) Ask any national high street retailer whether they are currently test marketing any products. Research the market and segment in which the product is placed and write a brief article for the trade press.

6.3.6 Product Branding

The term *branding* refers to brand names, trademarks, symbols, logos, and designs. In competitive markets it is essential for consumers to be able to exert their preference for particular brands. They must be able to recognise a brand, understand the product or service benefits and identify with its image. Successful brand names are acceptable in the market-place, pronounceable, easy to recall and convey the correct message to the trade and consumers.

The benefits of *branding* to the manufacturer are:

- commercial success depends on repeat purchases;
- 80 per cent of sales usually come from 20 per cent of customers;
- a brand is a vehicle for communication and promotion;
- it has a research identity;
- a brand is an investment, it has goodwill value;
- brands facilitate consumer recall and self-selection;
- the distribution chain wants brands;
- display space is obtained more easily;
- importance of price differentials may be diminished;
- branding facilitates market segmentation;
- the level and cost of personal selling is reduced.

The benefits of *brand loyalty* to the consumer are:

- consistency of product performance;
- assurance of satisfaction;
- quality reassurance;
- fewer time-consuming buying decisions;
- less post-purchase dissonance.

Packaging is of major importance in establishing a brand and has five major functions:

- facilitating the production process;
- protecting the product;
- enabling display;
- as a form of promotion;
- as a form of communicating.

Inner packaging forms an integral part of the mass-production process, as well as protecting the product during transit. Ease of display is a very important consideration in modern retail outlets and the outer package design should fulfil the following functions:

- ease of identification at point of sale;

- consumer appeal;

- on-shelf impact vis-a-vis competitive products;

- suitability for its domestic (or other) location;

- utility of outers for conversion for display;

- ease of use as a promotional vehicle;

- information source on product's uses;

- environmentally acceptable.

Own label brands are those goods which are branded under the retailer's name rather than the manufacturer's name. The advantage of this arrangement for the manufacturer is the utilisation of excess production capacity.

Own label products are always sold at a lower price than the manufacturer's brands. This is possible because the retailer has limited distribution and promotional costs. An exception to this norm is Marks & Spencer's *St Michael* brand which has no in-store competition. However, it appeals to a large and well-defined target market on the basis of quality and reliability.

Consumer brand loyalty allows the profitable survival of the branded goods which sell alongside the own label goods in-store. The principal marketing strategies used against own label products rely on the reassurance of a known brand name and the continuity of product quality and reliability. This is supported by advertising which is designed specifically for the branded product.

Task

Conduct a brief survey to ascertain which brand names are most familiar to students and what images they convey.

Assignment 6.3: Picking a winner

A national journal, *Food and Drink* , is running a competition for the best business idea of the year with a prize of £5,000. You have decided to use your marketing knowledge to identify significant gaps in the market and suggest a product to fill the gap. In keeping with the title of the journal, you have decided to limit your search to either health food snacks or low-alcohol drinks.

Student activities

(i)   Divide the market into segments.

(ii) Plot the brands and own-label products within the segments.

(iii) Identify the characteristics of the significant products, branded and own-label, considering such aspects as product benefits, substitution effects, corporate image, and promotional objectives.

(iv) Describe the type of product you think might fill a gap in the market.

6.4 The Role Of Pricing

6.4.1 Price Determinants

The *price* of a product or service is the mechanism through which most exchange transactions are effected, although some international transactions contain elements of barter. Price, therefore, represents a profit objective to the supplier and value to the buyer. Prices can be either fixed or negotiable.

Prices are charged at all stages along the distribution chain. The more links in the distribution chain, the larger the *mark-up* the price to the end-user, the consumer, must cover. The rationale behind this is that effective distribution can often only be achieved through extensive distribution. The use of intermediaries between the producer and the consumer is frequently the most cost-effective way of achieving this.

A number of factors act as *price determinants*:

- supply and level of market demand;
- competition;
- market segmentation and consumer types;
- consumer attitudes and behaviour.

Research can indicate the role of price in determining consumer perceptions of value for money, the contribution of a proposed price in determining consumer attitudes to a particular product and the role of price in assessing the *effective demand* for a product. Consumer sensitivity towards price change is known as price *elasticity of demand*.

Tasks

(i) Select five well known products and identify the various stages in the distribution chain for each product.

(ii) What is the relative importance of the price determinants on each product?

6.4.2 Costs

The most common method of fixing a price in the UK is to establish the costs and add the required *profit margin*. This is not ideal, as will be discussed later, but the establishment of true costs is essential, no matter what pricing policy is ultimately followed. There are two basic methods of defining costs: *absorption costing* (Sections 1.7.1 and 1.7.2) and *marginal costing* (Section 1.7.3).

The profit margin imposed is known as the *mark-up* and is usually expressed as a percentage of the costs. Total cost plus mark-up gives a selling price (although not one necessarily acceptable to the market place).

Costs are also defined by whether they are *fixed* or *variable* (Section 1.6.2). Examples of fixed costs include rent, light and heat. Examples of variable costs include manufacturing labour and salesmen's commissions. The calculation of the sales level needed to cover costs is known as the *break-even point* (Section 1.7.5).

Task

Identify the advantages and disadvantages of using absorption costing as a method of fixing prices.

6.4.3 Pricing Policy

Skimming is a new product introduction pricing policy. A high price allows early recovery of all costs and profit required before competition enters the market. It is suitable for short-life and high-tech products.

Penetration is a new product/on-going product pricing policy. It requires a lower price and lower profit margins. The objective of this policy is to build distribution and market penetration. It is suitable for long-life, high volume products.

A *mixed* policy is one in which product introduction begins with skimming the market and then the price is reduced to penetrate the market.

In a *cost-plus* policy all costs are calculated and the desired profit margin added. This is a mechanical policy which takes no account of current or potential demand, or of marketing opportunities. However, cost-plus pricing is the policy most commonly pursued in the UK.

In a *differential* policy different prices are charged for the same product on the basis of:

- different types of customer;
- different locations of customer;
- different sizes of purchase.

This type of policy takes account of distribution costs and bulk buying and can be used in conjunction with other pricing policies.

In a *single* policy one price is charged to all customers on the basis of units consumed; for example, power and transport.

A *variable* policy is common in industrial markets and takes into account such aspects as potential demand, knowledge of customer and costs. In a *variable for all* policy prices are altered for reasons of demand, but all customers pay the same; for example, train fares, computer time, telephones.

A *price lining* policy takes account of relationships between integrated products such as clothes or food.

Other forms of pricing policy relate to promotional activity where the price may be lowered temporarily. Pricing in commodity markets, where the seller's control over pricing is very limited due to the power of demand in the market, is known as *market pricing*.

Other factors which influence pricing policy include:

- government fiscal/economic policy;
- interest rate movements;
- tariffs and barriers;
- international agreements all influence price;
- government intervention.

Task

Analyse the pricing policies and the factors which influence the prices of the following products and services:

- petrol
- scheduled airline flights to New York
- package holidays to Kenya
- tumble driers
- baked beans

Assignment 6.4: An environmentally-friendly pricing policy

You are an assistant in a firm of management consultants which has just completed a marketing audit for a client. The client sells environmentally-friendly cleaning products to both industry and the consumer market. One of their main problems concerns pricing policy and you have been asked to prepare a preliminary report for the senior consultant.

Student activities

Write a word-processed report covering:

(i)   the factors influencing the client company's pricing policy decisions;

(ii) methods of market research which could be used in price decision-making.

6.5 The Role Of Promotion

Promotion covers the following areas of activity:

- advertising
- sales promotion
- public relations
- direct marketing
- personal selling

Through these activities the seller communicates with all buyers in the distribution chain, the consumer and the public in general.

6.5.1 Advertising

This high-profile industry specialises in *persuasive and/or informative communication* through *controllable media* such as:

- commercial and cable television
- national and local newspapers, free-sheets
- magazines
- commercial radio
- outdoor media, such as hoardings and Adshell
- cinema

The advantages and disadvantages of various media can be summarised as follows:

- *Printed media*: effective targeting on consumer types/market segments; difficult to gain and hold reader's attention, although the printed media readership usually exceeds its circulation.
- *Broadcast media*: powerful, especially television with great creative possibilities; dynamic but expensive; more difficult to target accurately; use of video increasing; use of hand-held controls allow commercial to be avoided.
- *Cinema*: good visual impact due to creative possibilities; accurate targeting possible but attendances variable; in competition with video.
- *Outdoor media*: good size, high visibility and impact; cheap but noise and informational barriers. Sites vary in terms of image and visibility.

Advertising is an *above-the-line* activity, which means that the agency's main source of income is commission on billings. The agency receives commission on advertising placed in the above media, from the media concerned. Modern advertising agencies are capable of fulfilling many functions, although not all are able to offer such a wide range:

- *Creative*: art, copy, print;
- *Account handling*: client liaison and advice;
- *Market research*: analysing marketing data, commissioning research, on-going industry research, economic analysis and forecasting;
- *Media buying*: for example, buying space and time;
- *Packaging*: design and artwork;
- *Sales promotion*: integrated promotional activity;
- *Public relations*: usually carried out by a sister organisation.

Both clients and agencies value the continuity of their relationship as this permits great expertise and knowledge of markets and products to be built up on both sides. One of the keys to establishing such a relationship is the client's brief to the agency. It should cover:

- market size and value;
- market segments;
- brands in the market and their characteristics;
- competitors and their recent activity;
- summary of market analysis data;
- client brand analysis and rationale;
- distribution summary;
- summary of research findings to date;
- summary of promotional history and evaluation;
- analysed sales data;
- organisational objectives;
- marketing objectives;
- sales targets.

The main sources of retail and media information are:

- *Nielsen reports*: the results of a retail audit giving a breakdown of sales by price, competitive activity and promotional response, for example;

- *TGI*: research into product consumers by socio-economic, demographic and lifestyle analysis;

- *JICNAR*: information on readership, viewing and listening data (commercial stations only) broken down by socio-economic, demographic and lifestyle analysis;

- *MINTEL*: periodic industry analyses.

An advertising agency may have access to more market research data than the client, which could be one of the reasons for employing it. However, the agency cannot, unless told, understand the client's corporate and marketing objectives.

Tasks

In groups, organise the following research:

(i) Log all the television commercials on one channel between 4 pm and 10 pm on one day. Analyse the relationship between audiences and the products advertised. At what other times during the week might you expect to see some of the commercials?

(ii) Collect a number of daily papers and analyse the relationship between audiences and the products advertised. Is the position of the advertisement in the paper significant? Look up the papers in BRAD.

6.5.2 Barriers to Communication

One of the objectives of advertising is to *inform*. This may be thought of as the *factual* element in advertising. The second element is *persuasion* and the third *reassurance*.

Much advertising is aimed at reducing *cognitive dissonance*. In rudimentary terms this is the feeling of uncertainty which often afflicts consumers after they have been through the decision-making process and are not sure whether they have made the right decision. This may be due to a variety of factors such as:

- additional product information;

- lack of peer group approval;

- price movements;

- product performance failure;

- competitive activity.

Barriers to effective communication include:

- the tendency for consumers to screen out messages which are uncomfortable or inconvenient;

- inappropriate encoding of advertising message;

- distortion;

- noise in the media;

- semantic differences between encoder and receptors.

Task

Estimate the number of advertisements that you are typically exposed to each day and compare notes with others in your group. Discuss the advertisements you remember and the possible reasons for this.

6.5.3 Advertising Budgets

These may be based on:

- *Percentage of sales*: the budget is based upon forecasting next year's sales from estimates of this year's sales. This assumes that the organisation understands the relationship between advertising and sales volume achieved. This policy may result in advertising expenditure declining in line with falling sales, which may not make much sense if the falling sales are due to a rise in competitive marketing activity.

- *Matching competitive expenditure*: The organisation adopts a policy of spending as much as its competitors. This assumes that all advertising expenditure is equally effective. Advertising expenditure information is available through MEAL.

- *Spending what you can afford*: This haphazard method involves deciding what the organisation can afford. It may sound reasonable, but in practice it can involve brand managers in a process more resembling collective bargaining than careful consideration of objectives and tactics.

- *Budgeting by objectives*: This is a systematic method involving:
  - identifying target market segments;
  - identifying optimum media to reach target audiences within these segments;
  - setting advertising objectives for communication targets and levels of recall;
  - setting sales targets;
  - establishing time schedules;
  - establishing evaluation criteria.

Task

Make a list of the difficulties in setting an advertising budget and suggest how they might be resolved.

6.5.4 Sales Promotion

This form of promotion is known as *below-the-line* because sales promotions agencies do not earn commission from media. Clients pay agencies for concept, design and execution. Promotions may be targeted at the trade in the distribution chain or at consumers. The difference between trade and consumer promotions is one of objectives:

- promotions to the trade *push* the product through the distribution system;
- promotions to the consumer *pull* the product off the shelves.

Sales promotions can have considerable immediate effects upon sales volumes, although usually this is not long-lasting unless linked with other promotional methods. The most effective promotional of these are usually integrated advertising and sales promotion campaigns.

The effects of consumer promotions can be either immediate or delayed in terms of the benefit to the consumer. *Reduced price offers (RPOs)* are immediate, whereas any promotion involving the collection of proofs of purchase is delayed in its effect, and its purpose is to encourage increased purchase.

Sales promotions can usually be organised more quickly than advertising. Therefore, they can be more effective in shifting backlogs of unsold stocks. Other aspects of sales promotions include:

- *point-of-sale (POS) display*, the purpose of which is to attract customer attention and encourage inspection and examination of the product;
- *merchandising* which is the process of stocking retail and distribution outlets with goods in accordance with well-researched and tried principles to encourage and facilitate buying decisions;
- *exhibitions* which create awareness and promote recall through the creative scope of the modern exhibition;
- *sponsorship* which has enjoyed rapid growth in recent years. Sponsors fund an event in return for a guaranteed minimum level of media advertising or in order to establish a named event.

Task

Draw up a list of examples of trade and consumer sales promotions.

6.5.5 Public Relations

The aim of *public relations (PR)* is to improve and maintain an organisation's relationships with the various groups with which it is associated via the media, exhibitions, conferences or by lobbying. Such groups include:

- employees
- shareholders
- local communities
- trade unions
- pressure groups
- consumers

PR agencies use their skills to gain *favourable media coverage* of their clients' affairs, but not through the medium of paid-for advertisement. The purpose of PR is to benefit from the high credibility factor associated with editorial matter in the media as opposed to the lower credibility factor associated with advertising copy. PR is an *uncontrollable* form of communication because:

- Agencies are dependent upon their own reputations as providers of useful and dependable material.
- They can only provide material in the form of press releases etc and hope that it will be used favourably.
- They cannot know with what other news or editorial matter they have to compete with for space.
- They cannot be sure that the material they provide will not be edited.

Advertising exposure in the media is targeted and paid for, which is why it is described as *controllable*. Publicity cannot be bought, which is why it is uncontrollable in the normal course of events. PR agencies offer a range of services including the following:

- product or service PR
- corporate PR
- crisis management
- financial PR
- political/pressure-group PR
- internal relations PR

Task

Public relations plays an important part in limiting damage at times of commercial disaster. A recent example of this was when traces of benzine were found in Perrier water which led to a world-wide withdrawal of the product. Research and trace the role played by PR in this or any other case.

6.5.6 Direct Marketing

The purpose of *direct marketing* is to communicate with and sell direct to the consumer. This obviates the need for an expensive distribution chain and allows a lower price to the consumer. Methods include:

- door-to-door selling;
- party-plan selling;
- general or specialist mail order catalogues;
- direct response advertising;
- direct mail (junk mail).

The success of all direct marketing is dependent upon accurate *consumer targeting* using segmentation systems such as ACORN or PINPOINT in conjunction with *database management*. The latter involves the analysis of in-company sales and accounts records and customer purchasing records. The third crucial element is the use of *credit* in direct marketing.

Direct marketing is booming because response rates are cost-effective. Moreover, direct marketing in the UK is a long way behind the USA and parts of Europe. It is essentially an information-based operation. As the information stored on databases increases and the means by which it is analysed becomes more effective and sophisticated, the greater is the power of direct marketing likely to become.

Some people believe there are ethical and moral aspects of direct marketing which deserve wider discussion and, possibly, legislation. The *Data Protection Act 1984* gives some protection (Section 3.3.3).

Task

Make a collection of junk mail and identify the main methods used to make this type of communication appeal to the consumer.

Assignment 6.5: Saving for charity

Taking a walk one evening, you see a well dressed woman fall into the river. You dive in and rescue her. She is overcome with emotion and gratitude and takes your name and address. A few days later you receive a letter from her stating that she wishes to use her considerable wealth in charitable works, but is not happy with the existing charities. Impressed by your display of initiative, she wants to employ you to establish a new charity.

Student activities

Prepare a report for your benefactress based on the following tasks:

(i) Imagine any type of new charity you wish.

(ii) State the charity's objectives in order of priority.

(iii) Devise the marketing strategy by which the objectives will be achieved.

(iv) Draw up an outline programme of activities using the framework of the marketing mix to support your marketing strategy.

(v) Choose one of the proposed activities in the area of communications and prepare a more detailed analysis of the marketing rationale behind the proposal.

6.6 The Role of Distribution

Distribution is *place* in the four 'P's of the marketing mix. Physical distribution is responsible for the following functions:

- ordering/delivering correct quantities of goods;
- ensuring availability to meet demand;
- maintaining physical product quality;
- facilitating purchase through merchandising and POS;
- minimising costs whilst maintaining customer service;

6.6.1 Choice of Distribution Channel

The term *channels of distribution* is used to describe the marketing organisations through which goods are transferred from the producer to the consumer. They include retailers, wholesalers, agents and brokers, and distributors. Channels can be either long or short, the shortest channel being direct selling.

Marketing involves basic processes which influence the choice of distribution channel:

- bringing into contact producers and consumers;
- methods of physically protecting and distributing products to ensure product quality;
- offering choices of goods wide enough to attract customers to a distribution point;
- facilitating the development of favourable attitudes towards productsat the distribution point;
- facilitating purchasing decisions through effective merchandising and POS;
- ensuring an adequate and continuous flow of sales;
- providing credit, technical advice, other service aspects where appropriate.

All distribution channel decisions are a compromise between *cost* and *effectiveness*. Using a long distribution channel is likely to help an organisation realise the objective of market penetration, but it may increase the price of the product to the consumer and may involve the company in losing control over some aspects of effective marketing. More than one channel may be used to market a product.

Organisations frequently segment their distribution procedures according to customer type:

- Major multiples negotiate with company senior management direct, and may collect the product from the producer.
- Suppliers' salesmen may have no access to stores at all.
- Suppliers' salesmen may visit the individual stores of other large multiples to take centrally agreed orders or merchandise the shelves, or they may have no access at all.
- Suppliers' salesmen may visit other retail outlets to sell, take orders and merchandise by territory.
- Supplier's salesmen may sell to wholesalers or visit the small independents.
- Cash & Carry contracts are usually negotiated through senior management.

Task

Analyse the factors affecting distribution channel decisions concerning the following products:

- the export of paper handkerchiefs to the Gambia;
- the sale of branded baked beans to Tesco;
- the sale of Casio electronic personal organisers.

6.6.2 Personal Selling

The cost-effectiveness of *personal selling* is a key factor in the choice of distribution method. The increasing costs of distribution, together with the development of electronic data processing, have seen a considerable development in the *computer analysis* of the logistics of distribution. This covers such areas as:

- warehouse location;
- journey planning and transport utilisation;
- vertically integrated ownership of distribution systems;
- the total systems concept of physical handling and distribution services from the production line to the consumer's domestic environment;
- the analysis of on-costs of channel alternatives;
- valuing the service aspects of different channels.

From the supplier's point of view, the control of physical distribution costs entails analysis of:

- transport costs;
- warehouse costs;
- packaging costs;
- service costs;
- management costs.

Retailers are concerned with:

- sales of different products per square or linear metre of space;
- gross margin per unit of space/time;
- product promotional campaign expenditures and effectiveness;
- optimum product type space allocations;
- the effect of branded product sales on own label sales;
- merchandising and point-of-sale effectiveness;
- consumer behaviour in-store.

Such is the power of major multiple retailers, and so severe the battle for shelf space, that producers may have to work with the following factors:

- new product introductions will fail unless they accepted by the major multiples;
- the major multiples may demand certain levels of promotional expenditure, either on product or joint promotional activities;
- it may be necessary to alter or adapt products.

Modern distribution systems are heavily dependent upon computer technology for:

- logistical analysis;
- planning and scheduling;
- storing, locating and retrieving goods;
- production of management reports.

This trend has reduced costs, primarily by reducing manpower and system inefficiencies. Distribution development will continue to utilise modern technology in this same way, but added value to the consumer and increased profitability for producers and distributors are likely to come from enhancing the service elements of the distribution chain in future.

Another method of distribution that is gaining popularity is *franchising* (Section 4.3.10). Under this method the supplier provides the product, training, marketing support and sometimes financial support to the franchisee who buys the product and sets up a retail or servicing outlet. Suppliers sometimes experience quality control problems, but these tend to diminish as the franchised brand becomes better known and attracts a more ambitious and higher quality franchisee.

Task

You have been asked to advise a rather old-fashioned sales manager who is having problems with his conversion rates (leads to sales). Write a short report on the modern theories of personal selling and training methods.

Assignment 6.6: Managing the sales force

Your company has just bought a smaller subsidiary and has identified the need to restructure its sales force. The new chief executive of this subsidiary is an accountant.

Student activities

Write a word-processed report to the chief executive on the following areas of sales force management:

(i)   the role of the sales force and the determinants of that role;

(ii) the modern alternatives to cold-calling;

(iii) the relationship between sales objectives, the size of the sales force and controlling sales force activity;

(iv) the major problems encountered by sales force management in administrating and controlling the sales function.

6.7 Marketing Information and Decision-Making

Modern marketing methods are crucially dependent upon information management such as:

- data capture and processing;
- information analysis and dissemination;
- on-going review of information systems.

Electronic processing speeds many processes up, ranging from the transfer of money from bank accounts to consumer expectations that their needs and wants will be satisfied speedily. Fast, accurate and reliable information is a necessary to marketers because opportunities can only be exploited, and catastrophes avoided, if the marketer can act quickly and be first. Furthermore, there is so much information available that it requires a sophisticated system to manage it.

For these reasons, organisations should set up a *marketing information system (MIS)* to perform these vital functions. The first stage is to assess the information available from the various sources.

6.7.1 Internal Sources

The information necessary for *marketing decision-making* comes from the other *internal* organisational functions:

- *Production*: for example, labour costs, raw material costs, quality control statistics, capital investment requirements, and research and development.
- *Finance*: for example, financial and management accounting information, sales invoice analysis, credit control information, age of debt analysis, cost of sales data, budgetary information, sources of finance.
- *Personnel*: for example, staffing levels and costs, skills availability, training requirements and availability, potential labour problems due to scarcity or industrial action.
- *Sales and distribution*: such as analysed historical sales data, forecast sales data, channel costs and data, customer records analysis, discount structure data, sales and distribution management information and trade promotions costs.

• *Marketing*: for example, market share data, market growth/trends, product range data, pricing data, historical promotional evaluation, promotional expenditure and consumer complaints.

Task

Make a list of the internal documentation, which may already be available in a large organisation, from which marketing information can be extracted. Classify the documents by function.

6.7.2 External Sources

External information can be divided into *primary data*, such as research commissioned for the organisation's specific purposes, and *secondary data*. The latter is information published by others for purposes which may not coincide with those of the organisation. Secondary data is plentiful and very useful, but must be analysed carefully and with regard to its sources and objectives.

Market analysis ranges from highly sophisticated and reliable reports from Nielsen, MINTEL, TGI and JICNAR to smaller organisations which might, for example, be undertaking work for trade publications in the industry.

Government statistics range from census data which may be analysed further by other organisations to analyses of specific areas of trade or organisational interest; for example, population age forecasts, changes in environmental infrastructure, social habits, community structures or economic indicators.

Computer databases are of particular use in segmentation, positioning and targeting in both direct and indirect marketing. Other sources of external information include:

• trade publications;
• academic journals;
• customers and suppliers;
• sales force feedback;
• exhibitions;
• international publications;
• scientific and technological journals;
• legal and legislative processes;
• patent research.

Task

Design a guide to the sources of external information available in your college library, giving details of how they are used.

6.7.3 Constructing the MIS

The following questions must be answered in order to construct the MIS:
• What marketing decisions must be made?
• On what basis are these decisions made?
• Who makes these decisions?
• How often are these decisions made?

- What information is needed to make them?
- Does the information available need further processing or analysis to be of use in decision-making?
- Does the information need to be disseminated further than the decision-makers and task implementers?
- To whom and in what form are the decisions and associated information to be disseminated?
- How much does it cost to collect, process and disseminated the information?
- What financial benefit will ultimately be gained from using it?
- If the cost-benefit analysis is not favourable, can the actual decisions, and information associated with them be re-prioritised?
- How will the evaluation of marketing activities feed back into the MIS?
- How will the system be managed and how does dynamic marketing informational feed into and emerge from the MIS?

The establishment of an MIS and its maintenance is closely linked to the *marketing audit*, a preliminary to systematic and effective *marketing planning*, which is covered in the next section.

Task

Draw up an interview schedule which you could use with managers in an organisation to research the way they construct a MIS. Contact a local company and endeavour to obtain an interview with a manager.

This section shares a joint assignment with Section 6.8

6.8 Marketing Management and the Marketing Plan

Planning is an on-going process. Whilst plans must not be inflexible, they should state objectives, strategies and programmes of activities clearly so that only unexpected events, either good or bad, result in change.

The *marketing audit* is a method of scanning the environments in which marketers operate, both internal and external. It is usually undertaken in a format which facilitates its analysis through the means of *SWOT analysis* (Section 4.2.4). The marketing audit is the framework for the *MIS*; both systems make crucial contributions to marketing management and the marketing planning process.

6.8.1 Marketing Management

Marketing management is the organisation of the functions of marketing analysis, planning and control. The organisational functions within a marketing-oriented firm are *interdependent*, but there are practicalities to be considered in the way the marketing department organises itself. Depending on the size and culture of the organisation, the following functions must operate in some form:

- new product development;
- development of existing brands;

- market research;
- promotional management.

The size of an organisation affects how many individuals are involved in covering these functions; there may be specialists in each area. Smaller organisations may expect their managers to be more versatile or they may use outside agencies. The appointment of a *brand or product manager* is common. The *job description* (Section 5.2.5) of a brand manager would probably cover the following functions:

- planning brand strategy;
- supervising on-going brand development;
- integrating and co-ordinating activities of other organisational functions affecting the brand;
- market and informational research;
- segmentation and targeting analysis;
- briefing promotional agencies;
- motivating sales and distribution channels.

The brand manager is general manager for his or her product(s), although actual functional authority may be limited or non-existent. The system has the advantage of devoting the energies and loyalties of one manager to one product or group of products, but has the disadvantage in that brand managers are obliged usually to compete for company resources and friction and inefficiencies can result. This is because the traditional brand manager has no line authority over functional specialists.

A refinement of this system is the creation of *strategic business units (SBUs)* where the product marketing managers are responsible for a specific business area, including:

- marketing strategy;
- marketing mix;
- new product/business development;
- budgetary control.

The SBU holds its own budget, the disposition of which depends upon the recommendation of the product marketing manager. Functional specialists' time may be paid for out of the budget. Alternatively, they may be permanently or temporarily attached to the SBU.

Brand managers usually report to a marketing manager or marketing director, depending on the size and structure of the business. SBU's usually report at director or divisional level.

Task

Draw up a job description for a brand manager in a cosmetics company.

6.8.2 Marketing Planning

The preparation of the *marketing plan* is the culmination of the progressive informational results of:
- marketing research and the MIS;
- the marketing audit;
- the SWOT analysis.

It is a proposed programme of business activity having resource implications. Marketing planning can be scheduled as follows:

Marketing objectives: These must be established in accordance with organisational objectives. Ansoff identifies four possible courses of action:

- selling existing products to existing markets;
- extending existing products to new markets;
- developing new products in existing markets;
- developing new products for new markets.

These possibilities must be assessed in terms of profit objectives, resource and investment implications, and risk.

Gap analysis is a term commonly applied to two useful, but different aids to marketing planning. It can refer to the gap which may be identified between long-term sales/financial objectives and current long-range forecasts. Such a gap can be filled by:

- lowering objectives;
- improving productivity;
- increasing market share and/or product use;
- by extending markets through new segments (see below);
- by exporting.

Gap analysis also refers to the analysis of a market into *segments* by various criteria, in order to identify under-exploited segments for further consideration. Marketing objectives are usually stated in quantifiable measures to assist evaluation and should cover:

- product range;
- markets and market segments;
- market share;
- distribution;
- sales volume;
- turnover;
- profit.

The next step is to establish *marketing strategies*. For example:

- pursuing market opportunities;
- exploiting competitive weaknesses;
- exploiting technological advances;
- correcting an unbalanced product portfolio;
- defending market share against threats;
- reducing marketing weaknesses.

It is at this point in the marketing planning process that programmes of activities begin to evolve through the mechanism of the *marketing mix*, the tools of strategic achievement. Policies must be developed for *product, price, promotion and place*. These policies result in the evolution of subsidiary objectives for each product, involving such aspects as:

- product performance;
- product improvement;
- product positioning;
- product design;
- product packaging.

Budgets (Section 1.8) must then be established for the achievement of the marketing objectives, as must activity programmes and their management responsibility and timing.

The final states in the marketing planning process take place after approval of the plan and the execution of the programmes:

- *monitoring* of activities against targets and/or other measures;
- responses to decisions required as a result of the monitoring process;
- *evaluation* of marketing programmes;
- *feedback* of evaluation to senior management, other organisational functions, the MIS and the marketing audit.

There has been a great deal of academic and practical analysis of appropriate strategic responses to well defined marketing problems, usually following the marketing mix model.

Task

Construct a flow diagram to illustrate the various stages in establishing a marketing plan, showing the decisions to be made at each stage.

Assignment 6.7/6.8: Hi-Tech Communications Ltd

You are employed in the marketing department of Hi-Tech Communications Ltd. The company has just developed a new telephone for the domestic market with the following features:

- 20 number memory recall.
- Silent button.
- Automatic re-dial.
- Facility for entering into memory a number whilst using the line and dialling that number afterwards.
- Facility for enforcing the use of personal user four-digit codes. Up to eight personal codes can be designated.
- Users cannot make a call without first entering their code.
- A small LCD display can at any time scroll the numbers dialled by any user, and the length of the call. This facility can be enforced or cancelled by the use of a code unique to each telephone.
- The LCD display can also be used to show numbers in the memory, time spent on call so far, etc.

Student activities

Prepare a marketing plan for this dynamic and innovative product idea using a word processing package.

Section 7

Operations Management

by Peter Cox

MSc, MBA, MAPM, MRAeS, MIMechEng,
Senior Lecturer in Operations Management at Bristol Business School

Operations management is the process of creating products, responding to the needs identified by marketing and profitably or cost-effectively fulfilling the expectations created by promotion. It is generally the central activity in an organisation. In co-operation with other management teams, operations management helps achieve the objectives of the organisation.

Recommended Reading

Crosby, P. B., *Quality is Free,* Mentor, 1980.

Goldratt, E. M., & Cox, J., *The Goal,* Gower, Revised, 1989

Hill, Terry., *Production/Operations Management,* Prentice Hall, 2nd Edition, 1991

Hughes, Chris, *Production and Operations Management,* Pan, 1987

Voss, C. A., Armistead, C., Johnston, B., & Morris, B.,
    Operations Management in Service Industries and the Public Sector, Wiley, 1985

"Yes, sir, I can assure you we have a fully automated system."

Contents

7.1 The Operations Framework

7.1.1 Operations Management

Operations management has emerged from production management in recent years as the production of goods has become less labour intensive and service industries have become a dominant area of employment. It is concerned with the *production of goods and services* in the widest sense. It recognises the value of regarding other individuals and departments, and other organisations within the supply chain, as customers in addition to the end-user customer. It is as relevant to the management of a hotel chain as it is in a manufacturing company; on a smaller scale, an agency or even a students' disco.

Operations is generally the *central activity* in an organisation. The function of operations management might be regarded simply as keeping the organisation running, but it is much more than that. It is the process of creating products, responding to the needs identified by marketing and fulfilling the expectations created by promotion profitably or, at least, cost-effectively. In co-operation with other management teams, operations management helps achieve the objectives of the organisation.

The activity may be distinct and the product tangible, as in the operation of a production line making television sets. Alternatively it may overlap with other functional areas, as in retail management. It may provide a service rather than a tangible product, for example a holiday tour firm.

Operations management should be distinguished from *operations research* and *production engineering*. Operations research involves analytical techniques which can be used in a wide range of applications. Some of these are described in Section 7.4. Production engineering is the application of technology to enable a product to be generated effectively and efficiently. The nature of the technology depends on its application. *Operations technology* might be a more appropriate term in service industries such as transport or computing. These technological approaches tend to be the prime focus for specialisation within the operations area.

The main production or operations area within an organisation is generally the area of highest employment and therefore offers the greatest opportunity for managing staff. The traditional view of production is of boring repetitive work, but much of this is now automated. Opportunities for operations managers are found increasingly in service industries where the direct involvement of the customer creates a need for a close relationship between marketing and operations management.

Task

Draw up a list of types of industries and organisations. Distinguish between those primarily involved in the manufacture of goods and those where the product is essentially a service. Are some difficult to classify into one category or another?

7.1.2 The Operations Manager

The *operations manager's job* is not merely varied, it is complex. The tasks involved cover a wide range of issues and can seldom be managed in isolation. The key aspects of the operations manager's job are:

- to manage the operations area as a department which provides a set of specialist systems or functions, and as a cost centre in terms of asset management and cash flow;
- to consider long and short-term issues;

- to understand and make effective use of technology;
- to determine the time-cost-specification mix;
- to act as an interface between the practical activities implicit in operations management and the more abstract concepts and approaches of other functional areas.

It is important that the manager does not concentrate on any one aspect of the job at the expense of others. If the immediate concern is to get an overdue order delivered to an irate customer, it should not be at the expense of such matters as:

- keeping existing production going;
- ensuring that materials of an appropriate quality are ordered and delivered;
- checking that equipment is operating correctly and receiving necessary maintenance;
- ascertaining that health and safety regulations are being observed;
- seeing that any incentive payment systems are working effectively for the benefit of both the firm and the employees;
- ensuring that the introduction of future products, developments in technology and methods of production receive appropriate attention.

Task

Individually or in groups obtain an interview with an operations manager in a local industry and find out what tasks he or she carries out during a typical week. Prepare some specific questions in advance. How do the answers you have obtained relate to the operations manager's role described above?

7.1.3 Definition of a System

A *system* is a set of parts acting together in an organised way to achieve a purpose. In an engineering system, for example, the parts may be mechanical or electrical, but in operations management they generally include people. Concepts from systems theory can be helpful in understanding how organisations work. The term *socio-technical system* is used to describe a system in which the relationship between people and technology is of particular significance, as is often the case in operations management.

A system may be made up of *sub-systems*. In many cases systems overlap and have parts in common. For example, the members of a department and its equipment may form a sub-system which overlaps with the company and with members of the department.

Inputs and *outputs* of a system occur across the system boundaries; *transformation* occurs within the boundaries. In some cases, it may be worth adjusting the position of the system boundaries to simplify measurement of inputs and outputs. For example, a cost centre could be organised in such a way that the costs incurred can be easily identified and provide useful information for management.

Task

Consider any system with which you are familiar and define its parts, inputs and outputs. Can you identify the presence of any sub-systems within the system you have selected?

7.1.4 The Systems Approach

The *systems approach* encourages a view aimed at good overall performance, rather than concentrating simply on performance of individual parts. The preparation of a meal makes a good example of a systems approach to an operation. Although this is a common enough activity, it can be quite complex. The tasks or *processes* must be carried out in a particular order, materials or *inputs* are required and something results (the *output*); in this case a meal. The basic elements of the operation can be represented in the form of a diagram.

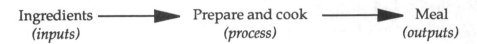

Ingredients ⟶ Prepare and cook ⟶ Meal
(inputs)   *(process)*   *(outputs)*

A good cook is not only concerned with how well the food was cooked, but also with the experience of those eating it. The output of the meal can be described at different levels:

- the cooked dishes;
- a pleasant experience;
- the satisfaction of those eating the meal.

Task

Consider how you would prepare a meal for some friends.

(i)   What materials are required?

(ii) What has to be done to them?

(iii) What is the result or output?

(iv) List the various people and parts that are necessary.

(v) Group together any parts that form a sub-system.

7.1.5 Types of Production

In studying operations it is useful to identify the range of basic types of production. In this way characteristic problems can be identified and common approaches developed. *Goods* can be simply defined as tangible products. *Services* imply a benefit received by a customer of an intangible nature.

Services are distinguished from goods by the fact that production and consumption are *simultaneous*. A service cannot be stored and the customer is involved at the time of production. However, in practice, most services include some physical element and most goods come with some sort of support service.

Production of goods and services can be *intermittent* or *continuous*. Production can be broken down into *unit, batch* and *mass production*; the choice depends on the nature of demand and the nature of the product. *Intermittent production* involves some extra effort and possibly wastage of materials in changing over from one product to another. It is appropriate where demand is lower and more varied. In true *continuous production* the product emerges as a continuous stream, as in an oil refinery.

Unit production may involve a simple product. Modern flexible automated manufacturing facilities are well equipped to manufacture in small volumes or even single items. Modestly complex products such as specialist electronic equipment may be assembled by hand, relying on the skill of the technician. But for an extensive and complex product, such as a power station or an international athletics

220

competition, particular care has to be taken to co-ordinate activities and ensure that the product emerges correctly first time. This involves a distinctive approach known as *project management*.

In some cases the production technology may necessitate producing the goods in *batches*. Fixed costs are usually lower than the costs of unit production, but the effort in planning and monitoring production is usually much greater

Mass production results in a continuous flow of identical or very similar products. It becomes viable when the demand for a product is not only large but can be expected to last for long enough to offset the cost of setting up a production line. It may be a single-stage process, as in injection moulding where a complex piece of plastic may be moulded in one operation, or it may involve an *assembly line*, on which previously manufactured components are assembled. Assembly lines are usually mechanised and often automated. The financial implications are indicated by a break-even curve with high fixed costs.

There is usually a close correspondence between the *type of production* and the *physical layout* of the production area. In batch production it is common for similar types of machines or processes to be grouped together, since successive jobs may require equipment or tasks to be used in different sequences. If different types of machine are regularly used in the same sequence, they may be grouped together using an approach called *group technology*. In mass production a typical layout minimises the movement of parts and assemblies during production.

Production involves the following distinct processes:

- generation
- storage
- inspection
- transport

In general each stage adds *value* to the product. Storage may simply be an unfruitful delay. But it can be valuable if availability from stock gives commercial advantage compared with generating the product when demand arises. The stages can occur in different sequences. In some cases the product is made to order and there may be some uncertainty as to whether the order will be fulfilled on time. In other cases production occurs in anticipation of sales and the operations manager has to cope with the uncertainty of the volume and timing of sales.

Bespoke or *jobbing production* is where the product is made to order and usually applies to unit production. The customer is able to specify the product in advance, but must wait for production to take place. It may be possible to anticipate customers' needs by providing some standard elements and yet still offer a customised product.

Tasks

(i) Identify the various ways in which you can obtain food, from vending machines to health farms. Put them in order of increasing proportion of service content.

(ii) Identify five types of goods and five types of service.

(iii) Identify examples of goods or services which are produced
- continuously;
- on an assembly line;
- in batches;
- one at a time.

(iv) Compare different retails outlets where food is served. Do any of them adopt a production line approach?

7.1.6 Operations Management in the Organisation

The *systems approach* stresses an *overall* view and may be used to identify the relationship between operations and other areas of the organisation. Whilst operations management should operate effectively and efficiently, this must be within the framework of the management of whole business organisation. The firm may have a number of policies which encourage consistency between the different management areas. Operations management usually depends extensively on support from accounting and personnel. But the key role of operations management is to *support* the business organisation in the market-place, and to *generate* and *deliver* what the customer wants *profitably*. Therefore, day-to-day co-operation is often most extensive with the marketing and design departments.

The problem is that it is often easy to deliver what the customer wants, but without making a profit. The sales department may only be able to get a large order by offering a discount, early delivery or a revised design. The costs of disrupting existing production plans or incorporating revisions may erode any profit. It is possible to change a brochure or price list quickly, but it generally takes much longer to install new machinery or recruit new staff; still longer to change attitudes and improve levels of quality.

It is important that mutual understanding exists between the operations, design, sales and marketing departments in recognising key customer requirements. Such requirements may differ from one customer to another, and circumstances may change for individual customers. For example, a customer who initially is only interested in a cheap computer may come to want more complex features and then learn the value of reliability. Whatever aspects are important to customers must be anticipated in time to bring production capability into line, provided this is consistent with profitability, at least in the long-term.

In many service industries, the involvement of the customer in the production process implies simultaneous sales and production activity, and may present a distinct marketing opportunity.

Tasks

(i) Obtain a copy of a car catalogue and make a note of the different ways in which customers can obtain a distinctive vehicle as opposed to a standard model. Find out how much preparation the manufacturer has made for fitting options or extras and how much work the agent garage has to do in carrying out fitting. A group visit to a car showroom may be helpful.

(ii) Consider several examples of services, including retail services. What opportunities are there for using the service transaction as:
- a further selling opportunity beyond the basic service offered?
- an opportunity for other related marketing activities?

Assignment 7.1: Visit to the country pub

You work for a brewery as a management trainee. The brewery owns a chain of public houses and is reviewing its policy banning all coach parties from the pubs. You have been asked to visit one of the country pubs owned by the brewery to find out what people's views are. You have been advised that you should consider in advance what the relevant issues are likely to be for each of the parties involved: the customers, the pub landlord and the brewery. Your manager realises that this will be the first time you have carried out a task like this and wants to check your approach before you leave.

Student activities

(i) Prepare a list of points you will be checking during your visit, whether by observation or in face-to-face interviews.

(ii) Write a brief report for your manager outlining your views on the merits of removing the coach ban from the pubs from the perspectives of each of the three parties concerned.

7.2 Operations Planning

7.2.1 The Planning Framework

Planning the activities of the operations area is normally carried out within a framework of *policies*, *budgets* and *plans* to ensure consistency of activity throughout the organisation. *Programmes* can be developed from plans by working back from when planned levels of production are required. Working from what needs to be done and when, the nature, timing and levels of resources necessary to fulfil the programme can be determined. For example, how early materials and components need to be ordered or the size and composition of workforce required.

There may be problems in developing a viable plan. New staff may have to be recruited or subcontractors hired. Production may have to start early because of other demands on specialist equipment.

Although broad plans can be turned into detailed programmes, the extent to which programmes can be carried out depends on the nature of the product and the demand for it. What is crucial is not so much the extent to which demand varies (whether in terms of variety or volume), but how early this can be *predicted* accurately. Reliable information is desirable before commitment becomes necessary. All firms in the market may be in the same position, but the operations manager who uses *technology* to achieve a more rapid response to changing requirements may be able to achieve a competitive advantage for the organisation. For example the Just-in-time approach detailed in Section 7.4.3 may be adopted to keep production in step with demand on a week-by-week or day-to-day basis.

Returning to the preparation of a meal example, you may not know how many guests to expect or which dishes they will choose. But this presents no problem provided they are prepared to listen to music or talk to each other while cooking proceeds. You may need to limit their choice to quickly prepared dishes, relying on frozen or microwave food.

Another example of production planning occurs when there is irregular demand for a product. A prolonged spell of hot weather increase sales of ice-cream dramatically and may reduce the range available in the shops. The manufacturer may only make to order and keep his customers waiting. He may have machinery that can manufacture fresh stock quickly, or enough stock to meet demand most of the time. He may ensure that he can always supply a limited range on demand. But he needs to decide whether the extra business he gets from holding stock justifies the cost, and whether he is justified in putting prices up when demand is high

The nature of the planning process depends on the type of production. If *continuous production* is involved, considerable complexity may be involved in designing and setting up the operation. Subsequent planning may involve little more than ensuring continuity of supply of materials. However, responsibility lies with the marketing department to ensure that production is effectively distributed.

With small scale or *unit production* of complex products the timing of availability of suitable workforce, equipment, components and materials is a large task. Planning and monitoring the process may be facilitated by use of *networks* or *critical path analysis* (Section 7.4.2).

Where production consists of small quantities of a wide variety of items, planning can be difficult. It may be necessary to use a *buffer stock* to ensure that response can be made to fluctuating demand. It is important to compare the cost of holding stock with the value of having it available (Section 7.4.3).

Task

(i)   Draw up a list of the tasks involved in preparing a meal. Identify those tasks which must occur in a particular sequence. Are there any key times that must be adhered to?

(ii) Identify another product where demand is liable to outstrip supply.

7.2.2 Product Life Cycle

A *product life cycle* (Section 6.3.3) has four stages:

- introduction
- growth
- maturity (incorporating saturation)
- decline

Early sales of a new product are low. During the stage of product *introduction* it takes time for knowledge of the product to become widespread and for demand to build up. Initial levels of production may be low to minimise risk. The price is likely to be set at a level to achieve a profit, despite the low sales volume, relying on the novelty or uniqueness of the product to justify the high price.

As demand builds up, increased sales are achieved, but at a lower price (the stage of product *growth*). However, confidence in persisting sales justifies corresponding increases in production volume, permitting reduction in cost due to economies of scale.

Once demand has built up, increased competition can be expected. Price competition (perhaps with styling change) becomes more important and effort is devoted to reducing production costs. The stage of product *maturity* can be extended by transferring production to low production costs areas, such as newly industrialised countries where labour costs are low.

There may be a final phase in the stage of product *decline* where there is a residual, dedicated, low-volume demand for the product, or for spare parts, which can only be satisfied profitably at high prices.

Design and initiation of production are themselves one-off operations which should be managed with a *project management* approach. Operations management needs to recognise the changing circumstances in the market during successive stages of the product life cycle. The dominant selling feature changes during the product life cycle thus:

- the initial volume is low, but prices may be high enough to permit expensive production, by batch for example;
- as production builds up, a move towards mass production may still be consistent with a premium price, but pressure for price reductions and increased production efficiency will grow;
- the final phase of production may involve small volume production in support of existing users; or often a transfer of production to a low cost producing area

Task

Select any well known consumer electronics firm and look at its current product range. To what extent do the different models on sale conform to the different stages of product life cycle as indicated by price and technical performance?

7.2.3 Forecasting and Managing Demand

There are various techniques available for *forecasting* demand which use historical statistics, but their level of accuracy depends on the application and the circumstances. Predictions attempt to distinguish *cyclical variations* and *trends*. *Cyclicality* is the term for the periodic variations that may occur for instance on a weekly, daily or annual basis. However, cyclicality does not necessarily follow the calendar; other influences may be involved. The operations manager must be able to cope with cyclicality, but long-term trends in demand can be used to make forecasts and anticipate the need to change capacity.

In cases where production capacity is inflexible and fixed costs are high, output may be maintained at a fixed level. Spare capacity might be acceptable for some of the year, but there could be scope to *modify* demand profitably rather than simply meet it. Examples include an oil refinery or a theatre

Task

In what way would you expect demand to vary in the following businesses?

- a newsagents;
- a supermarket;
- a holiday tour operator;
- a city centre hotel;
- a bank or post office.

7.2.4 Capacity Management

Effective production capacity depends on the *availability* of many things. At the simplest level this includes adequate capacity of production machinery, but anything which can limit output affects capacity. Lack of materials or capable workforce can halt production. More subtly, losses of various kinds can reduce effective capacity, whether they are generation of scrap, inadequate quality of components or the losses involved in changing over from one product to another.

In the short-term it may be possible to *vary* capacity, for example by using temporary staff. Such approaches are particularly important in service industries where it is impossible to store the product. Generally the aim is to achieve an acceptable *balance* between capacity and demand. Other approaches include:

- *premium pricing* or *streamlined service* at peak demand times;
- *self-service*, educating the customer if necessary;
- *queuing* with some customers returning later;
- *parallel services* which enable customers with urgent requirements
- *automation*, sometimes with limited service, but often with extended availability;
- *speed processing* through the use of standard forms, menus etc;
- relying on support from *sub-contractors*.

Capacity management is often a long-term consideration. New staff take time to recruit and train; machinery and facilities take time to set up; the minimum size of a new facility may need a substantial increase in forecast demand to justify commitment.

Predictions of future demand must consider the likelihood of *optimistic* and *pessimistic forecasts*, and their consequences. Long time scales also make it necessary to consider both changing technology and changes in the nature of demand so that appropriate type of capacity may be introduced. For example, manufacturers of chemicals must now take into account growing concern for the environment; new urban railways must allow for developing patterns of journeys to work.

Task

What mechanisms might the organisations listed in the task in Section 7.2.3 use to keep demand and supply in line?

Assignment 7.2: The new supermarket

A national supermarket chain is proposing to open a new outlet in a medium-sized town in which it currently does not have a presence.

Student activities

(i) Set out the range of issues that would need to be progressively considered in the evaluation and possible implementation of such a proposal.

(ii) If possible, identify a case where such a development is planned in your locality. Identify the interested parties and their respective points of view.

7.3 Organisation and Implementation

7.3.1 Purchasing

The purchasing department of a business may seem an unglamorous area, but it makes a distinctive contribution to the business. A *reliable* flow of materials is essential to smooth running of an organisation whether it is producing goods or services. In a manufacturing business the product price is controlled to a large extent by market conditions. Materials and components usually constitute a high proportion of the total cost of a product. The process of identifying *reliable suppliers* is now recognised as being of crucial importance to a business. This contrasts with traditional practices which concentrated on competitive bidding between suppliers.

The *vendor appraisal* approach is open to wide application. The process identifies the aspects of obtaining supplies which are of importance to the organisation and rates them numerically. Each potential supplier is identified and assessed in terms of actual or expected performance in the areas identified. It is then a routine process to multiply the importance rating by the score in that area for each firm, finally resulting in an overall score for each potential supplier

The process does not inevitably identify the best supplier, but is helpful in narrowing the selection. If there is a large number of potential suppliers and a wide range of changing requirements, the process can be computerised to allow personal effort to be concentrated on detailed evaluation and negotiation with the leading contenders.

Task

After identifying the ingredients for your meal, you should check whether you have any of them in stock. Next you should consider where it is best to do the shopping. Is the cost of a trip to the supermarket on the other side of town justified by the savings you would achieve? Is it worth buying some of the ingredients at a delicatessen because you can be sure that they will be of the right quality and will not spoil the occasion? Would it be worth buying a ready-made gateau to save time?

Carry out a vendor appraisal using the form below for a selection of ingredients and shops. Do the results of the calculation agree with your original choice? Would you adjust any numbers in retrospect?

Ingredient _____

Vendor characteristic	Weight	Shop 1	Shop 2	Shop 3
Product/brand availability				
Pack size suitability				
Product quality				
Price				
Ease of access				
Opening hours				

Overall scores _____

Key

Raw score ⬚ / Weighted score

7.3.2 Distribution

Achieving *effective* and *efficient distribution* of products forms a crucial element of the marketing mix (Section 6.6). It is an area that offers scope for reducing a business's dependence on competing on price. At a basic level the channels of distribution must effectively and economically meet market needs.

The *postal service* remains an extremely effective means of responding to a widely distributed, low level of demand. At the other end of the spectrum high volume suppliers with few customers may choose to *locate* their businesses near their customers. For certain products the problem of distribution is immaterial; an aircraft for example can distribute itself anywhere in the world.

Some services may be delivered via *telecommunication links*. *Travel* by the customer may also be a feature of distribution, whether to a discount warehouse or to a football match.

Comparative total costs for the various methods of distribution and different location of facilities can be evaluated, but cost is only one factor of several to be considered. The benefit of offering one-stop variety is crucial to the role of wholesalers and cash and carry organisations. As with vendor appraisal, evaluation should be based on those factors which are of importance to the business and its customers. If location of facilities is part of the evaluation, then long-term plans should be considered based on the length of time a facility is likely to be in use.

Management of distribution activity is itself an example of service operations management, whether the task is carried out within the organisation or by a specialist contractor. Specialist contractors are able to work economically by building adequate overall demand from many customers. However, they too can benefit from the knowledge of specialist management staff and others who may develop new approaches to achieve more efficient distribution.

Tasks

(i) Identify a range of products, both goods and services, and determine the methods by which they are distributed. Is there a dominant method?

(ii) List the merits of alternative approaches.

7.3.3 Scheduling

Scheduling is concerned with making effective use of the existing workforce and planning which jobs should be done and in what order. The process is used in drawing up detailed programmes from broad plans. A crucial aspect of scheduling is to allow for the effects of *constraints* on production in determining when activities must take place.

The nature of the process varies widely and depends on the nature of the production process, the nature of demand and the extent to which output needs to keep pace with demand. In industries where production requirements are highly predictable, such as in bakeries, the process is straightforward. Where demand is highly unpredictable and rapid production is possible, scheduling may be irrelevant; for example, in some fast food outlets.

Approaches to scheduling in more complex situations are discussed in Section 7.4.

Tasks

Consider a fairly complex activity with which you are familiar, such as redecorating a room.

(i) Prepare a list of the tasks involved.

(ii) Review the list and identify tasks which must occur in a specific sequence.

(iii) Distinguish those tasks which could take place simultaneously.

7.3.4 Managing Manpower

Managing manpower (Section 4.2.1) in the context of operations management is concerned with the process of *planning recruitment* to meet required production levels or product demand. This is of central concern to the operations manager. *Pay systems* (Section 4.4.2) may have a profound effect on production performance, but traditional piece-work systems which relate pay directly to individual output are now much less common.

The process is simple in principle but deserves care in implementation given the extent of uncertainties which may be involved. Benefits are clearest when unambiguous categories of products, staff and other resources are involved. Where there is a broad range of staff and levels of competence the assessment of manpower needs can only produce results of an indicative nature unless considerable effort is involved. The process involves the following stages:

First the overall demand, based on existing orders and forecast additional demand, is assessed, looking forward far enough so that resultant data is useful within the context of corporate plans.

Next the extent to which the demand should be met by in-house capacity is determined in the light of company strategy.

Then a common basis for cumulating demand for the various products product is determined, consistent with converting that demand into resource use. Where products are limited in number and work content well known, this presents little problem. But where the product range is varied or where the work content varies extensively, some level of approximation will be necessary to achieve useful results without excessive effort.

The fourth stage is to set out the resultant levels of the common basis for assessing load, and hence of resources which are of interest.

Finally, approaches must be developed to meeting the demand by moving production away from peaks and relying on storage to meet peak demand, by recruiting and, if necessary, training new staff or installing new equipment for example.

The emergent data will not be precise. More importantly, the emergent demand will *differ* from the plan, and short-term approaches to balancing supply and demand may be more appropriate.

Task

Contrast the problems involved in predicting the demands for staff and ensuring their availability in the following organisations:

- a take-away food shop;
- a department store;
- a design office of a high technology electronics firm;
- an assembly line of a high technology electronics firm;
- a construction company building housing estates;
- a seaside hotel.

Assignment 7.3: Planning recruitment

You are an assistant operations manager in a company which assembles parts manufactured by subcontractors. You have been asked to investigate the manpower requirements for the assembly operation.

Student activities

(i) Set up a spreadsheet based on the data below and determine a viable pattern of staff recruitment to meet demand.

Month	Forecast product demand	Start staff level	Number of recruits	Monthly output
March	5,000	30		4,000
April	6,000			
May	7,000			
June	10,000			
July	15,000			
August	9,000			
September	4,000			

You may assume that staff work 175 hours each month, that on average it takes an operator one hour to complete an assembly, and that new employees become productive in the month after recruitment to allow for training.

(ii) What problems emerge?

(iii) What other issues should be considered?

(iv) What alternative approaches are worth considering?

7.4 Operations Analysis

The range of techniques offered by operations research is extensive. Selected analytical approaches are used here to illustrate applications which have strong implications for operations management. A broader perspective of techniques which can be used to collect and analyse data to guide business decisions is given in Section 9.

7.4.1 Simulation and Models

Approaches to operations analysis generally depend on identifying critical aspects of a situation and representing them in the form of a *model*. A model can give an indication of physical appearance and layout, for example reduced-scale models, building models, mock-ups or three-dimensional computer graphics models. In addition they can predict product or system performance; for example functional reduced-scale models or computer performance *simulation* used in training. However, a model is not always a small-scale replica of something; it might be a formula or a spreadsheet.

The creation of a model allows the exploration of the outcome of a variety of different circumstances or decisions. Since the accuracy of representation in a model is limited, it is important to determine where those limitations exist, but the potential value of using models in simulation are extensive. The key benefits are:

- early availability of information;
- ability to explore a range of alternatives rapidly and cheaply;
- ability to explore unsafe situations or where a valuable specimen might be destroyed.

Flight simulators available for home computers can be very realistic because they draw on the technology used in commercial simulation and actual flight testing. Sometimes simulation is based on mathematical formulae which have been demonstrated to represent reality. In other cases the response of operating systems to typical random variations of circumstances can be illustrated by the use of *Monte Carlo* simulation, so called because the element of chance can be represented by the use of a roulette wheel or some similar process.

Task

Select six varied examples of a model or simulation. In each case identify:

(i) the characteristics it can be used to explore or demonstrate;

(ii) any likely or apparent limitations to the validity of its use;

(iii) the benefits arising from the use of the model or simulation.

7.4.2 Critical Path Analysis

Critical path analysis (CPA) is a simple concept which can be applied to complex tasks with the aid of appropriate computer software. It is used to determine the best way of scheduling a complex set of related tasks to reduce the time taken to a minimum. A set of lines drawn in the form of a network is used when the process is carried out manually. The method of evaluating a network is given in Section 9.5.6. The network, whether drawn manually or by computer, is a simplified model of the set of tasks or project. For example, the model enables the consequences of changing the sequence of tasks to be evaluated rapidly with the minimum additional effort.

The technique can be used to highlight the cost and potential value of computer-based data. If CPA is used simply to plan when tasks should be carried out, the essential information stored for each task is its duration, together with an identification label and sufficient data to represent the sequence in which it occurs. The cost of preparing, entering and maintaining such data for a significant project may be comparable with the cost of the type of desktop computer which can now effectively process such data.

It is possible to store additional data related to the task or the circumstances of the project using facilities provided by modestly priced commercial CPA packages, thus extending the complexity of the model and the information it is capable of generating. Typical CPA computer programs include the following:

> The facility to record the type and extent of resources needed for each task. A histogram can be generated to show the pattern of use, enabling task timings to be adjusted to reduce peaks. Such a facility is particularly useful where several project occur simultaneously and the overall pattern of use can be generated. Planned task costs can be used similarly to facilitate cash flow planning.

> Actual times, durations and costs can be entered together with planned value, enabling the model to act as a progress information system and an evaluation tool for investigating the consequences of modifying the pattern of uncompleted tasks.

The use of CPA as a management information system can be considerably enhanced by giving each task a label permitting the sorting and selection of data. Such selection might be based on the relative urgency of the task or on departmental factors. Selective tabular printouts are a valuable source of information, but bar charts or a network may be more helpful in presenting a summary.

> **Tasks**
>
> (i) Obtain access to a CPA system and use a demonstration network to familiarise yourself with the way in which information is presented on-screen and in printouts.
>
> (ii) Find out the range of facilities offered by three CPA computer programs.
>
> (iii) Which features would be important to you as a novice user if you had to use a system to plan an occasion such as a conference?

7.4.3 Stock Control and Scheduling

Critical Path Analysis (Section 7.4.2) is typically applied to forms of production where the product is extremely complex. In other forms of production a stream of products, either identical, similar or diverse, emerges from a less complex process in various quantities. There are several approaches to determining how many of an individual product should be produced or ordered at a time. Comparison of some of these approaches is useful in highlighting the importance of considering the assumptions and limitations that are implicit in using models to guide decision-making

In circumstances where the costs of setting up production are large compared with the marginal costs of producing an individual item, making a large quantity in a singe run minimises *set-up costs per unit*. Such an approach might be most apt, for example, in an organisation making standard plastic injection mouldings for a wide range of electrical equipment. The approach does not identify any maximum size of batch and leads to large stocks.

A more sophisticated analysis, known as *economic order quantity (EOQ)* evaluation, takes into consideration costs associated with the passage of time. Such costs range from the interest charged on the value of stock held, to the deterioration in the value of the product. It is possible to carry out a mathematical trade-off between costs associated with setting up a particular batch and the cost of holding stock over a period of time. The total costs do not vary widely with batch size so it is acceptable to use the emergent figure as an approximate guide. This approach lends itself to computerisation in supermarkets, for example, which hold a wide range of stock and operate on low profit margins. Itemised sales data is readily available, and manual calculations would be tedious.

On a smaller scale, the *two bin* concept can be applied to minimise administrative effort. Two bins or containers are used for each item stored: the first just large enough to be filled by one delivery batch, the second just large enough to contain safety stock and the amount used between order and delivery.

Computers have been applied extensively to assist planning operations, determining when things need to be done. *MRP* works backwards from planned product completion or delivery using the way the product is built up to determine when ordering of materials and components should take place in particular. Confusingly, MRP can either stand for *materials requirements planning (MRP I)* where lead times for deliveries are taken into account, or *manufacturing resource planning (MRP II)* where the time taken for the stages of production is also considered.

The process can be carried out manually but is usually computerised. Working backwards from the plan for emergence of the final product and the bill of materials, a programme is built up for each preceding stage of production. An output of quantities of components and the time they are required emerges. Allowance can be made for existing stocks and the EOQs for example. Although this approach takes has the advantage of the routine work being computerised, the underlying plan can become out-of-date and taking account of changes can be tedious.

The growing success of Japanese firms in recent years not only reflects their approach to international markets for mass-produced consumer durables, but also their approach to production and concern to minimise waste. This has led to product quality and availability. Stocks of materials, work-in-progress and finished goods are minimised. Each part of the production and delivery chain works just in time to meet the requirement of the next part of the chain.

In the *Just-in-time (JIT)* or *Kan Ban* approach the same understanding of product build up and production process is required as in MRP, but the process can be controlled simply by cards which move with the containers of parts. Such an approach makes it essential that components are available when needed; that they are of good quality and fit first time; that the workforce is properly trained and avoids mistakes; and that equipment works reliably. It implies that *quality is assured*, not simply checked at the end of the production line.

Instead of accepting things as they are and calculating optimum stock levels, the Japanese have found ways of working which make it practicable to work with low stock levels while achieving additional benefits. Making JIT work is demanding and takes time to implement effectively. The approach is most appropriate in cases where complex products are assembled from many components in several stages. It automatically responds to changes in demand, in contrast to MRP. Workers are encouraged to maintain equipment or find better ways of carrying out their work at times when demand is reduced. This may take place in *quality circles* (Section 7.5.6) where groups of workers adopt formal techniques to avoid delays in production or to improve product quality.

Optimised production technology (OPT) is a proprietary approach to the use of computer scheduling to achieve better results than the JIT approach outlined above. A wide range of available data is regularly re-evaluated to determine when and operations should be carried out. Like the JIT approach, OPT aims to minimise stock levels, but an overriding criterion is to ensure that *bottlenecks* do not occur. This may be achieved by using local buffer stocks for example. Bottlenecks are production elements which limit overall output.

Although this system may not be encountered very often in the workplace, it is worth mentioning because operations managers are expected recognise and adopt a formal philosophy as well as implementing the technology. (Such concern for recognising key issues is reflected in The Goal, a novel written by the author of the system (see recommended texts), intended to present the concepts in an informal manner.)

Task

Identify the specific sources of costs associated with holding stock, not having stock when required, and ordering/obtaining additional stock in the following organisations:

- a greengrocers;
- a hospital;
- a vehicle maintenance workshop.

7.4.4 Linear Programming

Linear programming (Section 9.5.1) is a mathematical tool which enables the user to decide how best to work with limited resources, such as machinery, labour or materials, which impose constraints on capacity. The approach can be used to determine the mix of products that can be made using the available resources to achieve maximum profit. Another application is to determine the mix of foodstuffs that can most economically provide adequate nutrition as the price of the ingredients varies. In this case the objective is to minimise cost rather than maximise profit.

Feasible combinations of the best use of resources available can be identified by means of a graph or with the aid of a suitable computer program (Section 9.5.1). The latter method offers scope for investigating the best mix of several products, whereas only two can be compared on a graph.

Tasks

You may wish to complete Section 9.5.1 before attempting this task.

You have two preparation machines and a freezer. One machine produces frozen fish, the other beefburgers. The freezer can cope with a maximum of 100 lbs per hour of either product. You have material supplies for 1,000 lbs of fish and 3,000 lbs of beefburgers each week. You make a profit of 30p per lb on fish and 20p per lb on beef and work a 40 hour week.

(i)   What is the maximum profit you can make per week?

(ii) Draw a graph showing lbs of beef per week on the horizontal axis and lbs of fish per week on the vertical axis. Identify the maximum amount of beef and of fish you can freeze, assuming that you are only producing one, not the other. You should end up with a triangle on the graph which represents the feasible combinations of meat and fish you could freeze in a week.

(iii) Put two further lines on the graph: one showing the limit imposed by availability of fish, the other showing availability of beef. The area showing feasible combinations of beef and fish will now be more constrained. Check the amount of profit you would make from the combination represented by the corners of the feasible area. The point associated with the highest profit shows the combination you should adopt. If you have access to simple linear programming software package, you should be able to work with a greater number of variables.

Assignment 7.4: Just-in-time production

You are working as an assistant to the manager of a firm making small electric motors. One of the firm's customers has decided to adopt the Just-in-time approach to product assembly and wants deliveries to be made at two or three day intervals, with quantities varying in line with demand for their products.

Student activities

You have been asked to prepare a word-processed report for your manager which should:

(i)   summarise the key elements of Just-in-time production;

(ii) identify the important areas to be considered in meeting the customer's requirements;

(iii) outline the sort of problems involved in implementing Just-in-time production.

7.5 Monitoring Control and Quality Assurance

7.5.1 The Objectives of Managing Operations Performance

It is a central management activity to monitor performance, identify any deviation from expectations and initiate corrective action where necessary. After plans have been set and implemented, monitoring, evaluation, replanning and revised implementation should be expected

Good management, in the form of careful preparation, minimises the need for corrective action. This is increasingly important as services and projects have become dominant commercial and industrial activities in developed countries, and as customers become increasingly sensitive to quality issues.

The output of operations can be measured in terms of *time, cost* and *product specification* or *quality*. An appropriate balance between these elements must be identified and maintained in the light of the nature of the market for the product and the capability of the producer. The variation in balance in different circumstances can be shown by comparing examples such as the following:

- a leisurely but expensive meal in a gourmet restaurant;
- a light snack eaten in time to catch a train;
- a cheap but substantial portion of fish and chips.

This can be expressed formally by identifying the *order qualifying, winning and losing features*. Used in this way, the term *feature* is any aspect of the product that influences the customer to buy or not to buy the product.

The supplier must be able to offer the order qualifying features so that the customer will considered purchasing the product. Order winning features then provide the basis for selection among the qualifying suppliers. Order losing features are more likely to become apparent after a purchase, and usually result in a reluctance on the part of the customer to make further purchases from the same supplier. Examples of order losing features include late delivery or product unreliability.

It is important to recognise the critical features for the target customer and ensure that they can be met. These features may vary with time and continual vigilance is essential. Simple corrective action may be rewarded with a continued match between the product and the market. Long-term effort may be required to develop new products or to improve operations capability. In some cases it may be easier to switch to markets which can be satisfied by existing capability.

Cost and *availability* are relatively straightforward. *Product quality* encompasses a wide range of issues. It tends to be increasingly important to customers as they become more sophisticated, and must be considered as part of competitive strategy. Product quality is multifaceted, offering scope for innovative approaches which avoid competition based only on price and availability. Management approaches leading to achievement of product quality may well lead to cost savings.

> **Tasks**
>
> (i)   Identify the features you would look for when purchasing a consumer durable product such as a midi Hi-Fi system, a camera or a car.
>
> (ii) Distinguish the order qualifying and order winning features.
>
> (iii) How do you think the importance of the features might have changed if you buy a replacement in five years' time?

7.5.2 Product Quality

In everyday usage the term *quality* refers to something with superior attributes. In business and management it refers more specifically to the extent to which a product fulfils its purpose: its conformance to specification or more generally, its consistency with *market expectation*.

In business-to-business transactions the customer generally prepares a formal requirement or specification to which the product must conform. In consumer markets the requirement is developed by the marketing department in anticipation of emergent market expectations.

In markets for consumer goods aggressive competition may make it difficult to define the appropriate standard of quality. It is useful to distinguish between:

- *quality of design*: the intended standard of the product as specified in design;
- *quality of conformance*: the extent to which the product as delivered conforms to the intended standard;
- *quality of performance*: the extent to which the product achieves the intended purpose;
- *reliability*: the extent to which a product maintains a defined performance over a period of time

The definitions of quality of design and quality of conformance allow for a distinction to be made between what a product is and what it does.

> **Task**
>
> Think again of the example of the meal you were preparing for friends in the task in Section 7.1.4.
>
> (i) How would you define what you think your friends might expect?
>
> (ii) What aspects of the meal and of the evening do you consider are important in fulfilling their expectations?

7.5.3 The Quality Control Approach

In the early stages of industrialisation achievement of quality depended extensively on the pride and skill of the craftsman. Later on the application of mass production techniques allowed less skilled workers to achieve consistent results repeatedly. However, pressure for high output, encouraged by incentive payment systems, is liable to result in poor quality, and this has remained a common concern in manufacturing.

Quality of the product is achieved by means of *quality control* which ensures that inadequate output is rectified or scrapped. Such an approach can be refined by examining the *costs of quality*. The total costs involved are those associated with:

- initial production;
- failure costs (scrap and rework);
- inspection.

Additional failure costs occur where unsatisfactory products get through inspection and are released to the customer. The additional costs involved in such cases include:

- customer liaison;
- further testing;
- rectification or replacement;
- loss of goodwill.

It make take considerable effort to assess these costs if a routine system for recording them is not in place. It is commonly found that quality costs are comparable with profits, offering substantial scope for savings. In principle it is possible to identify an optimum quality level at which the total cost of production, including failure, is minimised.

Task

Referring again to the example of the meal you were preparing for friends in the task in Section 7.1.4, how can you check:

(i)   that the meal you have prepared was cooked properly;

(ii) whether the friends you invited to the meal did enjoy themselves;

(iii) whether you have successfully completed your course?

7.5.4 Inspection and Control

In order to be able to decide whether the output of operations is acceptable, it is necessary to have standards against which comparison can be made. In almost all cases it should be possible to *measure* and *record* the critical aspects so that the uncertainty which is associated with judgement is avoided. In some cases a simple yes/no may be appropriate, but records of measurements enable trends to be identified, thus permitting problems to be anticipated and facilitating the location of their source.

Measuring the characteristics of output is crucial in triggering corrective action. Some care is needed in applying correction. The operating systems framework can be used to take into account some ideas from control system theory. Measuring *deviations* of the output of the system from requirements generates a *feedback* signal highlighting the need for correction. The feedback may suffer defects due to:

238

- incorrect initial measurement;
- spurious external signal (noise);
- delay in communication (lag).

This may lead to inappropriate corrective action. For example, a machine may have already been adjusted before defective output is identified. Proper records and an understanding of the way the system operates are essential to effective use of control.

In order to *control* operations, it must be possible to take *corrective action*. In continuous operations some problems may be resolved rapidly, whether by adjustment of machinery, change of raw material or advice to staff. In other cases resolution may require an extended period so that contingency plans must be applied. In short production runs or in unit production the option for adjustment or advice may be too late.

Task

It is important for national fast food chains to maintain consistency in the quality of the food and service they provide throughout their retail outlets.

(i)   In what ways can consistency be monitored by the head office?

(ii) Identify the problems which may be encountered in the process.

(iii) How do these problems conform to the categories of incorrect measurement, noise and lag?

7.5.5 Quality Assurance

In Section 7.4.3 it was noted that Just-in-time production highlights the importance of receiving quality parts in order to ensure that production is not held up. This contrasts with older approaches where acceptable levels of quality were defined: inspection of goods received were carried out and deliveries with an unacceptably high proportion of faulty goods rejected by the quality control department.

It is now increasingly common for a *quality assurance* approach to be adopted. The characteristics of this approach are:

- Deliveries are expected to be of the appropriate quality.
- Goods inward inspection is carried out only occasionally.
- The supplying/manufacturing organisation is organised in such a way that quality output is assured, and is subject to inspection to verify that this is achieved

This approach saves the receiving organisation time and trouble. It is likely to need care and effort on the part of the supplying organisation. This may extend over several years. The long-term benefits are summed up in the view that "quality is free": it is cheaper to get the job or product right first time rather that incur the costs and delays that result from failure.

When this philosophy is applied more widely, it is known as *total quality management*. Quality is not only considered in terms of the external customer and the final product, the savings achieved from getting the job right also apply in administrative and support areas. The onus for achieving quality lies with all staff, not only with the quality department. Quality staff become concerned with generating a framework to enable quality to be achieved, rather than with carrying out inspection.

> **Task**
>
> Think again of the imaginary meal you were preparing for friends in Section 7.1.4. How can you ensure that:
>
> (i)   the meal *will* be cooked properly;
>
> (ii) your friends *will* enjoy themselves;
>
> (iii) you *will* successfully complete your course?

7.5.6 Approaches to Quality

In addition to the broad principles of quality assurance (Section 7.5.5), there are a number of specific approaches.

British Standard 5750 has been developed by the British Standards Institute to provide a framework within which organisations can be certified as having a comprehensive quality management system. Certification can be relied upon by customers and the document can be invoked in contracts. Similar requirements are imposed on their suppliers by such organisations as Marks and Spencer, Ford Motor Company and the Ministry of Defence.

Statistical process control is widely used in mass production and is being introduced in other types of industry. It uses statistics measured during production rather at completion. It permits patterns and trends to be highlighted and their causes identified, even where deviations involved are not sufficient to render the product unacceptable. This reflects the view that absence of variations in process is important in achieving consistent quality.

Quality circles are formed by groups of workers in their workplace to identify problems and their causes, and to formulate and present solutions. The approach has been extensively applied in Japan within the context of Just-in-time production, where elimination of production holdups is critical, and where fluctuations in demand provide periods for operation. The support of management, the role of a facilitator and the use of formal problem-solving techniques are all essential. Successful applications in the UK have been more limited.

Industrial engineering may be mentioned in contrast to quality circles as the more conventional UK approach to improvement in production where the specialist observes current practice, identifies and evaluates alternatives for presentation to management. The approach brings makes use of specialist expertise, but may be less effective in drawing on knowledge of workers or in obtaining their commitment.

The *Zero Defects* approach and other similar schemes encourage the individual worker to develop a commitment to faultless work. Such schemes are typically associated with rewards or privilege clubs for qualifying workers.

Many of these approaches eliminate or alleviate existing problems. Design, whether of goods or services, of products or processes, has a key role in ensuring that quality is achieved. Solving problems on the drawing board is cheap; solving them on the shop floor is expensive; solving them when the product is in the hands of the customer may be too late.

Task

Identify the aspects of the operation perceptible to the customer at a typical fast food outlet which assist in the consistency of food and service throughout the retail chain.

Assignment 7.5: Hungry Jake's Take-away

The company you work for is acting as a consultant to Hungry Jake's Take-away, a fast food retail chain which wants to introduce a total quality policy. Your manager has asked you to assist in the preparation of draft recommendations.

Student activities

(i) Find out how local businesses address the issue. Formal statements regarding policies on quality are exhibited in many retail businesses. These may be useful in deciding who to approach for information.

(ii) Prepare a word-processed report which can be used to explain to the branch managers of Hungry Jake's Take-away what the quality assurance approach involves. Outline the benefits of this approach to customers, the firm and employees, and include examples of local practice from your survey of local businesses.

Section 8

People and Organisations

by Geoffrey Heaven

BSc (Hons), Senior Lecturer in Organisational Behaviour at Bristol Business School

The study of people and organisations is concerned with understanding the behaviour of people at work. It takes into account the influence of psychological processes, groups, technology, the organisation and society on individuals.

Recommended Reading

Bilton, T., *Introducing Sociology*, Macmillan, 1988

Buchanan, D. A., & Huczynski, A. A., *Organisational Behaviour*, Prentice Hall, 1985

Fincham, R., & Rhodes, P. S., *The Individual, Work and Organisation*, Weidenfeld & Nicholson, 1987

Handy, C., *Understanding Organisations*, Penguin, 1985

Wilson, D., & Rosenfeld, R. H., *Managing Organisations*, McGraw-Hill, 1990

Perhaps assertive training might help...

Contents

8.1 Psychological Processes and Individual Behaviour

8.1.1 Personality

This is a comprehensive, all embracing term. The way in which we understand the world and our place in it, the way we are motivated and the way in which we learn are all aspects of our personalities. The term *personality* is usually used to describe the characteristic behaviour and ways of thinking that determine a person's adjustment to the world. Personality is not necessarily stable and may change over time. This process of change is referred to as *personality development*.

Tasks

(i) Describe your own personality. On what dimensions do you differ from a colleague?

(ii) Is your behaviour a reflection of your personality? To what extent is your true personality suppressed in social situations and your behaviour a reflection of other factors, such as the role you currently occupy or group pressure?

8.1.2 Personality Assessment

Personality assessment occurs continually in organisations as people interact with one another. Individuals may be categorised by one dimension of their personality, such as whether they have an 'aggressive' personality or whether they have 'lots of personality' by which people usually mean they are extrovert. Research has shown consistently that individuals are very poor judges of each other's personalities.

In order to assess personality accurately, psychologists have attempted to devise various 'scientific' instruments or *tests* to measure personality. This more formal approach tends to be used in organisations when an accurate personality assessment is particularly important, such as when individuals are being recruited (Section 5.2.8) or when training needs are being explored.

Tasks

(i) Approach local companies and ascertain the use they make of personality tests. Collect various types of test.

(ii) Complete a personality test.

8.1.3 Perspectives on the Study of Personality

Major approaches to the study of personality and its development include:

• The *psychoanalytical perspective* which is closely identified with *Sigmund Freud*. Freud's ideas focus on personality structure (the nature and interrelationship of parts of personality) and personality development (how these parts develop during the course of life).

• The *behavioural perspective* which is closely associated with *B L Skinner*. It rejects the introspective approach of Freud and gives great emphasis to the part played by the environment in shaping personality.

• The *Phenomenological perspective* which has several sources, but the work of *C R Rogers* is representative of the general perspective. The focus of attention in this approach is on the individual's perception of his or her environment and on him or herself.

Tasks

(i) Identify the main influences on the development of your own personality since childhood.

(ii) Choose either the psychoanalytical, behavioural or phenomenological perspective on personality and relate the approach to the development of your own personality.

8.1.4 Motivation Theory

Motivation theory is concerned with the goals that individuals seek and the decision-making processes that lead individuals to pursue particular goals.

Tasks

(i) Interview members of an organisation about their personal goals. To what extent does their current position fulfil these ambitions?

(ii) In groups discuss why managers might be particularly interested in understanding motivation?

8.1.5 Content Theories of Motivation

Content theories of motivation give insight into people's needs and what they value or do not value as work rewards. *A Maslow* proposes that individuals seek to satisfy certain needs which can be classified hierarchically. In ascending order these are physiological, safety, social, esteem, and self-actualisation needs.

F Herzberg proposes a framework to distinguish between factors that lead to job satisfaction *(motivators)* and those that prevented dissatisfaction *(hygienes)*.

Motivators include:

- achievement
- recognition
- work itself
- responsibility
- promotion/advancement

Hygienes include:

- company policy and administration
- supervision
- interpersonal relations
- money
- status
- security

Tasks

(i)   Interview individuals from a range of occupations. Ask them to reflect on events in their work that either made them feel good about their job or made them feel dissatisfied. Clarify what made these events particularly motivating or demotivating?

(ii) Interview individuals in a range of occupations and try to determine the importance of money in their choice of job.

8.1.6 Process Theories of Motivation

Process theories of motivation attempt to understand the decision-making process in individuals, the thought processes of individuals which lead to certain acts or behaviour. *J S Adams* argues that people are motivated by perceived inequities. Inequities exist whenever people feel that rewards they receive for their work inputs are unequal to the rewards of others.

V H Vroom suggests that the force of an individual's motivation to behave in a particular way depends on the expectation that the behaviour will be followed by a particular reward, and the attractiveness of a particular outcome. The *expectancy equation* states that:

$$F = E \times V$$

where: F = motivation to behave

E = the expectation that the behaviour will be followed by a particular outcome

V = the valence or attractiveness of the outcome

Tasks

(i)   Examine an industrial dispute concerning pay. To what extent can the behaviour of the workforce be explained by reference to Adams' equity theory?

(ii) Using Vroom's expectancy equation, predict how hard you will work on your present course compared to putting your energies into some other activity.

8.1.7 Motivation and Job Design

A major area for the application of *motivation theory* is the way in which various tasks can be put together to form a particular job for an individual. Many jobs are designed using the *scientific management* approach of *F Taylor* who advocated the breaking down of jobs into small elements. This enables people to specialise and become very competent. Motivation theory suggests that this approach is not appropriate in many circumstances. *J R Hackman and G R Oldham* have developed a *job characteristic model* which helps assess the motivating potential of a particular job. The main dimensions are:

- skill variety
- task identity
- task significance
- autonomy
- feedback

The *motivating potential score (MPS)* is calculated as follows:

$$MPS = \frac{\text{Skill variety} + \text{task identity} + \text{task significance}}{3} \times \text{autonomy} \times \text{feedback}$$

Tasks

(i)   Observe a local fast food restaurant and relate the design of the various tasks performed to Taylor's approach. How successful is the design of jobs in this industry?

(ii) Calculate the motivating potential of various subjects you are studying on your course.

8.1.8 Perception

Perception is the process by which data is selected and categorised. Since our environment contains a wealth of activities, only a small amount of data taken in at any one time. First, data must be selected; then it must be interpreted and, finally, given meaning. We organise incoming data by reference to various concepts and categories based on past experience.

Tasks

(i)   Describe your journey to college. Explain why there were some events that you particularly observed whilst you ignored other events on your journey.

(ii) Look through any journal or magazine and explain why certain advertisements catch your eye.

8.1.9 Stereotypes

A *stereotype* is a preconceived and oversimplified idea of the characteristics which typify a situation, person or groups of people. It is constructed on the basis of distorted or incomplete knowledge. The process of stereotyping can be very useful since it allows us to make rapid judgments about situations and people. However, it can lead to over generalisations and inaccurate perceptions.

Tasks

(i)   Select a group of people (old age pensioners, an ethnic group, students on another course etc) with whom you do not normally mix and write down your perception of them. Interview members of your chosen group and compare your initial perceptions with your findings.

(ii) How do you think you are perceived by your colleagues? Ask them.

8.1.10 Perspectives on Learning

Learning is the process of acquiring knowledge through experience which leads to a change in behaviour. Changes in behaviour caused by maturation, aging, drugs and fatigue are not considered to be learning. Learning is facilitated by appropriate feedback.

Two major approaches to learning are the *behaviourist* (stimulus-response) and the *cognitive* (information processing) perspectives. Behaviourists emphasise the development of associations between stimuli and response through experience. Behaviour that is rewarded tends to be repeated.

The cognitive approach emphasises perception, interpretation and the giving of meaning to our experiences. For cognitive theorists reasoning and insight play a major role in learning.

Tasks

(i)   Try to remember two lists, one containing ten telephone numbers and the other containing ten words. Which list is easier to recall and why should this be?

(ii) List the factors which assist your own learning on your current course of study.

8.1.11 Learning Styles

It is suggested by many writers that individuals have preferences for different learning methods. *P Honey* and *A Mumford* classify individuals as:

- *activists*, who prefer a real experience from which to learn;

- *reflectors*, who prefer an opportunity to observe;

- *theorists*, who prefer to work with abstract ideas;

- *pragmatists*, who prefer to learn from practice and experimentation.

Tasks

(i)   Identify your own dominant learning style.

(ii) Choose an area in which you wish to develop some expertise. Approach the task using a learning style that you normally would not use.

8.1.12 Attitude

Attitudes reflect the different ways people respond to their environment. An attitude can be defined as a learned predisposition to think, feel and act in a particular way towards a given object. Attitudes involve a belief about an object (*cognitive aspect*), feelings experienced (*affective aspect*) and a predisposition to do something (*conative aspect*). It should be noted that the cognitive and affective aspects are not always closely related to overt behaviour. For example, someone who is racialist may believe that immigrants are inferior, but not always act towards them racially.

Tasks

(i) Consider your attitude towards the police. How has this attitude been formed?

(ii) Interview smokers on their attitudes towards smoking and the evidence that smoking is a danger to health. How do smokers cope with the evidence that they may be killing themselves?

8.1.13 Attitudes toward Change

Individuals' *attitudes toward change* (Section 5.6.1) vary according to how change is perceived. Resistance to change may be caused by:

- self-interest related to economic reasons such as unemployment, personal reasons such as resentment of implied criticism, or social reasons such as the dislike of outside interference;
- misunderstanding and lack of trust when the reasons for change or its nature and consequences are not understood;
- contradictory assessments, since individuals differ in the way they evaluate costs and benefits;
- low tolerance of change.

Tasks

(i) Consider your own attitude towards change.

(ii) Discuss what action management could take to make change more acceptable to individuals.

Assignment 8.1: Designing an awareness course

You are the assistant training officer in a large company which employs many clerical staff. Your boss has asked you to run a one-day training course to increase employees' awareness of the importance of health and safety in the office environment.

Student activities

(i) How would you approach this task? What information will you need to collect and what consideration would you give to psychological processes in planning your event?

(ii) Design a training programme for the day.

(iii) Produce the training materials needed to run the day using a desktop publishing package.

8.2 Interpersonal Skills

8.2.1 Assertiveness Training

Assertiveness training is about developing the ability to deal confidently with social situations. In assertiveness training a distinction is drawn between *assertion, aggression* and *passivity*.

Being assertive is about handling a situation openly and directly and about coming to a workable compromise with others. Being aggressive involves getting your own way at the expense of others; making them feel incompetent, stupid, worthless or tricked; manipulating them. Being passive means ignoring your own or other's interests and goals. It means not being proactive and involves waiting for others to initiate ideas.

Tasks

(i)   What are your basic rights as an individual in social situations?

(ii) Identify the situations in which you find it difficult to be assertive. Are these a particular type of situation or do you find it difficult to be assertive with particular individuals?

8.2.2 Self-image

A positive *self-image* is important for all interpersonal skills. *E Berne* suggests that we take one of four stances in our dealings with others:

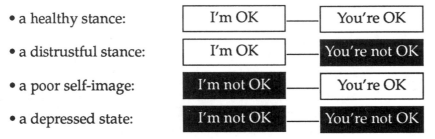

- a healthy stance: I'm OK —— You're OK
- a distrustful stance: I'm OK —— You're not OK
- a poor self-image: I'm not OK —— You're OK
- a depressed state: I'm not OK —— You're not OK

Tasks

(i)   Use Berne's framework to categorise your stance when dealing with particular situations or people.

(ii) Identify events in your life which have contributed to the formation of your self-image.

8.2.3 Impression and Role Management

E Goffman suggests that when we interact with others we constantly manage our own performance. We attempt to adjust the image people have of us to one that is appropriate for our particular objectives in the situation.

Tasks

(i)   List the aspects of your performance that can be controlled. What aspects are more difficult to manage and control?

(ii) Observe people in different occupational settings (lecturers, police officers, sales assistants etc) and assess the degree of impression and role management.

8.2.4 Verbal and Non-verbal Communication

Research indicates that *verbal communication* is less about content and words and more about tone of voice and visual images. It is suggested that *non-verbal communication (body language)* is of major importance in social situations. Non-verbal communication includes:

- physical appearance
- general posture/physique
- proximity
- body contact
- gestures
- facial expressions
- voice quality

Body language should be interpreted with care. Allowances should be made for individual and cultural differences. Judgements should be based on clusters of behaviour rather than any single action or gesture. Finally, it should be remembered that individuals may be actively managing their body language to create a particular impression.

Tasks

(i) Give examples of non-verbal communication in a classroom situation.

(ii) Collect examples of body language from different social settings (behaviour at interviews, in a pub, in a lecture etc).

8.2.5 Formal Presentations

Effective *public speaking* is based on good planning as well as giving consideration to the actual performance. When planning a talk you should:

- identify your personal objectives;
- identify the benefits for the audience;
- list the contents of your talk;
- organise the format and structure of the talk;
- identify any aids (films, handouts etc);
- prepare material (notes, overheads, slides);
- consider other administrative issues (need for projector);
- rehearse.

When giving a talk you should:

- consider the projection of your self-image;
- consider the audience (don't baffle, bore or insult them).

Tasks

(i) Give a talk on a topic of your own choice to your class.

(ii) Go along to a public meeting and collect examples of effective public speaking.

8.2.6 Chairing Meetings

The role of the *chairperson* is to preside, maintain order and ensure that the group does a constructive job of work. To ensure success a chairperson should plan the meeting in advance. He or she should be familiar with the agenda in order to identify the purpose of the meeting. At the start of the meeting the chairperson should communicate this to the group. Clear specific objectives from a well planned agenda forms the basis of control for the chairperson.

During the meeting the chairperson should give attention to both the *task* and the *nature of the group*. He or she should help define the limits of the discussion, keep people to the point, ensure that all views are considered whilst remaining as impartial as possible, summarise the various contributions and draw any conclusions from the discussions. Finally, the chairperson should ensure that a record is made of decisions, actions to be taken and responsibilities.

Tasks

(i)   Role play a meeting.

(ii) Visit your local authority and observe a committee meeting.

8.2.7 Interviewing

Interviewing skills are required in the recruitment and selection of staff (Section 5.3), the collection of market research data and in the control and disciplining of staff. The objective of interviewing is to obtain information. If the information is easily clarified and specific, some degree of structure to the interview (such as a questionnaire) may be appropriate. However, where the information sought is less specific, a more general structure might be needed since there is a danger in the agenda being set by the interviewer. Questions should be open-ended and the interviewer should be prepared to follow and explore the terms of reference provided by the interviewee.

Tasks

(i)   Design a questionnaire to discover how students spend their grant. Use your questionnaire to collect data.

(ii) Interview students concerning their attitudes to smoking.

8.2.8 Listening Techniques

Effective *listening techniques* include:

- clarifying (getting additional facts);
- restating (checking out the meaning);
- reflecting (showing that you understand feelings);
- summarising (bringing the discussion into focus).

Tasks

(i) List the reasons why some people are bad at listening.

(ii) Interview a friend about his or her career plans. Try to improve your listening skills by employing as many listening techniques as appropriate.

8.2.9 Negotiating

Effective *negotiation* (Section 5.5.5) requires a planning phase before the actual face-to-face encounter. In the *planning* phase you should:

- list all the negotiable issues;
- decide your priorities;
- estimate the other party's priorities;
- decide what would be the ideal outcome and the minimum you would accept;
- estimate what the other party's maximum and minimum limits are;
- compare the two ranges and look for a win/win situation;
- consider areas for trade offs/concessions;
- look for creative options;
- list the arguments and reasons that support your case;
- reflect on the arguments that the other party might use.

During the *encounter* you should:

- find out as much as possible about the other party's position, yet reveal as little as possible about your own;
- attempt to change your opponent's expectations;
- highlight strengths and minimise weaknesses of your own arguments.

Tasks

(i) What characteristics do you associate with a good negotiator?

(ii) Role play a negotiation encounter such as a pay claim or a selling situation.

8.2.10 Counselling

Counselling is concerned with helping another individual to solve personal problems. Personal problems often arise from the gap between an individual's current position and their desired state. Although there are different styles of counselling, most counselling techniques involve:

- Encouraging the other person to talk by:
  - offering reassurance;
  - asking open questions;
  - giving attention.

- Helping them to think it through by:
    - admitting your fallibility;
    - offering information rather than views or values;
    - establishing alternatives.
- Letting them find a solution by:
    - accepting their solution;
    - agreeing action;
    - establishing review.

Tasks

(i)   In groups discuss the reasons why counselling is an important managerial skill.

(ii) Explore a personal issue with a friend on which you would like to be counselled.

Assignment 8.2: Developing social skills

Identify a social skill you would like to improve in yourself.

Student activities

(i)   Describe the last occasion that you utilised the skill and analyse your performance.

(ii) Plan to improve your skill by researching the theoretical background to the skill and interviewing competent performers.

(iii) Practise the skill that you wish to improve as appropriate social situations occur.

(iv) Monitor and record your performance in a diary over a two-month period.

8.3 The Nature of Groups

8.3.1 Definition of a Group

A *group* is a number of persons or things gathered, placed or classed together, or working together for some purpose. According to *E Schein* 'a group is any number of people who interact with one another, are psychologically aware of one another, and perceive themselves as a group.'

Tasks

(i)   Which of the following would you consider to be a group?
   - a class of students
   - prison inmates
   - a football crowd
   - a department in an organisation
   - three people
   - passengers on a coach
   - a jury

(ii)   List at least three groups to which you belong.

8.3.2 Types of Groups

In organisations it is useful to distinguish between formal and informal groups. *Formal groups* are established by management to fulfil specific goals and carry out specific tasks which are clearly related to the total organisational mission. These include problem-solving and decision-making, co-ordination and liaison, negotiation and conflict resolution. *Informal groups* are created by organisational members in order to satisfy their affiliation needs and establish their self-concept.

Tasks

(i)   Examine an organisation with which you are familiar and identify the formal and informal groups.

(ii)   Identify the circumstances in which some managers might perceive informal groups to be a threat to their authority.

8.3.3 Characteristics of Groups

One of the most frequently observed characteristics of a work group is the way in which it quickly develops a *culture* of its own. We are able to think of a particular team or work group as if it has an identity of its own and as if the behaviour of its members is predictable. The major feature of this group culture is the development of *group norms*. Norms are standards or codes of behaviour to which members of that group conform. Several researchers and writers, such as *S E Asch, M Sherif, K Lewin, E Mayo and S Milgram,* have suggested that perception, attitudes and behaviour of individuals are all influenced by group pressures.

Because groups tend to foster conformity behaviour, they put pressure on members in decision-making. This conformity is called *groupthink* by *I L Janis*. Groupthink occurs when too high a price is placed on the harmony and morale of the group, so that loyalty to the group's previous policies or to the consensus of the group overrides the conscience of each member.

Risky-shift phenomenon is the tendency for individuals to accept higher levels of risk when taking decisions in groups. One explanation is that there is a diffusion of responsibility, since the group can be blamed if things go wrong.

Tasks

(i) Identify the group norms for a group to which you belong. Do group norms merely control overt behaviour or do they also influence group members' beliefs and values?

(ii) Interview someone who as part of their job works as a member of a group or team (for example, someone who serves on a committee). Discuss with them the advantages and disadvantages of using groups as opposed to individuals to carry out work in their organisation.

8.3.4 Stages of Group Development

Like individuals, groups develop and change over time. The following are the predictable stages through which most groups progress:

- *forming*, the stage of testing by group members to try and determine acceptable behaviour and attitudes;

- *storming*, the time of negotiation and conflict as power and status are allocated to individuals;

- *norming*, the stage at which group norms start develop;

- *performing*, the stage at which the group becomes self-managing. Task are assigned to those best fitted to do them and under the leadership of those best fitted to lead. Everyone knows what part they play in the group, the contribution they can make, and the strengths and weaknesses of the other group members.

Tasks

(i) Consider an occasion when you joined a new group (for example when you transferred from school to college). List the feelings and emotions you experienced.

(ii) Discuss with a work group the stage at which the group is at in terms of its development. Is it a mature group?

8.3.5 Observation of Group Content Versus Group Process

When we observe what a group is talking about we are focusing on the *content*. When we try to observe how the group is interacting we are focusing on group process. Analysing a group process, such as the pattern of communication, rather than focusing on content gives greater insight into how a group is operating.

Process behaviour in a group can be viewed from the point of view of what its purpose or function seems to be. When a member says something, are they primarily trying to get the group's objective accomplished *(task)*, are they trying to patch up some relationship amongst members *(maintenance)*, or are they primarily meeting some personal need or goal without regard to the group's problems *(self-orientated)*?

Tasks

(i) Observe and record the communication pattern in a group.

(ii) Observe and record the task, maintenance and self-orientated behaviours that occur in a group.

8.3.6 Group Dynamics

The term *group dynamics* refers to the forces operating in groups, factors that give rise to them and conditions that modify them. *C Handy* suggests that the determinants of group effectiveness are:

- the *group* (size, member characteristics, individual objectives, and stage of development);

- the *task* (nature of the task, criteria for effectiveness, salience of the task, and clarity of the task);

- the *environment* (the norms and expectations, the leader position, inter-group relations, and the physical location);

- the *intervening factors* (leadership style, process and procedure, and motivation).

Tasks

(i) Discuss with a group that has just completed a task how successful they think they have been. What criteria do they use to measure their effectiveness?

(ii) Use the model developed by Handy to analysis a successful or unsuccessful work group.

8.3.7 Team Roles

According to **R M Belbin**, group members can take various roles. A balanced group requires:

- a chairperson (the co-ordinator);

- a team leader (the shaper who gives the process direction);

- an innovator (the creative thinker);

- a monitor (the critical thinker);

- a company (the worker who gets the task done);

- a team worker (who manages the interpersonal interaction in the group);

- a completer (who keeps the team on its toes by always making reference to the end goal of the decision);

- a resource investigator (who keeps the team in touch with others in the organisation).

Too many of one type in a team indicates a lack of balance; too few roles and some tasks will not get done.

Tasks

(i)   Analyse the team roles adopted by a working group.

(ii) Identify the team roles you occupy and feel comfortable with when you are engaged in group work.

8.3.8 Perspectives on Leadership

The *trait approach* to *leadership* emphasises the characteristics of an individual leader. Traits such as intelligence, self assurance and initiative are considered typical qualities.

The *style approach* explores the impact of various styles of leadership (from autocratic to democratic) on subordinates. *D McGregor* suggests that many managers adopt a particular style due to their basic beliefs concerning human nature.

Theory X managers assume that:

- people dislike work and will avoid it;

- people must be coerced, controlled, directed and threatened in order to get them to work;

- the average person prefers to be directed.

Theory Y managers assume that:

- work is as natural as play;

- people can exercise self direction;

- people seek responsibility;

- the potential in people is not fully exploited by managers.

The *contingency approach* considers the range of factors involved in the leadership situation. In particular, contingency theorists emphasise the task, the work group and the position of the leader.

Tasks

(i)   List the characteristics and competences a good lecturer should display.

(ii) Consider your own beliefs regarding human nature. Are you a Theory X or a Theory Y manager?

8.3.9 Intergroup Conflict

An important objective for managers in organisations is to ensure that work groups are effective in fulfilling both *organisational goals* and the needs of their members. However, as groups become more committed to their own goals and norms they are more likely to become competitive with one another. Therefore, a further objective for managers is to establish conditions between groups that will enhance the *productivity* of each without destroying intergroup relations.

Tasks

(i) Identify departments in an organisation which might be in competition or conflict. What are the effects on a department that finds itself in competition with another part of the organisation?

(ii) Collect newspaper articles about an industrial dispute. Explain why the conflict has arisen.

8.3.10 Resolution of Intergroup Conflict

Research by *M Sherif* suggests various strategies for resolving *intergroup conflict*:

- stress total organisational effectiveness as the superordinate goal of all groups;
- locate a common enemy;
- locate a superordinate goal;
- stimulate high levels of interaction and communication between groups;
- allocate organisational rewards to groups which co-operate, emphasising the pooling of resources and co-operation to increase organisational effectiveness;
- avoid creating win/lose situations;
- rotate members of groups/exchange group membership on a temporary basis to foster mutual understanding between groups;
- bring groups together to analyse their own behaviour and to examine the gains and losses of their conflict.

Tasks

(i) What ideas and lessons do you think the research into the nature of groups and intergroup conflict has for the management of football supporters?

(ii) Suggest how you would reduce conflict between a production department and quality control inspectors.

Assignment 8.3: Provincial Travel

Provincial Travel, a small retail travel agency, has been established for some 20 years. The majority of the staff have been with the company since it was formed. One particular department is staffed by five young travel co-ordinators, three men and two women. The travel co-ordinators are assisted by three middle-aged women who are responsible for the secretarial duties and reception tasks.

Two of these secretaries have been with the company since its foundation and are very friendly with the owner, David Thomas. The third has worked at Provincial for 11 years. All three women are steady, reliable workers and they often do overtime when business is very busy. Although the office atmosphere is friendly and relaxed, the travel co-ordinators and the secretaries rarely mix socially. The three middle-aged women take their coffee breaks together and at lunch-time they eat their sandwiches in a back office or go into the town shopping. They rarely accept invitations from the travel co-ordinators to join them in the local wine bar.

A few months ago Provincial recruited a school leaver, on a temporary contract, to help the three secretaries with the increased summer workload. The school leaver, a girl aged 18, is extrovert with an attractive personality. She enjoys the company of the travel co-ordinators, particularly the three men who are closer to her own age, and she associates with them during coffee breaks and at lunch-time. She has made little effort to become accepted by the three middle-aged secretaries. Despite her limited experience, she handles all the tasks given to her by the travel co-ordinators in a competent manner. Office efficiency appears to have increased since she arrived and the backlog of work has been quickly cleared up.

Unfortunately there is growing unrest amongst the three original secretaries. They resent the new girl and the attention she attracts. They claim that the presence of the new girl is more of a hindrance than a help as they have to show her the office procedures and systems used to progress documentation. One of the older secretaries has expressed the view that if the young girl were to be taken on permanently, she would "have words" with David Thomas and even consider handing in her notice.

Student activities

(i)   Prepare a short word processed report on the causes of the hostility between the three middle-aged secretaries and the new girl.

(ii) In your report give advice to the office manager as to how the situation might be resolved.

8.4 The Impact of Technology

8.4.1 Technological Determinism or Strategic Choice

It is generally recognised that different technologies make different demands on those working with them. Taken to an extreme form, this perspective, *technological determinism*, contends that technology can be used to explain the nature of jobs, work groupings, hierarchy, skills, values and attitudes. Technological determinism is often closely associated with *economic determinism* since organisations may be forced to use new technologies as a result of competitive pressures. Companies which do not introduce the improved technologies that their competitors use inevitably fail.

An alternative approach to technological determinism is *strategic choice*. This maintains that the implementation and the impact of new technology is within the control of management and reflects the choices, based on ideological values, that they make.

Tasks

(i) Examine various manufacturing processes. Does the technology determine the work organisation or is there scope for other arrangements?

(ii) Compare working arrangements at Volvo with those of other car manufacturers.

8.4.2 Technology and Organisational Structure

J Woodward identifies three types of *production process* (unit, mass or process) and suggests that each category is associated with a particular *organisational structure*. The following all increase as the *technology* involved moves along the continuum from unit to process:

- the length of the line of command;
- the span of control of the chief executive;
- the percentage of turnover devoted to wages;
- the ratio of managers to others;
- the ratio of graduates to non-graduates;
- the ratio of indirect to direct labour.

C Perrow suggests that the extent to which the technology is *predictable* is the key factor in assessing the impact of technology on organisational structure. More routine technologies permit more bureaucratic organisational structures to be developed. The reverse is true for non-routine, ill-defined technologies.

Tasks

(i) List the characteristics of unit, mass, and process production processes.

(ii) Visit organisations that have unit, mass and process production processes and observe the organisational arrangements.

8.4.3 Technology and Job Satisfaction

Many observers suggest that the introduction of new technology frequently results in increased task specialisation and lower levels of skill on the part of the operator. When jobs are reduced to their simplest elements and the degree of skill is minimal, there is little scope for job satisfaction.

Tasks

(i) What are the advantages for management of introducing new technology?

(ii) Use J R Hackman's job characteristics model to analyse the impact of new technology on a particular job. Is deskilling an inevitable consequence of the introduction of new technology?

8.4.4 Technology and Alienation

R Blauner attempts to identify the degree of *alienation* associated with technology by exploring alienation in four dimensions:

- powerlessness (lack of control);
- meaninglessness (lack of co-ordinated activity);
- isolation (lack of social interaction);
- self-estrangement (loss of personal identity).

He concludes that alienation varies with the type of technology and that advanced technology would reduce alienation. With advanced technology all the boring, mundane jobs are done by robots and other automated tools, leaving individuals free to concentrate on more creative areas.

Tasks

(i) Use Blauner's framework to measure the degree of alienation you experience on your current course.

(ii) Do you agree with Blauner's optimistic conclusion?

8.4.5 Technology and Managerial Control

Many observers suggest that *technology* cannot be viewed as politically neutral. The kind of technology employed influences the patterns of interdependence in an organisation and thus the *power relations* between different individuals. The introduction of new technology can alter the balance of power.

In the labour process debate *H Braverman* proposes that the introduction of new technology could be used by management to extend control over a situation by deliberately increasing task specialisation, reducing the levels of skill required and increasing discipline in the workplace. Through the introduction of new technology it is suggested that management not only reduces costs and increases profitability, but also maintains and advances their own status as the controlling group in the organisation. Critics of Braverman claim that management is not as powerful as he suggests, that he romanticises the skilled craft worker of the past and that in many cases jobs are upgraded by new technology.

Tasks

(i) Review the introduction of new technology in the printing industry in the 1980s. To what extent were managers motivated by economic or political considerations?

(ii) Draw up a list of jobs which have been enhanced by theintroduction of the new technology.

8.4.6 The Socio-Technical Approach

E Trist suggests that any production system requires both material technology and a social organisation of its operators. This *social organisation* has social and psychological properties which are not dependent on the demands of the technology. Both the nature of the technical system and the social system should be taken into account when designing production.

Tasks

(i) For several years the typing and correspondence in an organisation has been carried out by personal secretaries using typewriters. Consider what problems might arise in changing to a centralised word processing typing pool.

(ii) Research suggests that experienced pilots do not always enthuse about the automated controls now fitted to aircraft. Explain why this should be the case.

8.4.7 New Technology - Microelectronics

Technological change has always been a feature of organisational life. However, in recent years with the development of *microelectronics*, in particular the *microprocessor*, very rapid changes in the design and manufacture of products and in the nature of jobs and work organisation have become possible.

Tasks

(i) What do you understand by the term *microprocessor*? List as many examples as you can of products that use microprocessors and identify their impact on jobs.

(ii) Do you view the microelectronic revolution as a positive or negative development? Examine in particular its impact on the balance of power between management and workers, employment opportunities, and skill levels.

8.4.8 Computer-based Technology in the Office

Office automation is a generalised, comprehensive term applied to the processes that integrate computer and communication technology with the traditional manual processes. Most office functions, such as typing, filing, and communications, can be automated.

- *Word processing* is the manipulation of written text.
- *Electronic mail* is the transmission of messages at high speeds over telecommunication facilities.
- *Teleconferencing* permits two or more individual in different locations to communicate.
- *Telecomputing* is the provision of online information services.

Sections 9.6 and 9.7 give further details of the application of computers and use of software packages.

Tasks

(i) What are the main characteristics of a successful word processing operator? How well do they fit your own idea of job satisfaction?

(ii) List the possible consequences for word processing operators of working at a keyboard for most of the working day.

8.4.9 Computer-Based Technology on the Shop-floor

- *Computer aided design (CAD)* allows engineers to design, draft, and analyse a product using computer graphics.

- *Computer aided manufacture (CAM)* allows engineers to analyse the manufacturing process.

- *Computer integrated manufacturing* links various departments of a company into a central data base.

- *Robotics* is the automation of manual tasks.

Tasks

(i) In groups discuss the impact and implications of introducing robotics in a production department.

(ii) Arrange to interview checkout operators in your local supermarket. What advantages are there for them of an electronic point of sale (EPOS) system? Are there any disadvantages?

Assignment 8.4: Introducing new technology

Arrange to visit a local bank or building society in order to collect information on the impact of new technology on their operations.

Student activities

(i) Interview the managers to establish their view of the use of technology and the problems and opportunities that it presents.

(ii) Interview members of staff who use the technology about the implications for how they do their jobs.

(iii) Write a word-processed report on the introduction of new technology into the organisation that you have visited.

8.5 The Nature of Organisations

8.5.1 The Classical Perspective

The main feature of the *classical perspective* is the attempt to study organisations with scientific and machine-like precepts. The classical approach assumes that the individual will always act in the interests of the organisation, is motivated primarily by financial incentives, and can be relied upon to act rationally. The classical perspective incorporates the ideas of *F W Taylor* (scientific management), *H Fayol* and *L Urwick* (administrative principles), and *M Weber* (bureaucratic model).

Tasks

(i) Analysis how your present course is managed. What assumptions are made about students? How are students controlled and rewarded?

(ii) List the advantages and disadvantages of a bureaucratic organisation.

8.5.2 The Human Relations Perspective

The main focus of the *human relations perspective* is on individuals and their social interaction. Human relations theorists emphasise needs, attitudes, values and emotional responses as key to understanding and managing organisations. In terms of its assumptions about human behaviour in organisations, the human relations approach assumes that individuals are not principally motivated by external financial rewards but by social, ego and self-actualisation needs. The human relations approach incorporates the ideas of *E Mayo* (research into groups at Hawthorne plant), *A Maslow* (hierarchy of needs theory) and *F Herzberg* (motivation-hygiene theory).

Tasks

(i) How would you organise the relationship between student and lecturer so that it reflected the human relations approach? Would it work?

(ii) List the various intrinsic and extrinsic rewards that motivate you. Which list is more important to you?

8.5.3 The Systems Perspective

The *systems perspective* sees an organisation as a collection of *interdependent sub-units*. It can be represented as a simple open system with inputs, some form of conversion process, and outputs. Rather than seeing organisations in mechanical terms like the classical approach, it uses biological analogies and metaphors. It also calls attention to a wide range of social, psychological, economic and technical forces operating on and within an organisation.

Critics of the systems perspective claim that the approach is too deterministic and that it does not give enough weight to the role that humans play in interpreting and creating their own environment.

Tasks

(i) Identify the inputs and outputs for a manufacturing organisation, a bank or a fast food outlet.

(ii) List the main environmental systems that impinge on a cigarette manufacturer.

8.5.4 Organisations as Political Systems

The *unitary perspective* regards organisations as a large family or a team: there is one source of authority and all individuals accept their place in the team so as to achieve a common goal.

The *pluralistic perspective* regards organisations as coalition governments. It is recognised that the organisation consists of many groups or stakeholders and therefore limited common purpose. The problem for the leaders is to balance the activities of the constituent groups so as to achieve the organisation's objectives.

The *Marxist perspective* regards organisations as an extension of the class power struggle in society. Managers in organisations are paid to achieve the best results for their shareholders. Invariably managers give greater priority to the needs of capitalists than they do to the needs of their employees.

Tasks

(i) How do you think people who adopt a unitary perspective would see the need for and role of trade unions?

(ii) Collect copies of companies' annual reports and accounts and see to what extent directors recognise any wider obligations they may have to other groups in addition to their shareholders.

8.5.5 Organisational Culture

The *culture* of an organisation consists of the *beliefs, values, norms and ideals* of members concerning the way in which the organisation operates. Culture is expressed by the way people do things in the organisation and is given a tangible form in the shape of rules, systems and structures. *R Harrison* identifies four distinct cultures and their associated rules, systems and structures.

- *Power culture* is typical of small entrepreneurial organisations. It depends on a central power source, has few rules and procedures, is power-orientated and risk taking.

- *Role culture* is typical of bureaucracies where organisation is arranged by function and specialities, and is controlled by rules and procedures.

- *Task culture* is typical of project-based matrix organisations where the emphasis is on getting the job done, using experts working as a team, and is a decentralised, adaptable, flexible externally focussed organisation.

- *Person culture* is typical of small professional organisations where the individual is the pivot around which the organisation revolves and structure is minimal.

Tasks

(i) Describe the culture in your college. How does it differ from other educational establishments you have experienced?

(ii) How would you classify the dominant culture in a small family business, a barrister's chambers, the civil service and an advertising agency?

8.5.6 Organisational Structure

The main function of *organisational structure* is to assist in the attainment of organisational objectives. It is concerned with allocating people and tasks and indicating to members what is expected of them (*operating procedures*). The basic structure of an organisation is usually represented by an *organisational chart*.

Although organisations may be structured in several ways (departments may be grouped by product, by customer, by location etc) the most common grouping is by *function*. A major problem in the design of organisations is achieving a balance between uniformity (reflected by standardisation and central control) and allowing for diversity (reflected by experimentation and autonomy).

Tasks

(i) Draw up a chart of the organisational structure of your college.

(ii) Visit a local organisation and draw up the organisational chart for that business. Explore alternative ways in which it might be organised and comment on the implications and consequences of a different structure.

8.5.7 Technology and Environmental Influences on Structure

J Child considers that the design of organisations is the outcome of strategic choice exercised by the management team. However, other researchers consider that the manager's freedom to act is limited. They believe that successful organisations develop a structure which reflects their technology *(J Woodward and C Perrow)* or their environment *(P Lawrence, T Burns and G Stalker)*.

- *Technological determinism* is founded on the belief that the complexity of production process (unit, mass or process) or technical predictability determines organisational relationships.

- *Environmental determinism* is based on the fact that an organisation is dependent on its environment for sales, labour, raw materials which places constraints on the choices an organisation can make about its structure. In complex and turbulent environments organic *organisational structures* are best; in less complex, more stable environments *mechanistic organisational structures* are appropriate.

Tasks

(i) Identify the technology used in a small jobbing foundry, a volume car producer and a large chemical company. To what extent does technology determine organisational structure?

(ii) What type of organisational structure would you need to be successful in the computer market?

8.5.8 Organisational Change

Change in organisations may be achieved by directly changing the attitudes, beliefs and values of individuals or indirectly by changing the structure, technology or goals of an organisation. *Change agents* are specialists in the facilitation of change. A range of change strategies may be utilised including the following:

- *power-coercive strategies* which reward or punish different behaviours;

- *rational-legal strategies* which appeal to logic and rules;

- *normative-re-educative strategies* which change values and norms.

Tasks

(i) List the factors that cause organisations to change.

(ii) In groups discuss the change strategies used by successive governments in changing people's behaviour with regard to drinking and driving, wearing car seat belts or the prevention of Aids.

Assignment 8.5: Using a systems model

Use the systems model to analyse your college.

Student activities

(i) Draw a systems model of your college. Distinguish the inputs into the system, clarify the conversion process and identify the outputs of the system.

(ii) List the main environmental systems that impinge on your educational establishment.

(iii) Identify the forces that are creating change in the system.

8.6 Organisational Power and Control

8.6.1 Perspectives on Organisations as Political Systems

Research into organisational power and control has been conducted along various dimensions. Some authors *(J French, B Raven)* focus on interpersonal power. Others focus at a structural level, either on the situational dynamics between departments *(G Strauss, D J Hickson)* or on the nature of managerial prerogative *(Karl Marx, A Fox)*.

The terms *politician* and *political* are often used in a negative manner to indicate double-dealing or dishonesty. However, politics and political individuals can be regarded in a more positive light if politics is defined as the decision-making process for deciding aims and objectives, and allocating scarce resources. The absence of politics results in the dictatorship of one group over another.

Tasks

(i) List the advantages and disadvantages of an organisation being a political system.

(ii) To what extent is your college a political institution?

8.6.2 The Concept of Power

The possession of *power* enables an individual to exercise some degree of *control* over others. Power is *relative* since people rarely have total power over others. In some cases another individual's power and source of influence may hold no importance for those they are trying to control; even the threat of death may not be significant.

Individuals may be able to exert *negative* power. In an extreme situation, such as a prison, individuals may still endeavour to exert their power by trying to escape or by being disruptive. Power is often located in a particular *domain*. Individuals who retire from powerful positions often find that they become powerless once outside of their former organisations.

> **Tasks**
>
> (i) What power do you have in relation to the teaching staff at your college and your parents?
>
> (ii) Interview employees at work and ask them how much power they feel that they have.

8.6.3 The Concept of Control

The *concept of control* has both positive and negative aspects. A degree of predictability, order, reliability and stability in a situation is often desirable. Control gives individuals feedback, a framework in which to work and is welcomed by those who enjoy dependency.

The negative aspects are coercion, domination, exploitation and manipulation. Marxists see control by managers as a form of social control exercised on behalf of capitalists.

> **Tasks**
>
> (i) Analyse how control is exercised on your current course. Who sets the standards, enforces them and measures them? How could the control process be improved?
>
> (ii) Do you believe that some individuals prefer to be controlled? If so, why should this be?

8.6.4 Sources of Interpersonal Power

J French and *B Raven* identify various sources of power and types of influence:

- *physical/coercive* where an individual has the ability to threaten or punish others and influence is through force;

- *resource/reward* where an individual has control over resources desired by others and influence is through bargaining and exchange;

- *positional* where a position in the organisation is regarded as being legitimate and therefore anyone occupying that role has rights over others; influence is through rules and procedures;

- *expert* where an individual has more knowledge or skill than others and influence is through logic and persuasion;

- *personal/charismatic* where the attractiveness of a person's personality causes others to defer to them and influence is through loyalty and faith.

Tasks

(i) Interview individuals in an organisation and establish which forms of power exercised by their bosses are most acceptable to them and why.

(ii) Compare military, commercial, non-profit making and voluntary organisations. Is there any difference between the types of power and methods of influence exercised in the various organisation?

8.6.5 Situational Sources of Power

D J Hickson suggests that in order to acquire power, individuals or departments need to be indispensable, in the right place at the right time and considered to be doing a critically important job. Power comes from:

- being able to cope with uncertainty;
- being non-substitutable;
- being central.

Tasks

(i) Use Hickson's model to analyse the power of different departments in your college.

(ii) Suggest ways in which an individual might increase their situational power.

8.6.6 Perspectives on Managerial Prerogative

A Fox outlines three different perspectives that individuals take regarding *managerial power* in organisations. The *unitary view* sees power and control residing with the owners of the organisation, or with their agents, who have the right to exercise control for the benefit of the shareholders. This view is regarded as legitimate since not only do shareholders legally own the business, but it is suggested that they bear a great deal of the risk.

The *pluralistic view* suggests that organisations are made up of coalitions of interest groups. Power is shared. Objectives and the way in which they will be put into operation are open to discussion and negotiation.

The *Marxist (radical) view* is that organisations should be controlled by their workers. The ability of capitalists to invest in organisations is a reflection of the unequal and unfair distribution of wealth in society. It is suggested that workers invest their lives in an organisation and therefore have a far stronger claim to control an organisation than those who merely have a financial interest.

Tasks

(i) Consider the following issues
- redundancy
- recruitment and selection
- investment policy
- wages
- working conditions
- health and safety
- introduction of new technology

Do you think workers should be consulted and be able to negotiate on these issues?

(ii) Who do you think has the greater claim to have ultimate power: shareholders or workers? Do you think that owning your own business would alter your perspective?

8.6.7 Frontiers of Control

R Hyman suggests that in every workplace there is an invisible *frontier of control* where management and workers contest power and control. Management strategies to enhance control include the use of:

- organisational structure and job descriptions;
- recruitment and selection;
- rewards and punishments;
- policies and procedures;
- budgets;
- technology.

Workers' strategies include:

- organisation of a trade union;
- demarcation;
- restrictive practices;
- control over jobs;
- control over recruitment;
- control over wage levels.

Tasks

(i) In groups debate whether trade unions have too much power.

(ii) Should trade unions deal only with wages and conditions or should they develop policies on wider issues of concern to their members?

Assignment 8.6: Bath Light Engineering plc

Bath Light Engineering plc is a large national engineering company with several thousand employees. The head office is based in Bath with six regional manufacturing sites and several sales offices around the UK.

The company is organised on traditional centralised, functional lines and is chaired by a chief executive with directors of operations, marketing, finance, research and development, personnel and purchasing. The directors are qualified professionals with a good deal of experience in the industry. All the directors are aged over fifty.

David Grey has had exceptional and striking success at Bath Light Engineering. At the age of 25, after experience primarily as a sales representative in Leeds, David was appointed as their Yorkshire regional sales manager. Within five years he became the youngest ever general manager of one of the production sites in Scotland.

One year the company's annual report and accounts contained a photograph of David (the only general manager ever to be honoured in this way). The caption described him as an example of what could happen to other aspiring young executives.

After four years he was promoted to the main board as assistant chief executive. He was given specific responsibility to assist the chief executive in developing a more decentralised organisation. This was to be achieved by conferring greater autonomy and decision-making power on production site general managers.

Student activities

(i)   Identify the problems David Grey might have in establishing himself in his new post.

(ii) What strategies would be useful in overcoming any problems he may encounter?

8.7 The Social Environment

8.7.1 The Nature of the Social Environment

Stratification is the idea that society is divided into a patterned structure of unequal groups. The basis of stratification in most societies is economic relationships (class societies), but other forms include those based on caste or age-set.

Patterns of *inequality* between groups are reflected in life-chances (such as wealth, income, health, job security), social status and political influences. Typical classifications of *social class divisions* are:

- an *upper class* which consists of the owners of the means of production who have advantageous life chances;
- a *middle class* comprising non-owners of wealth who have advantageous life chances due to education and skills;
- a *working class* also comprising non-owners of wealth but members of the working class have disadvantaged life chances due to limited market capacity for manual skills;
- the *poor* who have grossly disadvantaged life-chances due to the marginal position in labour market.

Tasks

(i) Using Social Trends, which is published by HMSO, examine the distribution of wealth and income in British society.

(ii) List the Registrar General's social classifications. Where would you place yourself?

8.7.2 Social Mobility

Social mobility has two aspects: *Intergenerational mobility* (offspring may have different social position to parents) and *intragenerational mobility* (individuals change their social position during their career). A major institution with the potential to assist social mobility is the educational system.

Tasks

(i) Conduct a local survey to find out the degree to which people feel there is social mobility.

(ii) Debate the extent to which the education system gives equal opportunities to all social groups.

8.7.3 Patterns of Women's Work

Participation: Women form over 40 per cent of the workforce. Over 40 per cent of women of working age work. Married women form over 40 per cent of the female workforce. In recent years more women have entered employment as a result of changes in women's expectations and economic requirements, and the fact that they live longer and have fewer children in a more concentrated period. At the same time there have been structural opportunities for them to find work, especially in the administrative and service sectors.

Job segregation: Although there has been some decline in numbers of occupations which are exclusively single sex in recent years, more than half of employed women work in three service sectors: distributive trades (shops, mail order, warehouses); professional and scientific (typing, secretarial, teaching, nursing); and miscellaneous (laundries, catering, dry cleaning).

Career progression: Men dominate authority structures in both predominantly male and predominantly female industries. For example, in banking where a high proportion of women are employed, only a very small percentage of branch managers are women. Similarly, in retailing only around one-third of managers are women.

Time at work: Compared with men, women work shorter hours, fewer work shifts and women are given less overtime. A high percentage of women work part-time compared to men.

Pay: There are still significant differences between men's and women's earnings, both in terms of hourly pay and weekly pay. To some extent this reflects the fact that women are grouped in a separate labour market. However, even in jobs where women are integrated with men and rates of basic pay are the same, men still earn more. This reflects the fact that men do more overtime, more men do shift work, men are likely to have been employed for longer and therefore qualify for length of service awards. In addition, men hold a disproportionate number of merit or responsibility positions.

Tasks

(i) Conduct research in your own college to establish what kind of jobs women do. Are their jobs as responsible, as satisfying, and as well paid as men's jobs?

(ii) Discuss the extent to which women work in female dominated occupations. Are they excluded from more prestigious and remunerative occupations?

8.7.4 Legislation and Gender

The *Equal Pay Act 1970* gives women a right to equal pay for work which is of the same or of a broadly similar nature or which has been given equal value with a man's under a job evaluation scheme. The *Sex Discrimination Act 1975* is a comprehensive framework of legislation which has made discrimination on the grounds of sex unlawful. The *Employment Protection Act 1975* includes provision for maternity pay and reinstatement rights.

See also Sections 3.3.3 and 5.2.6.

Tasks

(i) Discuss the impact of legislation on gender inequality at work.

(ii) Find out what maternity rights women have.

8.7.5 Employers and Gender

Recent research suggests that employers are now less likely to stereotype women than in earlier years. Most employers claim to operate *equal opportunity* policies, but evidence suggests that women are still not achieving their full potential. Employers complain that not enough female applicants apply for posts. When they do so, they do not always have the appropriate skills or experience, may not be physically strong enough for certain jobs or are not available for shift work.

It is significant that employers have moved very slowly in designing work to suit women. Nursery provision is rare. The expansion in part-time employment has not been designed to meet the needs of women. Instead it helps employers overcome difficulties in getting full-time workers or meets the need for additional labour at times of peak production.

Tasks

(i) Conduct a survey of crèche facilities in local companies. How easy is it for a woman to combine a job or a career with family commitments?

(ii) Interview employers about their equal opportunity policies. Find outhow the policy is monitored and enforced.

8.7.6 Gender Socialisation

Socialisation is the imposition of social patterns on behaviour. It is the process through which an individual learns to be a member of a society. Biological explanations (women by nature have a key child-bearing role) and cultural explanations (women traditionally are primarily responsible for child rearing) of the tendency of males to assert dominance and for women to take up a supportive role have been proposed.

Tasks

(i) List examples of how young boys and girls are treated differently.

(ii) Interview a female manager. List the problems she has faced. How does she explain her success?

8.7.7 Definition of Race and Related Concepts

Race is any of the major divisions of mankind with certain inherited physical characteristics in common, such as skin and hair colour.

The classification of people by *genotype* groups them according to their genes. Genes are the set of instructions for physical and intellectual development. Much of the biological research into race has been directed to locating and establishing the nature of genotypes.

Observers suggest that the establishment of whether or not there is a biological basis to race is not necessarily important, since the concept of race has also a social reality. Many people believe in the existence of race and the division of people into groups, and base their actions on this belief.

Racism is the idea that human abilities are determined by race. *Racialism* is the belief in the superiority of a particular race. This may lead to discrimination. An *ethnic group* is a racial group. Members are united because of their common background. An ethnic group is subjectively defined in that it is what the group members feel is important in defining themselves as a united people. There is frequently a coincidence between what others feel to be a racial group and what the members of the group think. For example, whites may think of Asians as a racial group; Asians may think of themselves as a united and therefore an ethnic group.

Tasks

(i) Conduct a survey to find out what people understand by the term *race*.

(ii) Interview members of an ethnic minority group and record their experiences of the attitudes of the majority white population towards them.

8.7.8 Race and Employment

Numerous studies on employment patterns conclude that *ethnic minority groups* experience greater difficulties in entering the labour market. In addition, they are less well represented in those occupations and positions that are usually considered most desirable. They are over-represented in those occupations considered most undesirable and they tend to face amuch higher risk of unemployment.

See also Sections 3.3.3 and 5.2.6.

Tasks

(i) List the occupations where ethnic minority groups have most easily found employment. Explain why this pattern has emerged.

(ii) Investigate the employment of ethnic minority groups in your own college.

8.7.9 Legislation and Race

The *Race Relations Act 1976* makes discrimination unlawful and victims were provided with redress. The *Commission for Racial Equality (CRE)* was established to work towards the elimination of racial discrimination and to promote equality of opportunity. The *British Nationality Act 1981* establishes three classes of British citizenship.

See also Sections 3.3.3 and 5.2.6.

Tasks

(i) To what extent do you think the law can be used to improve race relations?

(ii) In groups debate whether the quality of life in the UK is best enhanced by the integration of new groups and their cultures or by their total assimilation.

8.7.10 Employers and Race

The *role of employers* in ensuring good race relations is unclear. Many organisations consider that their prime function is to run their business, not act as social engineers. Other organisations, either out of a belief that there may be some economic advantage or from a genuine feeling that they have a responsibility to make a contribution, engage in a range of activities designed to change the situation. These includes:

- equal opportunity policies;

- ethnic monitoring;

- contract compliance;

- positive discrimination.

Tasks

(i) Interview local organisations to establish their attitude towards racial issues. Establish what policies they have and comment on their success.

(ii) In groups debate the justice of positive discrimination.

Assignment 8.7: Recruiting women

Over the next few years demographic changes will result in fewer young school leavers. In order to make up for this labour shortage organisations are having to consider the recruitment of more women into their workforce.

Student activities

Write an article for a local newspaper suggesting how a local company might attract and retain women workers. You should use diagrams and illustrations and support your arguments with relevant statistics. A spreadsheet or desktop publishing package should be used to prepare the material.

Section 9
Quantitative Methods and Information Technology

by Paul Goodwin

MSc, Senior Lecturer in Quantitative Methods at Bristol Polytechnic

Quantitative methods can be broadly divided into statistics and quantitative modelling. Statistics is concerned with the collection, analysis, interpretation and presentation of quantitative data. Quantitative models are usually simplified representations of problems which are designed to allow decision-makers to gain a greater understanding of the problems they face. Information technology is the technology used to gather, store, process and communicate information.

Recommended Reading

Francis, A., *Business Mathematics and Statistics, 2nd Edition,* DP Publications, 1988

French, C. S., *Data Processing and Information Technology, 8th Edition,* DP Publications, 1990

Morris, C., *Quantitative Approaches in Business Studies, 2nd Edition,* Pitman, 1989

Owen, F., & Jones, R., *Modern Analytical Techniques, 2nd Edition,* Pitman, 1988

Owen, F., & Jones, R., *Statistics, 3rd Edition,* Pitman, 1990

Rowntree, D., *Statistics Without Tears: a primer for non-mathematicians,* Pelican, 1981

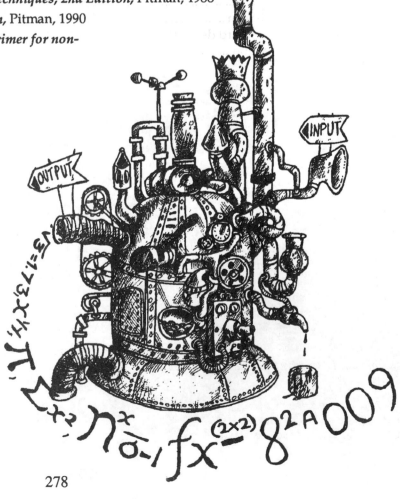

The quantitative model was working overtime...

Contents

9.1 The Collection of Data

9.1.1 Sources of Data

The main sources of *statistical data* are:

- surveys conducted for a specific purpose;
- published statistics supplied by the government or other organisations;
- internal records kept by companies and other organisations (for example personnel records).

Task

You are thinking of opening a record shop in your home town. Make a list of the statistical information which you would like to have before making your decision and identify possible sources for this information.

9.1.2 Terms used in Connection with Surveys

A *population* is the complete collection of people or objects which is relevant to the aims of the survey. A *sample* is a sub-group selected from the population.

A *sampling frame* is, ideally, a complete specification of the population in the form of a list, register or map etc (for example an electoral register, a telephone book) from which the sample is selected.

In *probability (random) sampling* every member of the population has a chance of being selected and the probability of any individual being selected can be measured. Probability samples require a sampling frame.

Tasks

(i) Identify a sampling frame which could be used to take a sample of:
- students attending your college;
- supermarkets in your town;
- streets in your town.

In each case make an assessment as to how accurately the sampling frame represents the population.

(ii) Make a list of business applications of sampling and in each case explain the advantages of using samples rather than surveys of the entire population.

9.1.3 Types of Sample

Simple random sampling gives every member of the population an equal chance of being selected. It may involve drawing names from a hat or using a computer to generate random numbers which can then be used to select individuals from the sampling frame.

Systematic sampling involves selecting every nth item from the sampling frame after a random start. For example, we might select every 50th name from the electoral register.

In *stratified sampling* the population is first divided into distinct groups (or strata) and a random sample is selected from each stratum. For example, if a company employs 700 men and 300 women, a stratified sample of 100 employees might involve randomly selecting 70 men and 30 women so that both sexes are adequately represented in the sample.

Quota sampling involves giving interviewers quotas of different types of people to question; for example 20 males aged under 21, 30 females aged over 60 etc. The sizes of the quotas are designed to reflect the make up of the population.

Cluster sampling involves making a random selection from a frame listing groups of individuals, rather than the individuals themselves. Every individual belonging to the selected groups is then interviewed or examined. For example, courses might be sampled from a college prospectus and every student on the selected courses interviewed.

Multi-stage sampling is used where the groups selected in a cluster sample are too large so that a sub-sample has to be selected from each group. For example, first select a sample of polytechnics; from each of these polytechnics select a sample of courses; from each of these courses select a sample of students.

Tasks

Explain how you would select the following samples and in each case, justify your choice of method:

(i)   a sample of 1,000 people aged over 18 living on the UK mainland to determine their views on a proposed new national television channel;

(ii) a sample of 30 train arrivals at your local station next month to determine the percentage of trains which arrive more than five minutes late.

9.1.4 Carrying out a Survey

The main ways of collecting data in a *survey* are:

- personal interviews;
- telephone interviews;
- mail questionnaires.

Tasks

(i)   List the pros and cons of using each of these collection methods in a survey of (i) in the preceding task.

(ii) Design a questionnaire to determine the views of students at your college *either* on the car parking facilities at the college *or* the college library.

9.1.5 Published Statistics

The main supplier of *published statistics* is the government whose publications include:

- The *Annual Abstract of Statistics* (and the associated Monthly Digest of Statistics) which covers a wide range of areas, including population, transport, education, retail prices and industrial production.

- The *Employment Gazette* which gives statistics relating to the labour market such as unemployment, vacancies and industrial disputes.

- The *Family Expenditure Survey* which gives details of spending patterns of private households.

Tasks

(i) Identify the publications which contain statistics on:

   - air traffic between the UK and abroad;

   - company insolvencies in England and Wales;

   - expenditure by households in Greater London on furniture;

(ii) Write a short article for a newspaper explaining the difficulties involved in making international comparisons of industrial relations statistics.

Assignment 9.1: Conducting a survey

You have been asked to conduct a survey of either the population of your town or city or the population of students at your college in order to assess attitudes to and usage of one of the following: the local public transport system; the sports and leisure facilities provided by the local council; facilities provided locally for recycling waste materials.

Student activities

(i) Design a questionnaire.

(ii) Decide upon a suitable sampling method.

(iii) Carry out the survey using personal interviews.

(iv) Present your results in the form of a word processed report. Your report should also include a justification of your survey method and a discussion of any reservations you may have about the reliability of your results.

9.2 Conveying Information

9.2.1 Using Graphs and Charts

Graphs and *charts* are often more effective than words in conveying quantitative data. To display information clearly the graph or chart should have:

- a clear title;

- clear labels for axes;

- an indication of the units being used, such as £s, tonnes, thousands of passengers;

- if the data is secondary, a reference to its source.

9.2.2 Pie Charts

Pie charts can be used to show how a total is made up. They are not effective when they contain too many sectors or when it is necessary to compare how different totals are made up.

Task

Obtain data for a recent period on UK exports (in £m) by countries. Construct a pie chart to show how total exports to EEC countries were divided between the member countries (group countries buying few exports under 'Other countries').

9.2.3 Bar Charts

There are a number of types of *bar chart* including:

- the *component (stacked) bar chart* which enables totals to be compared and also shows how these totals are made up (see Figure 9.1(a));

- the *multiple bar chart* which enables the size of the components to be compared when the totals are of no interest (see Figure 9.1(b)).

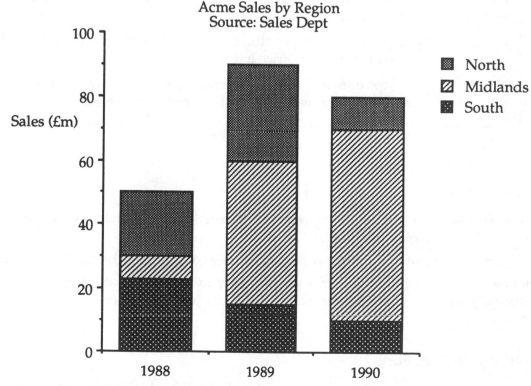

Figure 9.1(a)   Component (Stacked) Bar Chart

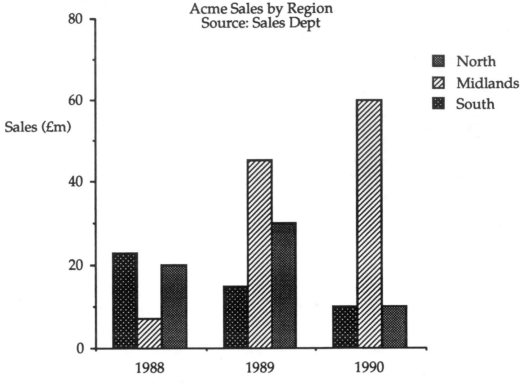

Figure 9.1(b) Multiple Bar Chart

Tasks

Obtain recent statistics on the following topics, and use an appropriate graph or chart to represent the information:

(i) the percentage of total expenditure by the 'average' household on the main categories used in the Retail Price Index;

(ii) the total number of motor vehicles licensed in each of the last five years, and how these totals were split between different categories of vehicle.

9.2.4 Other Types of Graph

Other types of graph include:

- *pictograms* where quantities are represented pictorially, rather than by bars or lines, in order to make the display more attractive;

- *semi-logarithmic graphs* which allow percentage rates of change to be displayed clearly;

- *Lorenz curves* which show the degree of inequality in the way a total figure is shared out (for example, 90 per cent of the market is supplied by just five per cent of the companies in that market).

9.2.5 Frequency Distributions

Large sets of data are often more easily comprehended when they are organised into *frequency distributions* like the one shown below:

Travel-to-work time of a sample of 70 London commuters

Travel time (minutes)	Number of commuters
0 to under 20	4
20 to under 40	18
40 to under 60	34
60 to under 120	14
Total	70

The categories of travel times (0 to under 20 minutes etc) are known as classes. The number of commuters belonging to a class is referred to as the frequency of the class.

Task

Given below is a set of raw data on the amount spent (to the nearest £) by a sample of 40 supermarket customers. Organise this data into a frequency distribution and discuss what it shows.

20	15	1	24	3	2	26	3	20	23
27	25	4	18	28	18	29	11	25	19
34	21	26	5	12	12	4	10	49	29
8	5	26	8	25	6	21	9	6	26

9.2.6 Histograms

A *histogram* is a graphical representation of a frequency distribution. Figure 9.2 shows a histogram for the commuter travel-to-work time data. Note that it is the area, rather than the height, of the bars which is proportional to the class frequencies; because the last class is three times wider than the others, its height has been reduced to one third of its frequency.

In this case, height $= \dfrac{14}{3} = 4.67$

The vertical axis is therefore labelled *frequency density*.

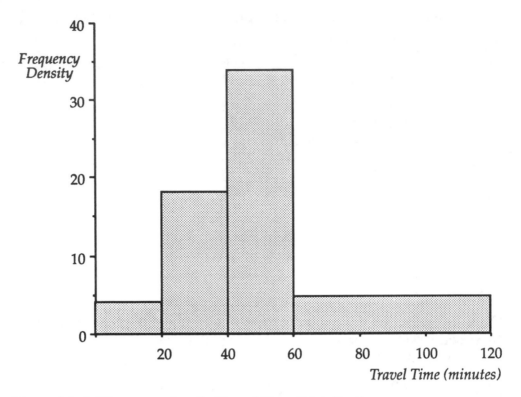

Figure 9.2 A Histogram for the Travel Time Distribution

Task

Construct a histogram for the supermarket expenditure data given in Section 9.2.5 and comment on its shape.

9.2.7 Cumulative Frequency Distributions and Ogives

A *cumulative frequency distribution* shows the number of observations which fall below certain values in a distribution.

Example

The cumulative distribution for the travel-to-work time data from Section 9.2.5 shows that 56 commuters had a journey of less than 60 minutes duration.

Travel time (minutes)	Number of commuters = cumulative frequency
under 20	4
under 40	4 + 18 = 22
under 60	22 + 34 = 56
under 120	56 + 14 = 70

An *ogive* is a graph of a cumulative frequency distribution. Figure 9.3 shows an ogive for the travel-to-work time data.

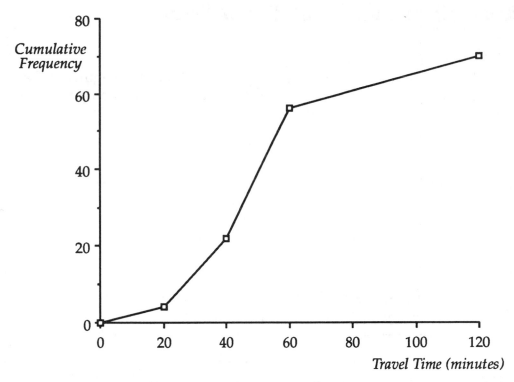

Figure 9.3 *An Ogive for the Travel Time Distribution*

Tasks

Construct a cumulative frequency distribution and an ogive for the supermarket expenditure data given in Section 9.2.5. Use it to estimate the following:

(i)   the percentage of customers who spent less than £15;

(ii) the expenditure level which half the customers fell below.

Assignment 9.2: Writing a chapter for a training manual

You have been asked by your company to write a chapter entitled *The Do's and Don'ts of Effective Data Presentation* for a company in-house training manual.

Student activities

(i)   Obtain or invent a set of data relating to a company's operations.

(ii) Write the chapter, basing your examples of good and bad practice on the data in (i).

Use a desktop publishing package if possible.

9.3 The Analysis and Interpretation of Data

9.3.1 Sigma Notation

The Greek letter Σ (sigma) means 'add up'. Thus Σx means 'add up all the figures in the column or row labelled x'. In the absence of brackets, adding up is always the last operation performed. For example, Σx^2 means square all the x's first and then add the resulting figures.

Example

Given the following data:

x	1	3	4	0	2
y	7	2	1	6	9

$$\Sigma x = 1 + 3 + 4 + 0 + 2 = 10$$
$$\Sigma x^2 = 1^2 + 3^2 + 4^2 + 0^2 + 2^2 = 30$$
$$\Sigma xy = (1 \times 7) + (3 \times 2) + (4 \times 1) + (0 \times 6) + (2 \times 9) = 35$$

Task

Given:

p	4	6	7	2
q	3	5	9	1

Calculate:

(i) Σp (ii) Σp^2 (iii) Σpq (iv) $(\Sigma p)^2$

9.3.2 Averages

An *average*, or measure of central tendency, is a value which is typical and representative of a set of data. The main averages are the arithmetic mean, the median and the mode.

The *arithmetic mean*, often represented by the symbol x (x bar), is found by dividing the sum of a set of observations by the number of observations. The main limitation of the mean is that it can be distorted by extreme values.

The *median* is the middle value when the data has been arranged in ascending order.

Example

Five sales staff receive bonuses of £30, £80, £20, £75 and £100. The bonuses in ascending order are: £20, £30, £75, £80 and £100 so the median is £75.

When there is an even number of observations the median is halfway between the middle two figures.

The *mode* is the most frequently occurring value in a set of data. For example, if the following figures represent the number of children in nine families, the mode is two children.

Number of children: 3, 2, 2, 2, 0, 1, 2, 2, 5

Task

The operating costs of seven identical machines over the past year are given below. Calculate the mean, median and modal costs and comment on your results.

Operating costs: £350, £390, £350, £370, £350, £380, £1,450

9.3.3 Calculating the Mean and Median from a Frequency Distribution

To calculate the *arithmetic mean* from a frequency distribution the formula is:

$$\bar{x} = \frac{\Sigma fx}{\Sigma f}$$

where: f = the frequency of each class

 x = the mid-point of each class

Example

Given the frequency distribution below, calculate the mean wage per week.

Wages per week	Number of workers		
	f	*x*	*fx*
£80 to under £100	12	90	1,080 (ie 90 x 12)
£100 to under £120	50	110	5,500
£120 to under £140	20	130	2,600
£140 to under £160	8	150	1,200
	$\Sigma f = 90$		$\Sigma fx = 10,380$

Therefore: $\bar{x} = \dfrac{\Sigma fx}{\Sigma f} = \dfrac{10380}{90} = £115.33$

The *median* can be estimated by constructing an *ogive*. It is the value which has a cumulative frequency which is equal to half the total frequency.

Task

Thirty engineers are asked to estimate how long a major construction project will take to complete. Their estimates are given below. Find the mean and median estimates and interpret your results.

Completion time of project (Years)	Number of estimates
2 to under 3	4
3 to under 4	14
4 to under 5	6
5 to under 6	4
6 to under 8	2
Total	30

9.3.4 Quartiles

The *upper quartile* (Q_3) is the value which exceeds three-quarters of the observations in a set of data. For example, a student who has the third quartile height in a class will be taller than 75 per cent of his or her colleagues.

The *lower quartile* (Q_1) is the value which exceeds one quarter of the observations.

Quartiles are usually calculated from frequency distributions rather than raw data. An ogive can be used for this purpose. For example, the first quartile is the observation which has a cumulative frequency equal to 25 per cent of the total frequency.

Task

Determine the quartiles for the estimated project completion times (see previous task) and interpret your results.

9.3.5 Measures of Dispersion

Measures of dispersion are designed to show the amount of variation in a set of data (for example, how much variation there is in the prices charged by garages for unleaded petrol). The main measures are the *range*, the *interquartile range*, the *standard deviation* and the *variance*.

The *range* is the difference between the highest and lowest values in a set of data. For example, the range of the numbers: 3, 100, 34, and 6 is 100 minus 3, ie 97.

The *interquartile range* is the difference between the upper and lower quartiles (ie Q_3 - Q_1) and therefore measures the spread of the middle 50 per cent of observations.

The *standard deviation* (s) is calculated by using the following formula:

$$s = \sqrt{\frac{\Sigma(x - \bar{x})^2}{n}}$$

where x = an observation

$\bar{x}$ = the mean

n = the number of observations

Example

The weekly sales of a product over a five week period are 10, 15, 32, 16 and 27 units. Find the standard deviation.

Here $\bar{x}$ = 20 units and n = 5 so we have:

x	x - $\bar{x}$	(x - $\bar{x}$)^2
10	-10	100
15	-5	25
32	12	144
16	-4	16
27	7	49

$$\Sigma(x - \bar{x})^2 = 334$$

So, $s = \sqrt{\dfrac{334}{5}}$ = 8.17 units

The *variance* is the square of the standard deviation.

Task

The marks achieved by five students on an aptitude test are 62%, 44%, 76%, 84% and 59%. Calculate the range and standard deviation of the marks.

9.3.6 Calculating the Standard Deviation from a Frequency Distribution

The following formula can be used for this:

$$s = \sqrt{\frac{\Sigma fx^2}{\Sigma f} - \left(\frac{\Sigma fx}{\Sigma f}\right)^2}$$

where: f = the frequency of each class

x = the mid-point of each class

Example

Given the frequency distribution below, calculate the standard deviation of the weekly wages.

Wages per week	Number of workers			
	f	x	fx	fx²
£80 to under £100	12	90	1,080	97,200
£100 to under £120	50	110	5,500	605,000
£120 to under £140	20	130	2,600	338,000
£140 to under £160	8	150	1,200	180,000
	90		10,380	1,220,200

That is: $\Sigma f = 90$; $\Sigma fx = 10,380$; $\Sigma fx^2 = 1,220,200$

Therefore, $s = \sqrt{\dfrac{1220200}{90} - \left(\dfrac{10380}{90}\right)^2} = £16$

Task

Calculate the standard deviation of the engineers' estimates of project completion time (see task in Section 9.3.3).

9.3.7 Correlation

Correlation is concerned with measuring the strength of association between two variables (for example, how close is the association between the absenteeism and pay of a company's employees?).

Positive correlation occurs where an increase in the value of one variable is associated with an increase in the value of the other (for example, more advertisements may be associated with higher sales).

Negative correlation occurs where an increase in the value of one variable is associated with a decrease in the value of the other (for example, higher temperatures outside are associated with lower office heating costs).

Task

Identify two business related variables which you would expect to be positively correlated and two which you would expect to be negatively correlated.

9.3.8 Scatter Diagrams

Scatter diagrams are used to illustrate the relationship between two variables. Figure 9.4 shows four typical patterns which can occur:

    (a) strong positive linear correlation;

    (b) perfect negative correlation;

    (c) no correlation;

    (d) non-linear correlation.

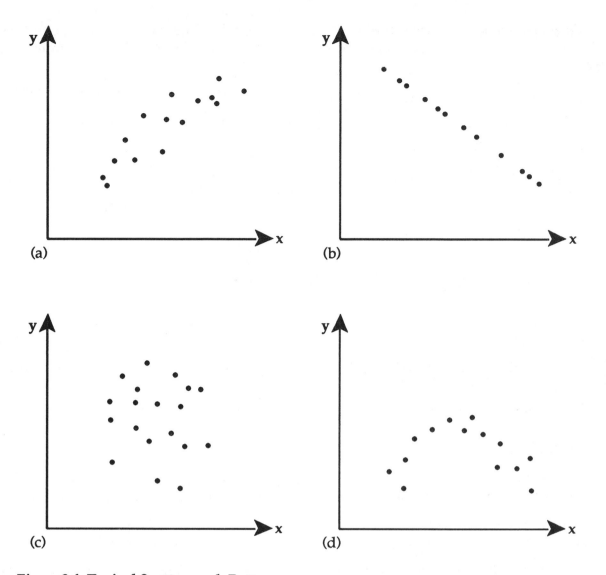

Figure 9.4 Typical Scattergraph Patterns

Task

The sizes of advertisements placed in a newspaper by an insurance company and the number of enquiries resulting from each advertisement are shown below. Plot the data on a scattergraph and comment on what the graph shows.

Size of advertisement: (*column inches*)	1	3	2	4	6	5
Number of enquiries:	30	60	42	56	76	82

9.3.9 Measuring Correlation

Two widely used *measures of correlation* are:

- Pearson's product moment correlation coefficient (r);
- Spearman's rank correlation coefficient (r').

Both measure correlation on a scale from -1 (perfect negative correlation) to +1 (perfect positive correlation) with 0 representing no correlation (for example r = -0.9 implies strong negative correlation).

Correlation coefficients should be interpreted with care. A correlation between two variables does not prove the existence of a causal link between them. Often two causally unrelated variables are correlated because they both relate to a third variable (for example, sales of ice-cream and sales of sunglasses).

9.3.10 Calculating Pearson's Product Moment Correlation Coefficient

This is more conveniently calculated by computer. However, the formula is:

$$r = \frac{n\Sigma xy - \Sigma x \Sigma y}{\sqrt{[n\Sigma x^2 - (\Sigma x)^2][n\Sigma y^2 - (\Sigma y)^2]}}$$

where one variable is labelled x and the other y

and n = number of pairs of observations

Example

Calculate r for the following data which relates to the advertising expenditure and sales of the XYZ company for five periods.

Advertising expenditure (£m)	x	0	1	4	2	3
Sales (£m)	y	20	19	25	24	26

For this data $\Sigma x = 10$; $\Sigma y = 114$; $\Sigma xy = 245$; $\Sigma x^2 = 30$; $\Sigma y^2 = 2638$ and n = 5.

Therefore, $r = \dfrac{5(245) - 10(114)}{\sqrt{[5(30) - (10)^2][5(2638) - (114)^2]}} = 0.86$

suggesting a strong positive correlation.

Task

Calculate r for the size of advertisement and number of enquiries data from the previous section. Interpret your result.

9.3.11 Calculating Spearman's Rank Correlation Coefficient

The formula for this is:

$$r' = 1 - \frac{6\Sigma d^2}{n(n^2 - 1)}$$

where d = the differences between the pairs of ranks

n = the number of pairs of ranks

Example

Calculate r' for the XYZ company's advertising expenditure and sales data from the previous section.

Advertising expenditure (£m)	Rank (1 = highest)	Sales (£m)	Rank (1 = highest)	d	d^2
0	5	20	4	1	1
1	4	19	5	-1	1
4	1	25	2	-1	1
2	3	24	3	0	0
3	2	26	1	1	1
					—
			n = 5		$\Sigma d^2 = 4$

Therefore, $r' = 1 - \dfrac{6(4)}{5(5^2 - 1)} = 0.80$

Task

Calculate r' for the size of advertisement and number of enquiries data and interpret your result.

9.3.12 Regression Analysis

Regression analysis is used to describe the *nature* of the relationship between two variables (for example, what increase in sales can be expected for each £1,000 spent on advertising?). It is mainly used to predict the value of one variable (the dependent variable) from a knowledge of the other (the independent variable).

The analysis involves finding the equation of the line which best fits the points on a scattergraph (the regression equation). This equation will have the form:

$$y = a + bx$$

where: y = the variable to be predicted (the dependent variable)
      x = the independent variable
      a = the intercept (ie the height at which the line passes above the origin on the scattergraph)
      b = the slope of the line

9.3.13 The Line of Best Fit

Finding the *line of best fit* is most easily done on a computer. However, the formulae for calculating the slope and intercept are:

$$b = \frac{n\Sigma xy - \Sigma x \Sigma y}{n\Sigma x^2 - (\Sigma x)^2}$$

and

$$a = \frac{\Sigma y}{n} - b\frac{\Sigma x}{n}$$

where: x = the values of the independent variable

y = the values of the dependent variable

n = the number of pairs of observations

Example

With reference to the XYZ sales and advertising data (Section 9.3.10), find the regression equation which can be used to predict sales from advertising expenditure and interpret your result.

Sales are to be predicted so y = sales and x = advertising expenditure.

From Section 9.3.10 we know $\Sigma x = 10$; $\Sigma y = 114$; $\Sigma xy = 245$; $\Sigma x^2 = 30$ and n = 5.

Therefore, $b = \dfrac{5(245) - 10(114)}{5(30) - (10)^2} = 1.7$ and $a = \dfrac{114}{5} - \dfrac{1.7(10)}{5} = 19.4$

So the equation is: y = 19.4 + 1.7x

In words: Sales (£m) = 19.4 + 1.7(Advertising expenditure £m)

Thus, if £0 is spent on advertising, sales of £19.4m will be expected; each £1m spent on advertising will increase expected sales by £1.7m.

Using the line of best fit for prediction simply involves substituting the appropriate value of the independent variable into the regression equation.

Example

Predict XYZ's sales for a period when they will be spending £1.5m on advertising.

y = 19.4 + 1.7(1.5) = £21.95m of sales

Predictions of sales for advertising expenditure levels outside the observed range £0m to £4m (*extrapolation*) should be treated with caution since the observed relationship may no longer apply (for example, each extra £1m spent on advertising may eventually lead to smaller increases in sales).

Task

The percentage of total rent in arrears and the percentage of rent collected door-to-door is shown below for a sample of six local councils.

Percentage of rent collected door-to-door	1	12	16	11	20	6
Percentage of rent of total rent in arrears:	13	10	8	12	7	11

Calculate a regression equation which can be used to predict the percentage of total rent which will be in arrears from the percentage of rent collected door-to-door. Interpret the equation.

9.3.14 Index Numbers

Index numbers are useful for monitoring variables like prices, wages and costs, normally over periods of time. The *base period* of an index is the period against which all other periods will be compared.

Normally, the index for the this period is set at 100. Thus for a price index, if 1989 = 100 and the index for 1992 = 108, then 1992 prices are eight per cent higher than those in the base year.

A *price relative* is an index number which measures the change in price of just one item. The formula is:

$$\text{Price relative} = \frac{p_n}{p_0} \times 100$$

where p_n = price in current year

p_0 = price in base year

Example

The price of a product was £40 per tonne in 1988 and £45 in 1990. Calculate the price relative for the product in 1990 if 1988 is the base year.

$$\text{Price relative} = \frac{45}{40} \times 100 = 112.5$$

indicating a 12.5 per cent price increase.

A *weighted average of price relatives* index number measures the average change in price of several items. Each item is weighted according to its importance. The formula is:

$$\text{Index number} = \frac{\Sigma(\text{price relative} \times \text{weight})}{\Sigma(\text{weights})}$$

Example

Calculate a weighted average of price relatives index for 1990 from the data below, using 1989 as base year.

Commodity	1989 Price	1990 Price	Weight
A	£80 per tonne	£100 per tonne	10
B	£5 per metre	£8 per metre	50
C	£6 per litre	£9 per litre	20

The price relatives are 125 for A, 160 for B, 150 for C, so the index is:

$$\frac{(125 \times 10) + (160 \times 50) + (150 \times 20)}{80} = 153.1$$

Task

Assume that the government is proposing to award students grants with future increases being linked to the Retail Price Index (RPI). Find out how RPI is calculated and write an article for a student newspaper arguing either in favour of, or against, the fairness of the proposal.

9.3.15 Using Index Numbers for Deflation

Index numbers can be used to assess whether variables like costs or wages are increasing in 'real terms' (when the effect of inflation has been removed). To **deflate** a figure, first divide the figure by the index number for that year and then multiply by 100. The result will be expressed in terms of the value of money in the base year.

Example

A local authority spent £20m on roads in 1987 and £23m in 1990. If the RPI had the following values: 1987 = 100 and 1990 = 120, determine whether the expenditure has increased in 'real terms'.

$$\text{Deflated 1990 expenditure} = \frac{23}{120} \times 100 = \text{£19.2m}$$

which suggests reduced expenditure in 'real terms'.

Task

Obtain data on the average weekly earnings of full-time manual employees in the UK for the last few years and use the RPI to assess whether their wages have increased in 'real terms'.

9.3.16 Time Series Analysis

A **time series** is a set of data recorded at intervals over a period of time (for example, quarterly sales figures for the last five years). **Time series analysis** involves decomposing the data into a number of components to establish if a pattern exists.

The main components of time series observed in business time series are:

- the **trend** which represents the long term underlying movement in the time series;

- the **seasonal pattern**;

- the **cyclical component** which reflects swings in the economy from boom years to years of depression;

- the **random component**, which appears as **irregular** movements on a graph, reflecting the many unpredictable factors which affect time series.

Tasks

Obtain data on the following variables for several recent years, plot the time series on a graph and identify which of the above components appear to be present:

(i)   number of live births per quarter in the UK;

(ii) quarterly sales of footwear in the UK;

(iii) quarterly number of passengers travelling into the UK by air.

9.3.17 Measuring the Trend in a Time Series

Moving averages are used to smooth out short run fluctuations in time series to obtain the underlying trend. For quarterly data a four period moving average is normally used. This needs to be 'centred' in order to align the values with actual time points.

Example

Use a four period moving average to measure the trend of the sales figures in Table 9.1. Figure 9.5 shows a graph of these figures. Note that the centred average values have been plotted for the trend.

Table 9.1 Time series analysis

Year	Qtr	Sales (units)	Moving Average	Centred Average	Seasonal deviation = sales – centred average
1988	1	56			
	2	88			
			66		
	3	100		67	+33
			68		
	4	20		70	-50
			72		
1989	1	64		76	-12
			80		
	2	104		82	+22
			84		
	3	132		87	+45
			90		
	4	36		92	-56
			94		
1990	1	88		95	-7
			96		
	2	120		99	+21
			102		
	3	140			
	4	60			

	Quarter 1	Quarter 2	Quarter 3	Quarter 4	Total
1988			+33	-50	
1989	-12	+22	+45	-56	
1990	-7	+21			
Average	-9.5	+21.5	+39.0	-53.0	-2
Adjustment	+0.5	+0.5	+0.5	+0.5	
Average seasonal deviation	-9.0	+22.0	+39.5	-52.5	

299

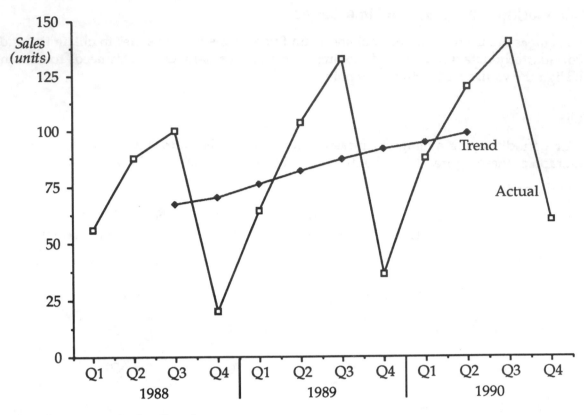

Figure 9.5 Time Series Graph

To calculate the moving averages:

(i)   Average the first four sales figures (56,88,100,20). Note that the result is written halfway between the middle two periods.

(ii) Drop the 1988 Q1 sales figure, replace it with the 1989 Q1 figure and average the new set of figures (88,100,20,64).

(iii) Repeat the process of moving down a quarter at a time until the last four sales figures have been averaged.

The results, which are shown in Table 9.1 and plotted in Figure 9.5, indicate an upward trend.

Task

Select one of the variables from the task in the last section, calculate a four period moving average to represent the trend and superimpose this on to your original graph.

9.3.18 Types of Seasonal Variation

Figure 9.6 illustrates two types of seasonal variation.

300

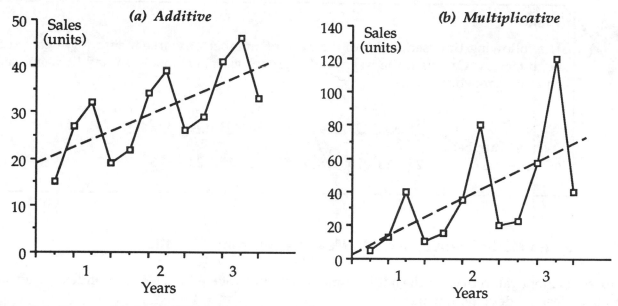

Figure 9.6 Types of Seasonal Variation

Figure 9.6(a) shows seasonal variation which can be represented by the *additive model*. For each season the distance of the actual figure from the trend is approximately the same from year to year.

Figure 9.6(b) shows seasonal variation which can be represented by the *multiplicative model*. For a given season the actual figure equals the trend multiplied by a constant factor so that, as the trend rises, the seasonal swings become more marked.

9.3.19 Using the Additive Model to Measure Seasonal Variation

Example

Use the additive model to measure the seasonal variation for the sales in Table 9.1.

To measure the seasonal variation:

Stage (i)   Centre the moving averages so that each actual value can be compared with the trend. These centred averages are the values midway between the pairs of moving averages.

Stage (ii)   Calculate the seasonal deviations where:

$$\text{seasonal deviation} = \text{actual value} - \text{centred average}.$$

Stage (iii) Put the seasonal deviations into a table so that the deviations for corresponding seasons appear in the same column and average the columns.

Stage (iv)   If necessary, adjust the averages of the columns so that they sum to zero (for example in Table 9.1 $\frac{1}{4}$ of 2, ie 0.5, has been added to each of the figures).

Table 9.1 shows that, on average, quarter 3's sales are 39.5 units above the trend, while quarter 4's are, on average, 52.5 units below the trend.

301

Task

The following time series shows the average number of workers absent per day at a large factory. Calculate the trend and seasonal variation (using the additive model) and interpret your results.

	Year 1				Year 2				Year 3			
	Q1	Q2	Q3	Q4	Q1	Q2	Q3	Q4	Q1	Q2	Q3	Q4
Average number of absentees	25	13	20	28	29	11	16	23	26	9	14	21

9.3.20 Using the Multiplicative Model to Measure Seasonal Variation

The process is identical to that for the additive model except at Stage (ii) a seasonal index is calculated instead of a seasonal deviation, where:

$$\text{seasonal index} = \frac{\text{actual value}}{\text{centred average}}$$

and at Stage (iv) the averages of the columns should sum to 4 (assuming the data is quarterly). If they do not, multiply each figure by an adjustment factor, where:

$$\text{adjustment factor} = \frac{4}{\text{actual sum}}$$

Applying these calculations to the sales data in Table 9.1 we have Q1: 0.89; Q2: 1.25; Q3: 1.52; Q4: 0.34; showing, for example, that sales in Q3 are, on average, 52 per cent higher than the trend.

Assignment 9.3: Forecasting

You have been asked by a manager who is unfamiliar with the technique to demonstrate, explain and evaluate forecasting based on time series analysis.

Student activities

(i) Obtain a set of quarterly time series data, covering at least three years, for a variable which has a seasonal pattern. Plot the data on a graph and analyse it using an appropriate model.

(ii) Plot the trend on your graph and use your judgement to extrapolate the trend into the next year.

(iii) By taking into account the seasonal variation, make forecasts for each quarter of the next year.

(iv) Draft some notes for the manager explaining your analysis and discussing its strengths and limitations.

9.4 Probability and its Applications

Probability is measured on a scale from 0 (impossible) to 1 (certain). The notation p(A) means the probability of event A occurring.

9.4.1 Approaches to probability

There are three approaches:

The *a priori* approach:

$$p(A) = \frac{\text{number of ways in which event A can occur}}{\text{total number of possible outcomes}}$$

where all of the outcomes are assumed to be equally likely.

Example

What is the a priori probability of obtaining an odd number score in one throw of a die?

$$p(\text{odd number score}) = \frac{3}{6} = 0.5$$

The *empirical approach* which requires either past or experimental data:

$$p(A) = \frac{\text{number of times event A occurred}}{\text{total number of observations or experiments}}$$

Example

Out of 400 light bulbs tested from a batch 15 were faulty, hence:

$$p(\text{bulb from batch faulty}) = \frac{15}{400} = 0.0375$$

The *subjective approach* where a person uses judgement to assess the probability. For example, "I estimate that there is a 0.9 probability that this product will make a profit next year."

Tasks

How would you assess the probability of:

(i) a packet of frozen food, filled by an automatic process, being underweight;

(ii) a woman being the next US president;

(iii) you being selected in a simple random sample of thirty students taken at your college;

(iv) a sales forecast having an error of less than 10 per cent?

9.4.2 Mutually Exclusive Events

Two or more events are *mutually exclusive* if the occurrence of one of the events means that the simultaneous occurrence of the other events is impossible (for example, the simultaneous occurrence of a head and tail in one throw of a coin is impossible).

Tasks

One card is to be drawn from a shuffled pack of 52 cards. Which of the following pairs of events are mutually exclusive?

(i)   the card is a club, the card is a diamond;

(ii) the card is a queen, the card is a spade;

(iii) the card is a queen, the card is an ace.

9.4.3 The Addition Rule

This gives the probability of *either* one event *or* another occurring. If the events are mutually exclusive then:

$$p(A \text{ or } B) = p(A) + p(B).$$

If they are not mutually exclusive then:

$$p(A \text{ or } B) = p(A) + p(B) - p(A \text{ and } B)$$

Example

One card is drawn from a well shuffled pack. Find the probability that it is (i) either an ace or a jack; (ii) either a king or a diamond.

(i) $p(\text{ace or jack}) = \dfrac{4}{52} + \dfrac{4}{52} = \dfrac{8}{52}$

(ii) $p(\text{king or diamond}) = \dfrac{4}{52} + \dfrac{13}{52} - \dfrac{1}{52} = \dfrac{16}{52}$

Tasks

One person is to be selected at random to represent your class. What is the probability that this person:

(i)   travelled to college most recently by either car or by motorbike;

(ii) is either a male or a person who travelled to college most recently by car?

9.4.4 Independent Events

Two events A and B are *independent* if the probability of A occurring is not affected by the occurrence or non-occurrence of B.

> **Tasks**
>
> Which of the following pairs of events would you judge to be independent?
>
> (i) in a marriage, the husband having group 0 blood, the wife having group A blood;
>
> (ii) the occurrence of a drought in the UK next year, the rate of inflation exceeding 8 per cent next year;
>
> (iii) a road vehicle having defective brakes, the vehicle having defective tyres.

9.4.5 Conditional Probability

This is denoted by p(A | B) which means 'the probability of A occurring *given that* B has occurred'. For example, a manager might judge:

p(delivered goods are OK) = 0.9

but p(delivered goods are OK | packaging is damaged) = 0.3

9.4.6 The Multiplication Rule

This gives the probability of one event *and* another occurring. If the events are independent then:

$$p(A \text{ and } B) = p(A) \times p(B)$$

Example

Find the probability of obtaining a double six when two dice are thrown.

$$p(6 \text{ on first die and } 6 \text{ on second die}) = \frac{1}{6} \times \frac{1}{6} = \frac{1}{36}$$

If they are *NOT* independent then:

$$p(A \text{ and } B) = p(A) \times p(B \mid A)$$

Example

A box contains 100 electronic components of which 20 are defective. If two components are removed from the box without replacement what is the probability that they will both be defective?

p(both components defective)

= p(first defective) x p(second defective | first was defective)

$$= \frac{20}{100} \times \frac{19}{99} = 0.0384$$

Tasks

Two machines, A and B, operate independently in a factory. A is out of order 10 per cent of the time and B for 5 per cent of the time. What is the probability that at midday tomorrow:

(i)   both the machines will be out of order;

(ii) neither of the machines will be out of order?

9.4.7 Expected Values

An *expected value* can be interpreted as a long run average result (for example, the average score on a die over a large number of throws should be close to 3.5). To calculate an expected value first multiply each value by its probability of occurrence and then add the resulting figures.

Example

Find the expected weekly sales, given the probability distribution below:

Number of units sold per week:	4	5	6
Probability:	0.4	0.5	0.1

Expected sales = $(4 \times 0.4) + (5 \times 0.5) + (6 \times 0.1) = 4.7$ units

9.4.8 Decision Trees

Decision trees are diagrams which are used to represent decision problems. They involve two symbols:

- a square represents a *decision node* - the decision-maker can choose which course of action to follow here;
- a circle represents a *chance node* - the branch followed here is determined by chance.

Figure 9.7 shows a simple decision tree for a decision concerning the purchase of a machine. Also shown are the payoffs for each possible outcome and the probability of each outcome occurring if a given course of action is chosen.

If the *expected monetary value (EMV)* criterion is adopted, the course of action offering the 'best' expected pay off is chosen. Figure 9.7 shows that buying the small machine offers the highest expected payoff.

Tasks

A company's managers have to choose one of two venues, A or B, for a forthcoming exhibition. If they choose A they estimate that they will make a profit of either £40,000, £15,000 or -£10,000 with probabilities of 0.2, 0.5 and 0.3 respectively. If they choose B they estimate that profits will be either £60,000 or -£30,000 with probabilities of 0.6 and 0.4 respectively.

(i)   Draw a decision tree and identify the venue offering the highest expected profit.

(ii) Discuss the limitations of your analysis.

306

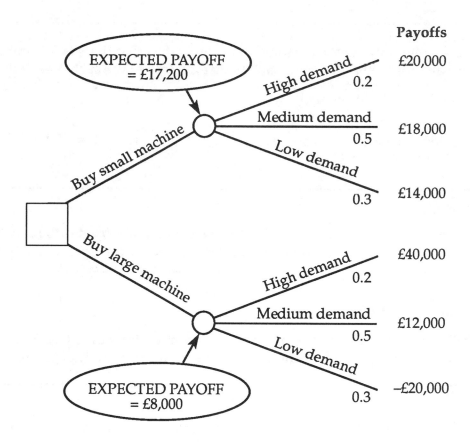

Figure 9.7   *A Decision Tree for the Machine Purchase Problem*

9.4.9 The Binomial Distribution

The *binomial distribution* is used to determine the probability that an event will occur a given number of times when it has a certain number of opportunities to occur (for example, a coin is to be tossed five times, what is the probability that just three of the tosses will result in heads?). Each occurrence of the event is called a *success* and each opportunity for it to occur is called a *trial*. To use the distribution, the probability of a success must be the same for each trial.

Binomial probabilities can be obtained by using either published tables or a formula. For both methods it is necessary to identify n, p and r where

n = the number of trials

r = the number of successes

p = the probability of a success occurring in a single trial

The formula is:

$$p(r \text{ successes in } n \text{ trials}) = \frac{n!}{r!(n-r)!} p^r (1-p)^{n-r}$$

where, for example, 4! (4 factorial) = 4 x 3 x 2 x 1 = 24

Example

A salesman is due to call on six customers tomorrow. He reckons that there is 0.7 probability that each customer will place an order. What is the probability that just four of the customers will place orders?

Here, n = 6, r = 4, p = 0.7 so the formula gives:

$$p(4 \text{ customers place orders out of 6 visited}) = \frac{6!}{4!(6-4)!}(0.7)^4(1-0.7)^{6-4} = 0.3241$$

Task

Ten per cent of a company's customers live in Scotland. What is the probability that in a random sample of eight customers, three live in Scotland?

9.4.10 The Normal Distribution

The *Normal distribution* is represented by a bell shaped symmetrical curve (see Figure 9.8). The exact characteristics of the distribution are determined by its mean and standard deviation.

Task

Identify two business-related variables which you would expect to be at least approximately normally distributed.

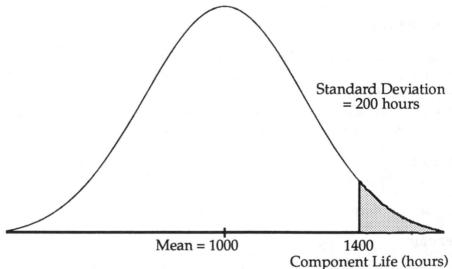

Standard Deviation = 200 hours

Mean = 1000   1400
Component Life (hours)

Figure 9.8   A Normal Distribution

9.4.11 Areas under the Normal Curve

If a variable is normally distributed the probability of it taking on a value in a given range is represented by the proportion of the area under the curve which falls in that range. This proportion can be obtained from published tables. These require the calculation of Z values where

Z = the number of standard deviations of a point from the mean

$$= \frac{x - \mu}{\sigma}$$

where: x = the original value of the point
μ = the mean of the distribution
σ = the standard deviation

Example

The lifetime of a component is normally distributed with a mean of 1000 hours and a standard deviation of 200 hours. What is the probability that the component will last for more than 1400 hours?

Figure 9.8 shows the required area which is known as an 'area in the tail' of the distribution.

$$Z = \frac{1400 - 1000}{200} = 2$$

Published tables show that because $Z = 2$ the required probability is 0.02275

Tasks

The weights of food cartons leaving a production line are normally distributed with a mean of 500 grams and a standard deviation of 12 grams. Find the probability that a carton will weigh:

(i)   more than 530 grams;

(ii) less than 488 grams;

(iii) between 500 and 520 grams.

9.4.12 Confidence Intervals

Confidence intervals are used when a random sample is used to estimate statistics relating to a population. The estimate is expressed as a range of figures, together with a statement of the probability (level of confidence) that the interval contains the true population value.

Two statistics which are often estimated are the *mean of the population*, the mean salary earned by doctors for example, and the *percentage of the population* with a given characteristic, the percentage of the population owning a microwave oven for example.

9.4.13 Confidence Intervals for the Population Mean

If the sample is at least size 30, the population standard deviation unknown and the population large relative to the sample, the formula for a 95 per cent confidence interval for the population mean is:

$$\text{sample mean} \pm 1.96 \frac{s}{\sqrt{n}}$$

where s = the sample standard deviation
n = the sample size

For a 99 per cent confidence interval 1.96 is replaced by 2.58.

The expression $\dfrac{s}{\sqrt{n}}$ is known as the *standard error of the mean*.

Example

A mail order company monitors a random sample of 50 deliveries in May. These have a mean delivery time of 18 days and a standard deviation of five days. Estimate the mean delivery time of all orders during May at the 95 per cent level of confidence.

$$95\% \text{ interval} = 18 \pm 1.96 \, \frac{5}{\sqrt{50}} = 18 \pm 1.4 \text{ days}$$

This means that we are 95 per cent confident that the mean delivery time of all the orders was between 16.6 and 19.4 days.

Task

Forty bus journeys in a town are monitored at random during a given week. The mean number of passengers per bus was 16.5 and the standard deviation was 3.5. Estimate the mean number of passengers carried on all buses during that week at the 95 per cent level of confidence.

9.4.14 Confidence Intervals for the Population Percentage

The formula for a 95 per cent confidence interval for the population percentage is:

$$p \pm 1.96 \sqrt{\frac{p(100-p)}{n}}$$

where p = the sample percentage

n = the sample size

The expression $\sqrt{\dfrac{p(100-p)}{n}}$ is known as the *standard error of percentages*.

Example

A random sample of 250 television sets produced at a factory contained 50 sets with minor faults. Estimate, at the 95 per cent level of confidence, the percentage of all sets produced at the factory which had minor faults.

$$p = \frac{50}{250} = 20\%, \text{ so the 95\% confidence interval is:}$$

$$20 \pm 1.96 \sqrt{\frac{20(100-20)}{250}} = 15.04 \text{ to } 24.96\%$$

Task

A random sample of 400 of a company's customers contained 34 who were dissatisfied with the service they had received. Estimate the percentage of all of the company's customers were dissatisfied with the service at the 95 per cent level of confidence.

9.4.15 Significance Tests

Significance tests are used to test the plausibility of a hypothesis about the population on the basis of the results of a sample. For example, a company claims that 80 per cent of its deliveries are made within a week. However, when a sample of 100 deliveries is monitored only 50 per cent arrive within a week. Is it beyond the likelihood of chance that the claim is true?

The following are some of the terms used in significance tests:

- *Significant* means beyond the likelihood of chance.
- The *null hypothesis* (H_0) is the idea to be tested (for example, H_0: 90 per cent of employees support the pay award).
- The *alternative hypothesis* (H_1) is accepted when the H_0 is rejected (for example, H_1: Less than 90 per cent of employees support the award).
- In a *one tail test* the H_1 involves either a 'greater than' or a 'less than' statement (for example, H_1: Greater than 10 per cent of output is defective).
- In a *two tail test* the H_1 simply involves a 'not equal to' statement (for example, H_1: The percentage of defective output is not equal to 10 per cent).
- The *significance level* is the probability of rejecting a true H_0 (values of 5 per cent or 1 per cent are often used).

A procedure for hypothesis testing is as follows:

- Set up the hypotheses.
- Decide on the significance level.
- Calculate the appropriate test statistic (for example, Z or χ^2).
- Compare the result with a critical value.
- Decide whether to reject the H_0.

9.4.16 Tests Based on the Normal Distribution

These involve the calculation of Z for which the general formula is:

$$Z = \frac{|\text{ sample result } - \text{ value specified in } H_0 \ |}{\text{appropriate standard error}}$$

where | | means ignore a minus sign if it occurs.

At the 5 per cent significance level the H_0 is rejected if Z exceeds:

1.65 (for a one-tail test)

1.96 (for a two-tail test)

Examples of these tests include:

- **The Z test of means** which is used to test a hypothesis about the mean of the population when the sample size is at least 30. The test can also be used for smaller samples when the population standard deviation is known and the population normally distributed, but this is rare.
- **The Z test of percentages** which is used to test a hypothesis about the percentage of the population having a given characteristic.

Example

A component should have a mean diameter of 22 cm. However, a sample of 40 components taken from today's output had a mean diameter of only 21.8 cm with a standard deviation of 0.5 cm. Does this suggest that the component is not meeting specifications?

This is a Z test of means:

H_0: mean diameter = 22 cm

H_1: mean diameter $\neq$ 22 cm

Significance level to be used: 5%

$$Z = \frac{|\text{ sample mean} - \text{mean specified in } H_0 \; |}{\text{standard error of the mean}}$$

$$= \frac{|\; 21.8 - 22 \;|}{\dfrac{0.5}{\sqrt{40}}} = 2.53$$

So the H_0 is rejected at the 5 per cent significance level.

> **Task**
>
> A type of battery is claimed to have a mean lifetime of 400 hours. However, a sample of 50 batteries had a mean lifetime of only 376 hours with a standard deviation of 70 hours. Should the claim be rejected at the 5 per cent level of significance? Explain the reasoning behind your answer.

9.4.17 Chi squared Tests

Chi squared tests (χ^2) are used to compare the **observed** frequency of the occurrence of events with the frequencies which would be expected if the H_0 was true. The formula for χ^2 is:

$$\chi^2 = \sum \frac{(O - E)^2}{E}$$

where: O = the observed frequencies

E = the expected frequencies

The H_0 is rejected if χ^2 exceeds a critical value which can be obtained from published tables.

Example

A sample of a hundred components contained 40 from factory A (of which 11 were defective), 30 from factory B (5 were defective) and 30 from factory C (9 were defective). Is there evidence that the proportion of defectives produced varies between the factories?

H_0: There is no difference between factories in proportion of output which is defective.

H_1: There is a difference.

The observed frequencies are shown below. The expected frequencies, in brackets, were calculated by finding the total proportion of output which was defective (that is, 25 per cent) and assuming that each factory will have this defect rate if the H_0 is true.

Number of components

	Factory A	*Factory B*	*Factory C*	*Total*
Defective	11 (10.0)	5 (7.5)	9 (7.5)	25
Not defective	29 (30.0)	25 (22.5)	21 (22.5)	75
Total	40	30	30	100

Therefore, $\chi^2 = \dfrac{1^2}{10} + \dfrac{2.5^2}{7.5} + \dfrac{1.5^2}{7.5} + \dfrac{1^2}{30} + \dfrac{2.5^2}{22.5} + \dfrac{1.5^2}{22.5} = 1.64$

For this test:

number of degrees of freedom $= $ (number of rows $- 1$) (number of columns $- 1$)

$$= (2-1)(3-1)$$

$$= 2$$

At the 5 per cent significance level, tables show that the critical value $= 5.991$, so the H_0 is not rejected.

Task

The table below shows the results of a survey of 200 people who were asked if they liked or disliked a proposed design for a new car. Is there evidence that the proportion of people liking the design differs between the age groups?

Age groups

	under 21	*21 to 30*	*31 to 45*	*over 45*
	Number of people			
Liked design	10	23	26	39
Disliked design	20	37	24	21

Assignment 9.4: An investment decision

You work as a financial consultant and you have been asked by a client to advise him on how he should invest £100,000 for a two-year period.

Student activities

(i)   Identify a set of alternative investment opportunities (business supplements of newspapers may be helpful here).

(ii) For each alternative, use your judgement to assess a probability distribution for the possible values of the investment at the end of the period (for simplicity, assume a high, medium and low return, where appropriate).

(iii) Use a decision tree to represent the problem.

(iv) Write a word-processed report for the client explaining your analysis, providing a rationale for your probability estimates and advising him on his decision. You should also mention any reservations you may have about the analysis.

9.5 Quantitative Models for Decision-Making

A *quantitative model* is usually an attempt to represent the complexity of a real problem or situation in a relatively simple and manageable form. By ignoring minor details, models allow the fundamental aspects of problems to be analysed.

9.5.1 Linear Programming Models

Linear programming models are often used in decision problems where it is necessary to make the best use of limited resources, such as limited cash, production time or raw materials. The problem is represented by a mathematical model. The model is formulated by:

- *Identifying the decision variables* which are the variables whose value the decision maker wants to determine. For example, how many units of A and how many of B should be produced to maximise profit?
- *Formulating the objective function;* this represents the objective to be achieved and shows how it relates to the decision variables.
- *Formulating the constraints* which show the how the possible values of the decision variables are restricted by factors like limited production time.

Example

The PQR company produces two components, the deluxe and the standard, which both require time on a lathe and a polishing machine. The times needed on the two machines for each unit produced are shown below, together with the hours available each week and the contribution earned by each unit.

	Deluxe	Standard	Hours available per week
Lathe time	4 hours	3 hours	60
Polishing machine	2 hours	4 hours	40
Contribution	£600	£500	

314

Formulate a model which can be used to determine the number of Deluxe and Standard components which should be produced per week to maximise contribution.

Identify decision variables:

Let D = the number of deluxe components produced per week

S = the number of standard components produced per week

Formulate the objective function:

Maximise contribution = 600D + 500S

Formulate the constraints:

$$4D + 3S \leq 60 \text{ (lathe)}$$

$$2D + 4S \leq 40 \text{ (polishing machine)}$$

Also, since negative output is impossible:

$$D \geq 0$$

$$S \geq 0$$

Task

A manufacturer produces a component for diesel engines and a similar part for petrol engines. Both parts must pass through a machine centre and a testing centre. The number of hours required in each centre are shown below, together with the contributions per unit.

	Diesel part	Petrol part	Hours available per day
Machine centre	4	2	16
Testing centre	2	2	12
Contribution	£60	£45	

Formulate a model to determine the number of units of each part which should be manufactured each day in order to maximise contribution.

9.5.2 Solving Linear Programming Problems

Problems involving two decision variables can be solved using the graphical method. For larger problems it is advisable to use a computer package.

Example

Use the graphical method to solve the PQR company problem in the previous section.

This method involves the following steps (see Figure 9.9):

Stage 1   Assign an axis on the graph to each product.

Stage 2   Plot the constraints as if they were equations.

Stage 3   Shade the feasible sides of the constraints (for the $\leq$ constraints the underside is shaded).

Stage 4   Identify the feasible area (this represents the combinations of output of the two products which do not violate any of the constraints.

Stage 5   Identify the corners of the feasible area (one or rarely two of these will represent the optimal combination of output).

Stage 6   Find the corner which generates the highest contribution.

Here, the combinations of output at the corners of the feasible area and their associated contributions are:

D	S	Contribution = 600D + 500S
0	0	£0
0	10	£5,000
12	4	£9,200
15	0	£9,000

So PQR should produce 12 deluxe and 4 standard components per week.

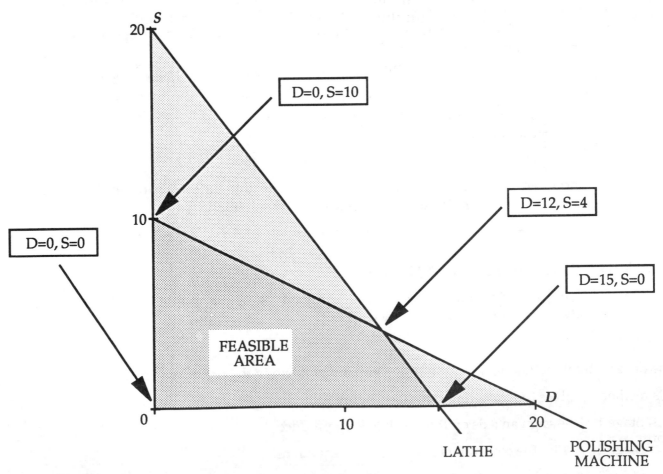

Figure 9.9 Solving the Components Problem

Task

Use the graphical method to solve the diesel and petrol engine components problem in Section 9.5.1.

9.5.3 Stock Control Models

The following terms are used in *stock control:*

- the *lead time* is the time between placing an order and receiving the goods;
- *holding costs* are those costs incurred by holding goods in stock such as storage, insurance cost or the cost of tying up capital in stock;
- *ordering costs* are those costs incurred each time an order is placed such as administrative or delivery costs;
- a *stock out* occurs when an item is required which is not in stock.

9.5.4 The Economic Order Quantity Model

The *economic order quantity (EOQ) model* can be used to determine the size of order which will minimise the total cost incurred each year through holding and ordering stocks. This optimum size of order is known as the economic order quantity. The assumptions of the model are:

- demand for the item of stock is constant;
- the lead time is either zero or constant;
- no stock outs are allowed;
- annual holding costs are proportional to the amount of stock held (for example, doubling the stock level leads to a doubling of holding costs);
- the cost of placing an order is the same for any size of order.

If these conditions are met:

$$EOQ = \sqrt{\frac{2cd}{h}}$$

where: c = the cost of placing an order

d = the annual demand for the item of stock

h = the cost of holding one unit in stock for a year

Example

The annual demand for a product is 40,000 units. It costs £0.40 to hold one unit of the product in stock for a year and £20 to have an order delivered. Determine the EOQ (assuming that the model is appropriate).

$$EOQ = \sqrt{\frac{2(20)(40000)}{0.4}} = 2,000 \text{ units}$$

Task

The annual demand for a product is 2000 units. The cost of holding a unit in stock for a year is 20 per cent of the cost of the unit. Each delivery costs £20 and the supplier charges £10 per unit for the product. Determine the EOQ (assume that the model is appropriate).

9.5.5 Critical Path Analysis

A *project* is a set of activities which must be carried out in a defined order. *Critical path analysis (CPA)* is widely used in the planning and control of projects, ensuring that the resources associated with the project are used effectively. In CPA a project is represented as a network diagram. An activity-on-the-node network has two symbols:

- *nodes* which represent the activities;
- *arrows* which show the sequence of the activities.

Figure 9.10 shows how information about an activity can be displayed on a node including:

- the *earliest start time (EST)* of the activity;
- the *earliest finish time (EFT)*, that is the EST + the duration;
- the *latest start time (LST)*, that is the latest time an activity can start without delaying the project's completion;
- the *latest finish time (LFT)*, that is the latest time an activity can finish without delaying the project's completion;
- the *float*, that is the amount of time an activity's start or finish can be delayed without delaying the project: float = LST - EST

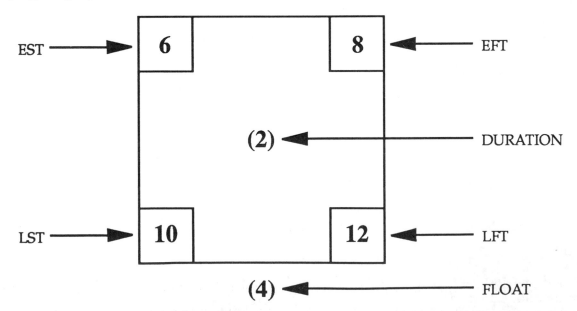

Figure 9.10 Displaying Activity Information on a Node

Figure 9.11 shows a network for a machine overhaul project which is detailed in the following table.

318

	Activity	Estimated duration (days)	Preceding activities
A	Transport machine to workshop	1	none
B	Replace electrical components	4	A
C	Service cooling system	2	A
D	Clean and repair fuel pump	3	A
E	Test and adjust controls	1	B, C and D
F	Transport back to factory	1	E

The earliest start and finish times are calculated by moving forward through the network.

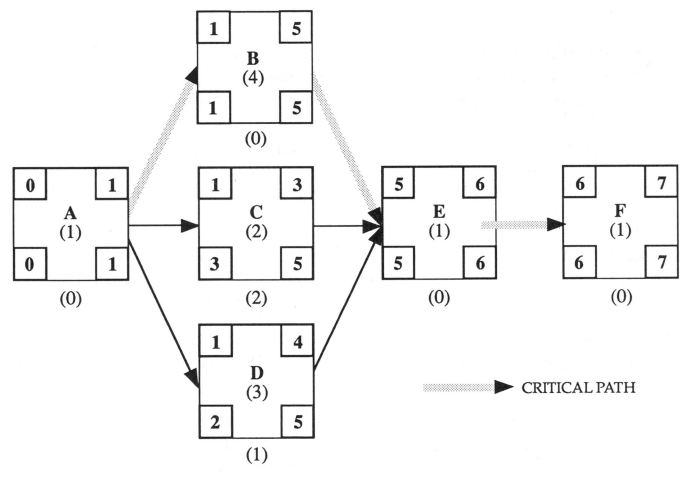

Figure 9.11 A Network for the Machine Overhaul Project

Note:

- The EST for activities B,C and D is 1 day since they are all waiting for A to be completed.
- Activity E cannot start until **all** its predecessors have been completed. B is the last of these to finish so the EST for E is 5 days.
- The earliest finish time for the last activity, F, gives the **duration of the project**, ie 7 days.

The latest start and finish times are calculated by moving backwards from the last activity.

Note:

- F's latest finish time must be 7 days, so its latest start time is 7 - 1 ie. 6 days.
- This means that E must have a latest finish time of 6 days.
- A's latest finish time must be such that it does not delay the most urgent of its successors. B, C and D have latest start times of 1, 3 and 2 days respectively, so A's latest finish time is 1 day.

The *critical activities* are those which have zero float, that is they cannot be delayed without holding up the project. The path they lie on (A-B-E-F in this case) is called the *critical path*.

Extensions of critical path analysis include:

- *Gantt charts* which show which activities will be taking place at any one time and therefore allow resource requirements such as labour, machines etc to be planned in advance;
- *crashing* which can be used to determine which activities should be speeded-up to meet a deadline for example.

Task

Details of a project are given below. Draw a network and calculate for each activity the earliest and latest start and finish times and the float. Which activities are critical and what is the estimated duration of the project?

Activity:	A	B	C	D	E	F	G
Duration (weeks):	6	7	9	3	1	7	2
Preceding activities:	-	A	A	B,C	C	A	D,E,F

9.5.6 Monte Carlo Simulation Models

Monte Carlo simulation models are designed to imitate the random behaviour which occurs in real systems so that the effects of alternative courses of action can be evaluated. For example, simulating the arrival patterns of customers at a bank in order to compare the effect on queues of operating different numbers of cash desks.

Simulation is often applied to problems where a mathematical model would be too complex and, in practice, normally involves the use of a computer.

9.5.7 Using Random Numbers in Simulation

Random numbers are used in simulation to determine the occurrence of events. They are generated by a process, such as spinning a roulette wheel or running a computer program, which ensures that each number in a specified range, say from 00 to 99, has an equal chance of being selected at any one time.

Example

The number of requests for help reaching a motoring organisation's office each hour during the night follows the distribution shown below. Simulate the number of requests reaching the office over a five-hour period.

Number of requests:	6	7	8
Percentage of hours:	40	50	10

When a random number is generated, the event it implies must be determined. As shown below, two-digit random numbers can be assigned to events by:

- cumulating the percentages;
- allocating the numbers by starting with 00 and ending each range with a value equal to the cumulative percentage less one.

Number of requests	Percentage of hours	Cumulative percentage	Random numbers
6	40	40	00 - 39
7	50	90	40 - 89
8	10	100	90 - 99

For example, if the following random numbers were generated: 23, 91, 45, 40, 27 it would imply 6, 8, 7, 7, and 6 requests in hours one to five respectively.

Task

A stock controller finds that 35 per cent of orders are for one item, 40 per cent for two items, 15 per cent for three items and 10 per cent for four items. Explain how two-digit random numbers could be used to simulate the size of orders received by the controller.

Assignment 9.5: A queuing problem

The manager of a small supermarket is concerned about the length of the queues that form at the single checkout desk on Saturday mornings. She is therefore considering opening a second desk. Each desk will cost £5 per hour to operate. The following information is available:

	1	2	3	4
Customer inter-arrival times at checkout (minutes):	1	2	3	4
Percentage of customers	50	40	9	1
Servicing times (minutes):	3	4	5	6
Percentage of customers:	2	50	30	18

Student activities

(i) Carry out a simulation, using a computer if possible, of the system if (a) one and (b) two desks are open.

(ii) Write a brief word-processed report to the manager advising her on the decision. Your report should also include a discussion of any reservations you may have about your results.

9.6 The Application of Computers

9.6.1 Hardware and Software

Hardware is the equipment used in a computer system such as the electronic components, printer, keyboard and monitor. *Software* refers to the programs which are the sets of instructions which tell the computer what to do.

System software refers to the programs which are used to maintain and operate a computer system. It includes:

- the *operating system,* a program which controls the computer's internal functions, performing tasks such as managing the information flow between the computer and peripheral devices;
- *utility programs* which perform routine functions such as copying files or restoring data which has been deleted in error.

Applications software refers to programs which perform specific tasks such as word processing, stock control or invoicing.

Task

Identify the main items of hardware in a computer system to which you have access and explain the function of each item.

9.6.2 Applications best suited to Computers

Computers are particularly useful in tasks which involve:

- the need for a speedy response;
- the need for high levels of accuracy;
- large volumes of data;
- complex calculations;
- repetitive operations;
- the need to access information from remote locations;
- the need for several users to access the same data.

Task

Consider a task which has been computerised, such as a stock control system or a customer record system, and discuss the advantages that computerisation has to offer.

9.6.3 Routine Business Applications of Computers

These include:

- payroll calculations;
- bookkeeping;
- word processing (Section 9.7.1);
- customer billing;
- maintaining stock records.

Often these applications are dealt with by an *integrated system.*

Task

Discuss the advantages of using a computer system which integrates stock control, order processing and sales accounting.

9.6.4 Applications of Computers in Planning and Control

Applications of computers in planning and control include:

- project management;
- production planning;
- sales forecasting;
- statistical analysis for market research;
- financial modelling such as using a spreadsheet package (Section 9.7.3).

Assignment 9.6: Purchasing a computer system

The owner of a shop which sells a wide range of car accessories, parts and tools has asked for your advice on the purchase of a computer system for his business. Two full-time staff and one part-timer are employed by the shop, which attracts customers from a wide area. The businessman has indicated that he would not wish to spend more than £3,500 on the hardware and software

Student activities

(i) Identify areas of this business where a computer would be useful.

(ii) Identify a make and type of computer and brand names of any other hardware you think the businessman should buy. This information can be obtained by studying computer magazines for example.

(iii) Write a report to the businessman explaining the role a computer could play in his business, and recommending what he should purchase, giving your reasons.

9.7 The Use of Software Packages

9.7.1 Word Processing Programs

Word processing programs are designed to assist in the creation, editing and printing of text. They are widely used in the production of standard letters, reports and memos. Typical facilities enable the user to:

- *insert and delete* text so that changes can easily be made and mistakes corrected;
- *move* a section of text to another part of the document;
- *search and replace* text, for example replace every £ with a $;
- *spell check* text;
- design the *page layout*, including margin widths, page length and justification of text.

Task

Use a word processing program to type and print your curriculum vitae.

9.7.2 Database Management Programs

A *database* is a collection of information which is organised in a useful form such as an address book or a file of customer records. A *database management program* is used to create, access, expand and update a computerised data base. The advantages over a manual filing system include:

- the *speed* with which records can be sorted;
- the *variety of ways* in which records can be sorted;
- the *different criteria* which can be used to select records.

> **Task**
>
> Discuss how a data base management program could be useful to a video rental shop.

9.7.3 Spreadsheet Programs

Spreadsheet programs perform calculations on data which is entered into a worksheet. A worksheet is a large matrix of rectangles called cells. These can contain numbers, words (labels) or formulae. The latter are useful for 'what if' analysis, for example instantly calculating what would happen to net cash flows if material costs doubled. Typical applications of spreadsheets include budgeting, financial modelling and forecasting.

Facilities available on most spreadsheets include:

- *graphics*, such as bar and pie charts;
- *statistical and financial functions*, such as standard deviation, regression, net present value (NPV).

9.7.4 Other Packages

Other packages include:

- *desktop publishing packages* which are used for producing high quality documents and usually allow text and diagrams to be merged on the same page.
- *accounting packages* which perform functions such as bookkeeping.

Assignment 9.7: Using a computer to produce a report

Your boss has asked you to provide a statistical report to assist in the preparation of an important business meeting. The title of the report is: *A comparison of the prosperity of the regions of Britain* and is to take into account such factors as unemployment, and the percentage of households with certain durable goods.

Student activities

(i)   Obtain relevant data from appropriate statistical publications.

(ii) Use a spreadsheet package to analyse the data and produce graphs and charts to illustrate key elements.

(iii) Produce a word-processed report containing a concise interpretation of the results of your analysis.

Appendix A
Integrated Assignments

The following seven assignments have been designed to integrate a number of core subjects. Students should not think of them as a 'marketing' assignment or a 'law' assignment, for example, but as illustrations of typical problems found in the workplace where a range of knowledge and skills is required to seek a solution.

Students should also be cautious of seeking a 'right' solution. There are often a number of viable solutions. Achievement is measured in the approach adopted to analysing the problem, the identification of possible alternative solutions, and the selection of the one which best fits that specific context.

When preparing answers to these assignments students should constantly bear in mind that an integrative approach is required. The index can be used to refer to the various sections in this manual, so that the different facets which may be relevant to the assignment can be explored and examined.

ASSIGNMENT 1. INTERNATIONAL CONFERENCES LTD

You have recently been appointed as assistant promotions manager at International Conferences Ltd. Before being promoted, your predecessor had drawn up a proposal to sell badges bearing the date and location of the conference, which would be sold as a souvenirs whilst at the same time promoting the company.

It was suggested that one of three grades of badge should be sold: bronze, selling price 30p each; silver with coloured lettering, selling price 50p each; and gold with fancy coloured lettering, selling price £1.25 each. All the badges would bear the company's name and logo.

The costs for each grade of badge are estimated at:

	Bronze badge	Silver badge	Gold badge
	£	£	£
Metal	0.10	0.10	See below
Fastenings	0.02	0.02	See below
Enamel	0	0.06	0.10
Presentation box	0.05	0.08	0.20
Certificate	0.04	0.06	0.08
Envelope	0.02	0.06	0.04

There is some uncertainty about the costs of the metal and fastenings for the gold badge. There is a 0.6 probability that the metal for each badge will cost £0.60 and a 0.4 probability that it will cost £0.65. It is thought that the cost of each fastening will be either £0.08 or £0.10. It is estimated that there is a 0.3 probability that the higher of these two costs will apply.

The proposal suggests that the badges could be made on portable equipment at each conference venue and the equipment hired on a monthly basis. A room would be set aside at each conference to make, package and store the badges during the conference. The following table shows estimates of these costs:

Monthly costs

	£
Equipment hire	60.00
Light and heat	50.00
Rent	60.00
Wages	200.00
Delivery charges	45.00

International Conferences Ltd holds 20 one-day conferences on average a month. Details of the number of delegates attending the most recent 100 conferences organised by the company are as follows:

Number of delegates	*Number of conferences*
100 - 299	10
300 - 399	14
400 - 499	23
500 - 599	32
600 - 699	10
700 - 799	8
800 -999	2
1,000 and over	1
	100

So far no decision has been taken as to which of the three grades of badge should be sold at the conferences, but one morning, shortly after joining the company, the following memo arrives on your desk.

```
                        M E M O R A N D U M

From: Promotions Manager

To: Assistant Promotions Manager
─────────────────────────────────────────────────────────────────

We need to take a decision soon on whether to go ahead with the sale
of souvenir conference badges. I wish to obtain Board approval to
conduct some market research as a first step. Could you therefore
please prepare a draft proposal for me covering the following points:

(i)     detailed proposals of how market research might be
        conducted;

(ii)    the break-even point for each of the bronze and silver
        badges and the possible break-even points for the gold
        badge, together with an assessment of the probabilities that
        these break-even points will apply;

(iii)   an appraisal of the strategic and marketing advantages and
        disadvantages of the project;

(iv) any other factors you think should be taken into consideration
        when arriving at a decision.


                        Promotions Manager
```

Student activities:

Prepare a word-processed draft proposal as requested in the promotions manager's memo.

ASSIGNMENT 2. BILKO'S BIKES

Your friend, John Bilko, is a sole trader. In January 1990 he started up his small business, Bilko's Bikes, selling custom-made mountain bikes. He works from a garage, which he rents at £425 per quarter, close to where he lives. Unfortunately he has not kept proper books of accounts, but what records he has show that in the first year of business he had total sales of £85,600, of which he is still owed £12,160. During the year he has paid cash for frames and other parts to the value of £34,420. He still has £3,190 worth of stock left. He has bought tyres and accessories totalling £5,230 on credit and still owes £470. At the end of the year there is £235 worth of this stock left.

John's main expense is advertising, which totals £813 for the year, and he still owes £745 of this. He believes that his home telephone bill has increased by £644 over the year as a result of business use; £172 of this is still outstanding. In addition, there have been various miscellaneous cash expenses which amount to £438 for the year.

Bilko's Bikes was started with a capital sum of £7,000; £4,000 was used to buy equipment and tools which John thinks will last about ten years. He has not kept any record of the money he has personally drawn from the business, but at the end of the year he has £13,200 in the bank and £560 cash.

Elated with the apparent success of the business, John shows you these records, knowing that you are a business student, and tells you that he wishes to expand by employing two lads to help him. He also thinks that there may be a market for selling cycling clothes and other accessories.

Student activities:

Advise John on the following:

(i)   What are the main factors he has to bear in mind when employing the two lads?

(ii) How can be find out if there is a market for cycling clothes?

(iii) What is his profit for 1990?

ASSIGNMENT 3. THE SANDWICH COURSE

At the beginning of term your college announces that due to financial constraints the refectory and bars are to be closed indefinitely. Not unexpectedly, this meets with considerable opposition. However, an enterprising group of engineering students decides to attempt to remedy the situation by making and selling a variety of filled rolls and sandwiches.

They approach the branch manager of the bank on the campus for an overdraft. However, unimpressed by their lack of business acumen, he tells them that he would be willing to consider an application for a loan on condition that a business student and a catering student are recruited to the team, and a proper business plan drawn up.

The engineering students ask you if you would be prepared to join them.

Student activities:

(i)   Construct a survey to explore the potential market among students at the college.

(ii) Draw up a word-processed business plan for submission to the bank.

ASSIGNMENT 4. NOSTALGIA LTD

You are a personal assistant in the chairman's office at Nostalgia Ltd, a small company which manufactures and sells reproduction Victoriana. The operations statement for the month of April 1991 shows a loss of £40,000 which the chairman has declared is unacceptable; in his view the company should be achieving a monthly profit of £80,000. He calls a management meeting to discuss the results and seek solutions.

The meeting is extremely acrimonious; the senior managers are in total disagreement as to the best way forward. To allow tempers to cool, the chairman decides to halt the meeting and reconvene it in a fortnight's time. However, within 24 hours he receives the following memo from the production manager, a man who he values highly.

```
                        M E M O R A N D U M

From: Production Manager

To: Chairman
_____

Further  to  yesterday's  meeting  I  feel  I  really  must  make  the
following  points.  As  was  revealed  at  the  meeting,  at  present  we  are
only  working  at  50  per  cent  of  total  production  capacity.

Clearly  we  must  increase  our  sales  volume  so  that  we  can  achieve
maximum  production  capacity  and  thus  the  lowest  cost  per  unit.  I
really  believe  that  we  have  no  choice  but  to  reduce  selling  prices  by
10  per  cent  to  boost  sales.

I  am  truly  dismayed  at  the  direction  the  company  is  going  in  and  I
attribute  much  of  our  present  difficulties  to  the  new  marketing
manager.  Unless  he  resigns,  I  am  certain  that  a  number  of  us  will  be
reconsidering  our  commitment  to  the  company,  despite  our  personal
loyalty  to  you.
```

Production Manager

The chairman has already discussed strategies for increasing sales with the marketing manager, who has put forward a very plausible argument, unfortunately not backed with hard figures, for a budget of £50,000 per month to spend on advertising. He claims that this will increase sales sufficiently to achieve the target profit.

Next the chairman consults with the accountant, a personal friend of long standing. He advises that by renting additional warehousing at £25,000 per month, raw materials could be purchased in bulk and a discount of 10 per cent obtained. He also believes that at April's production levels, the variable factory overheads could be reduced by £11,000 simply by implementing cost controls. He implies that the production manager has been somewhat lax in this area.

The figures for Nostalgia Ltd for April 1991 are shown opposite.

Operating statement for April 1991

Output	550,000 units	
	£	£
Sales		1,100,000
Direct materials	660,000	
Operatives wages	220,000	
Factory overheads:		
fixed	35,000	
variable	55,000	
Administration and selling overheads:		
fixed	60,000	
variable	110,000	
		1,140,000
Profit/(loss)		(40,000)

Student activities:

At the next management meeting the chairman wishes to put forward specific proposals for improving the company's performance and find a strategy that will reduce the management conflict and lead to a more coherent management team. Prepare word-processed draft proposals.

ASSIGNMENT 5. SPICE OF LIFE STORES

Sarah Spicer is a sole trader and has owned Spice of Life Stores for eight years. She became worried recently after reading that two other sole traders in the area, also in the health food trade, have gone out of business as a result of intensive competition from a large new store which opened in the area some six months ago.

Spice of Life Stores has not been seriously affected by the competition from the new store as fortunately it is some five miles away. The business is not only solvent but trade is expanding. However, Sarah is considering turning the business into a limited company to protect her personal assets in the event of a similar disaster befalling the shop. In addition, she has plans to open a second shop and wants to borrow £250,000. She believes that this may be easier to obtain as a limited company.

Although she has an accountant to deal with the tax affairs of the business, Sarah finds it very difficult to understand the explanations he gives her and the accounting terms he uses. For this reason, when introduced to you as a business student by a mutual friend at a party, she asks you a number of penetrating questions on accounting. Sensing that you have a clear grasp of the subject, she asks you whether you would be interested in drafting a report in clear language for her for a modest fee. You agree.

Student activities:

(i) Prepare a word-processed written report for Sarah Spicer covering the following:
- the advantages and disadvantages of private limited companies;
- any factors that should be taken into consideration when forming a private limited company;
- an outline of the main legal requirements involved when forming a private limited company.

(ii) Provide an example of the type of accounts that Sarah's company would be required to produce under Format I of the Companies Act 1985 (give illustrative figures).

(iii) List the various sources of finance open to a private limited company, indicating which sources you consider would be most appropriate to Sarah's plans.

ASSIGNMENT 6. COUNTRYWIDE BUS COMPANY LTD

Countrywide Bus Company Ltd is a large organisation offering a public service. No matter how efficiently the service is run, there are always a substantial number of complaints which are dealt with by some 20 clerks. Personal complaints are received by the receptionist on duty, who writes down the complaint on a complaints form, which is then passed to the head of the complaints department. There are two telephonists who take down details of any complaints received by 'phone on complaints forms, which are also passed on to the head of the complaints department.

The clerks in the complaints department sit in four rows of five desks. The head of the department sits at the front, facing the clerks. Each morning the head of the department sorts all the complaints, whether personal or postal, into piles according to the nature of the complaint and distributes them to the clerks. The individual clerks then investigate the complaints and look up any records. Their findings are pinned to the front of the complaint form and the papers passed along to the clerk at the head of the row, who is known as the letter-writer. The letter-writer is responsible for replying to the complainant.

Recently there have been some serious disputes between the clerks in the complaints department, and the telephonists and receptionists. The latter claim that they are at the sharp end and have to deal directly with the public. The staff in the complaints department argue that they are never provided with all the details and therefore cannot investigate the complaints fully.

Despite his best endeavours, the head of the complaints department can see that the department's productivity is going down. He decides to keep a record of the number of complaints each clerk investigates a day. After three months his records show that output has decreased by 20 per cent. Unfortunately his records are seen by one of the letter-writers and this leads to some emotional exchanges. In the end five of the most dissatisfied clerks leave the company and find jobs elsewhere.

The head of the complaints department discovers that it is very difficult to find replacement staff and tries to keep productivity levels up by working overtime during the evenings and at weekends. But the strain of working at this level proves to be too much for him and he suffers a nervous breakdown.

Student activities:

You work for a firm of management consultants who have been called in to advise Countrywide Bus Company Ltd. Write a word-processed report to the personnel manager including the following:

(i) an analysis of the reasons for the poor motivation in the complaints department and the reasons for staff leaving;

(ii) the way in which the complaints department could be redesigned to improve motivation;

(iii) what to do about the head of the complaints department;

(iv) how best to go about recruiting new clerks for the complaint department.

ASSIGNMENT 7. METROPOLITAN BANK LTD

Metropolitan Bank Ltd, one of the major banks, is planning to move its head office out of London. It is looking for a provincial site with good communications where modern, purpose-built premises are available or could be erected.

At present some 1,000 members of staff are employed at the London head office, but with the introduction of new technology at the time of the move, staffing levels will be reduced to 850. The following table gives details of existing head office staff employed in London and estimates of those required after the move.

Staff	Numbers of existing head office staff	Estimated numbers of head office staff after relocation
Senior managers	20	20
Professional specialists	30	50
Middle managers	100	80
Supervisors	170	150
Technicians	30	30
Clerks	600	480
Ancillary workers	50	40
Total	1,000	850

Senior managers at the bank have had extensive discussions with another financial institution which has recently relocated. This has helped them draw up the following estimates of how many of the present members of staff would be prepared to relocate.

Staff	%
Senior managers	50
Professional specialists	50
Middle managers	40
Supervisors	20
Technicians	20
Clerks	10
Ancillary workers	5

The move is planned to take place over a three-year period. Despite the confidential nature of the plans, news of the move has been leaked and has met with a very hostile reaction from the staff. It is thought that the person responsible for the leak, and who was consequently dismissed, was one of the secretarial staff. The secretary's boyfriend, a computer analyst at the bank, went to see the personnel manager about her dismissal and angry words were exchanged, leading to a scuffle. In no time, the computer analyst had been dismissed.

Student activities:

You work in the public relations department of Metropolitan Bank Ltd. The chairman is convinced that relocation is the right move to make and asks you to prepare a draft report on the strategies of relocation, how it should be handled and the key aspects of the move. To improve communications with the head office staff he also wants you to write an article for the staff newspaper explaining the reasons for the move and how it will be implemented. You should use a desktop publishing package to prepare the material.

Finally, the chairman wants your advice on the cases of the secretary and the computer analyst who were dismissed. It transpires that in fact the leak was made by one of the senior management team and the chairman is concerned to put matters right.

Appendix B
Present Value Factors

Present value of 1 at compound interest: $(1 + r)^{-n}$

Rate of discount (r)

Years (n)	1%	2%	3%	4%	5%	6%	7%	8%	9%	10%	11%	12%	13%	14%	15%	16%
1	0.990	0.980	0.971	0.962	0.952	0.943	0.935	0.926	0.917	0.909	0.901	0.893	0.885	0.877	0.870	0.862
2	0.980	0.961	0.943	0.925	0.907	0.890	0.873	0.857	0.842	0.826	0.812	0.797	0.783	0.770	0.756	0.743
3	0.971	0.942	0.915	0.889	0.864	0.840	0.816	0.794	0.772	0.751	0.731	0.712	0.693	0.675	0.658	0.641
4	0.961	0.924	0.889	0.855	0.823	0.792	0.763	0.735	0.708	0.683	0.659	0.636	0.613	0.592	0.572	0.552
5	0.952	0.906	0.863	0.822	0.784	0.747	0.713	0.681	0.650	0.621	0.594	0.567	0.543	0.519	0.497	0.476
6	0.942	0.888	0.838	0.790	0.746	0.705	0.666	0.630	0.596	0.565	0.535	0.507	0.480	0.456	0.432	0.410
7	0.933	0.871	0.813	0.760	0.711	0.665	0.623	0.584	0.547	0.513	0.482	0.452	0.425	0.400	0.376	0.354
8	0.924	0.854	0.789	0.731	0.677	0.627	0.582	0.540	0.502	0.467	0.434	0.404	0.376	0.351	0.327	0.305
9	0.914	0.837	0.766	0.703	0.645	0.592	0.544	0.500	0.460	0.424	0.391	0.361	0.333	0.308	0.284	0.263
10	0.905	0.820	0.744	0.676	0.614	0.558	0.508	0.463	0.422	0.386	0.352	0.322	0.295	0.270	0.247	0.227
11	0.896	0.804	0.722	0.650	0.585	0.527	0.475	0.429	0.388	0.350	0.317	0.288	0.261	0.237	0.215	0.195
12	0.887	0.789	0.701	0.625	0.557	0.497	0.444	0.397	0.356	0.319	0.286	0.257	0.231	0.208	0.187	0.169
13	0.879	0.773	0.681	0.601	0.530	0.469	0.415	0.368	0.326	0.286	0.258	0.229	0.204	0.182	0.163	0.145
14	0.870	0.758	0.661	0.578	0.505	0.442	0.388	0.341	0.299	0.263	0.232	0.205	0.181	0.160	0.141	0.125
15	0.861	0.743	0.642	0.555	0.481	0.417	0.362	0.315	0.275	0.239	0.209	0.183	0.160	0.140	0.123	0.108
16	0.853	0.728	0.623	0.534	0.458	0.394	0.339	0.292	0.252	0.218	0.188	0.163	0.142	0.123	0.107	0.093
17	0.844	0.714	0.605	0.513	0.436	0.371	0.317	0.270	0.231	0.198	0.170	0.146	0.125	0.108	0.093	0.080
18	0.836	0.700	0.587	0.494	0.416	0.350	0.296	0.250	0.212	0.180	0.153	0.130	0.111	0.095	0.081	0.069
19	0.828	0.686	0.570	0.475	0.396	0.331	0.277	0.232	0.195	0.164	0.138	0.116	0.098	0.083	0.070	0.060
20	0.820	0.673	0.554	0.456	0.377	0.312	0.258	0.215	0.178	0.149	0.124	0.104	0.087	0.073	0.061	0.051

Rate of discount (r)

Years (n)	17%	18%	19%	20%	21%	22%	23%	24%	25%	26%	28%	30%	35%	40%	45%	50%
1	0.855	0.848	0.840	0.833	0.826	0.820	0.813	0.807	0.800	0.794	0.781	0.769	0.741	0.714	0.690	0.667
2	0.731	0.718	0.706	0.694	0.683	0.672	0.661	0.650	0.640	0.630	0.610	0.592	0.549	0.510	0.476	0.444
3	0.624	0.609	0.593	0.579	0.565	0.551	0.537	0.525	0.512	0.500	0.477	0.455	0.406	0.364	0.328	0.296
4	0.534	0.516	0.499	0.482	0.467	0.451	0.437	0.423	0.410	0.397	0.373	0.350	0.301	0.260	0.226	0.198
5	0.456	0.437	0.419	0.402	0.386	0.370	0.355	0.341	0.328	0.315	0.291	0.269	0.223	0.186	0.156	0.132
6	0.390	0.370	0.352	0.335	0.319	0.303	0.289	0.275	0.262	0.250	0.227	0.207	0.165	0.133	0.108	0.088
7	0.333	0.314	0.296	0.279	0.263	0.249	0.235	0.222	0.210	0.198	0.178	0.159	0.122	0.095	0.074	0.059
8	0.285	0.266	0.249	0.233	0.218	0.204	0.191	0.179	0.168	0.157	0.139	0.123	0.091	0.068	0.051	0.039
9	0.243	0.226	0.209	0.194	0.180	0.167	0.155	0.144	0.134	0.125	0.108	0.094	0.067	0.048	0.035	0.026
10	0.208	0.191	0.176	0.162	0.149	0.137	0.126	0.116	0.107	0.099	0.085	0.073	0.050	0.035	0.024	0.017
11	0.178	0.162	0.148	0.135	0.123	0.112	0.103	0.094	0.086	0.079	0.066	0.056	0.037	0.025	0.017	0.012
12	0.152	0.137	0.124	0.112	0.102	0.092	0.083	0.076	0.069	0.063	0.052	0.043	0.027	0.018	0.012	0.008
13	0.130	0.116	0.104	0.094	0.084	0.075	0.068	0.061	0.055	0.050	0.040	0.033	0.020	0.013	0.008	0.005
14	0.111	0.099	0.088	0.078	0.069	0.062	0.055	0.049	0.044	0.039	0.032	0.025	0.015	0.009	0.006	0.003
15	0.095	0.084	0.074	0.065	0.057	0.051	0.045	0.040	0.035	0.031	0.025	0.020	0.011	0.006	0.004	0.002
16	0.081	0.071	0.062	0.054	0.047	0.042	0.036	0.032	0.028	0.025	0.019	0.015	0.008	0.005	0.003	0.002
17	0.069	0.060	0.052	0.045	0.039	0.034	0.030	0.026	0.023	0.020	0.015	0.012	0.006	0.003	0.002	0.001
18	0.059	0.051	0.044	0.038	0.032	0.028	0.024	0.021	0.018	0.016	0.012	0.009	0.005	0.002	0.001	0.001
19	0.051	0.043	0.037	0.031	0.027	0.023	0.020	0.017	0.014	0.012	0.009	0.007	0.003	0.002	0.001	0.000
20	0.043	0.037	0.031	0.026	0.022	0.019	0.016	0.014	0.012	0.010	0.007	0.005	0.002	0.001	0.001	0.000

Index